本书获得 贵州大学社科学术出版基金 经费资助
        贵州大学学科建设

Through Trials to Triumph:
Exploring Revolutionary Landmarks

- 中英对照 -

砥砺征途：
革命历史景点故事

主　编　周　杰
副主编　宁　梅
编　者　田　婷　吴　雯
　　　　黎晓容　陈恒娇
　　　　贾海波　杨　敏

南京大学出版社

图书在版编目(**CIP**)数据

砥砺征途：革命历史景点故事：汉文、英文 / 周杰主编. -- 南京：南京大学出版社，2025.1.
ISBN 978-7-305-28665-0

Ⅰ. K201

中国国家版本馆 CIP 数据核字第 2024JC6684 号

出版发行	南京大学出版社
社　　址	南京市汉口路 22 号　　邮　编　210093

书　　名　砥砺征途（中英对照）：革命历史景点故事
　　　　　　DILI ZHENGTU(ZHONGYING DUIZHAO): GEMING LISHI JINGDIAN GUSHI
主　　编　周　杰
责任编辑　孙　辉

照　　排　南京紫藤制版印务中心
印　　刷　盐城市华光印刷厂
开　　本　718 mm×1000 mm　1/16　印张 15.5　字数 262 千
版　　次　2025 年 1 月第 1 版　2025 年 1 月第 1 次印刷
ISBN 978-7-305-28665-0
定　　价　75.00 元

网　　址：http://www.njupco.com
官方微博：http://weibo.com/njupco
官方微信：njupress
销售咨询热线：(025)83594756

* 版权所有，侵权必究
* 凡购买南大版图书，如有印装质量问题，请与所购
　图书销售部门联系调换

国家级一流本科英语专业建设成果；

教育部首批新文科研究与改革实践项目"'全人'教育理念下的西部高校英语专业人才培养创新与实践"研究成果。

前　言

当今世界,中外人文交流日益频繁,文明交流互鉴不断深入,不同文化背景的人们跨越地域界限,频繁互动,相互学习借鉴,共同推动着人类文明的进步。在这一宏大背景下,语言,作为文化的桥梁和纽带,其重要性愈发凸显。外语学科的人才培养目标,已超越单纯的语言技能掌握,更在于培养能够讲好中国故事,传播好中国声音,塑造可信、可爱、可敬的中国形象的国际传播人才。往昔,翻译仿若一扇望向世界的窗,让国内领略异域风情,如今,它更是一座沟通内外的桥,将中国的深厚底蕴精准输送至全球。

2025年是一个具有特殊意义的年份,我们迎来了中国人民抗日战争暨世界反法西斯战争胜利80周年,同时也是遵义会议召开90周年。在这样的时间节点上,我们更应深入挖掘中国革命历史中的宝贵精神财富,传承红色基因,汲取奋进力量。为此,我们精心编写这本承载着中国革命历史厚重篇章的书籍,旨在通过详实的历史回顾、生动的红色故事以及丰富的红色景点介绍,带领读者走进那段波澜壮阔的革命岁月,深刻体会中国共产党从诞生到壮大的光辉历程,学会用外语讲好中国共产党的革命历史故事。

本书以新民主主义革命时期形成的中国共产党人精神谱系为纲,沿着中国革命历史发展脉络,选取了上海、江西、长征、遵义、延安、重庆、西柏坡等关键节点,详细介绍了这些地方在中国革命进程中的重要历史事件、红色故事以及红色景点。在每个章节中,我们都精心设置了"历史回眸""红色故事""红色景点"以及"专栏"等板块。"历史回眸"带领读者回顾那段波澜壮阔的历史,感受革命先辈们在艰苦卓绝的斗争中所展现出的坚定信念与不屈意志;"红色故事"则以生动的语言、感人的细节,讲述了一个个鲜活的革命故事,让读者仿佛身临其境,与故事中的人物一同经历那段峥嵘岁月;"红色景点"则为读者提供了实地参观、缅怀先烈的场所,让读者在游览中接受红色文化的熏陶与洗礼;而"专栏"更是深入挖掘了与各章节主题密切相关的革命精神,如伟大建党精神、井冈山精神与苏区精神、长征精神、遵义会议精神、延安精神与伟大抗战精神、红岩精神、西柏坡精神等,这些精神是中华民族宝贵的精神财富,也是我们在新时代不断前行的动力源泉。

  在本书编写过程中,贵州大学学生处龙汶处长和贵州大学历史与民族文化学院郭红军教授为本书中文内容的编写提供了宝贵建议;加拿大编辑Robert Orth对本书的英文部分进行了审校;南京大学出版社杨金荣老师、孙辉老师和田甜老师为本书的编辑出版给与了大力支持,在此深表感谢。

  本书不仅适合广大读者阅读,还可作为高等院校英语、历史、国际传播等相关专业的辅助教材,同时,也适合国际学生用以了解中国革命历史、学习中国文化。为确保术语的精准无误,本书重点参考了《毛泽东选集》(中文版、英文版)、《习近平谈治国理政》(中文版、英文版)和中央编译出版社2021年推出的《中国共产党史》(中文版、英文版)等权威著作。然而,由于编者学识有限,书中难免存在疏漏和不妥之处,恳请各位方家不吝赐教,予以指正。

编 者

2024 年 12 月

目 录

第一章 上海：开天辟地 党的创立 …………………………………… 1
Chapter Ⅰ Shanghai：Emergence and Establishment of the Communist Party of China ………………………………………………… 1

    第一节 历史回眸 ………………………………………………… 1
    Section Ⅰ A Glimpse of History ……………………………… 1
    第二节 红色故事 ………………………………………………… 9
    Section Ⅱ Red Stories ………………………………………… 9
    第三节 红色景点 ………………………………………………… 21
    Section Ⅲ Red Tourism Attractions ………………………… 21
    专栏1：伟大建党精神 ………………………………………… 29
    Special Column Ⅰ：The Great Founding Spirit of the CPC …… 29

第二章 江西：革命摇篮 红都瑞金 …………………………………… 32
Chapter Ⅱ Jiangxi：The Cradle of the Revolution with Ruijin as the Capital ……………………………………………………… 32

    第一节 历史回眸 ………………………………………………… 32
    Section Ⅰ A Glimpse of History ……………………………… 32
    第二节 红色故事 ………………………………………………… 39
    Section Ⅱ Red Stories ………………………………………… 39
    第三节 红色景点 ………………………………………………… 53
    Section Ⅲ Red Tourism Attractions ………………………… 53
    专栏2：井冈山精神与苏区精神 ……………………………… 70
    Special Column Ⅱ：The Jinggangshan Spirit and the Spirit of the Soviet Areas …………………………………………………… 70

第三章　长征：伟大壮举　革命奇迹 …… 72
Chapter Ⅲ　The Long March: An Unprecedented Feat and a Revolutionary Miracle …… 72

第一节　历史回眸 …… 73
Section Ⅰ　A Glimpse of History …… 73

第二节　红色故事 …… 79
Section Ⅱ　Red Stories …… 79

第三节　红色景点 …… 91
Section Ⅲ　Red Tourism Attractions …… 91

专栏3：长征精神 …… 103
Special Column Ⅲ: The Long March Spirit …… 103

第四章　遵义：历史转折　出奇制胜 …… 104
Chapter Ⅳ　Zunyi: A Surprising and Victorious Turn in History …… 104

第一节　历史回眸 …… 105
Section Ⅰ　A Glimpse of History …… 105

第二节　红色故事 …… 110
Section Ⅱ　Red Stories …… 110

第三节　红色景点 …… 126
Section Ⅲ　Red Tourism Attractions …… 126

专栏4：遵义会议精神 …… 146
Special Column Ⅳ: The Spirit of the Zunyi Meeting …… 146

第五章　延安：革命圣地　抗战中心 …… 147
Chapter Ⅴ　Yan'an: The Chinese Revolutionary Holy Land and the Command Center of the CPC …… 147

第一节　历史回眸 …… 147
Section Ⅰ　A Glimpse of History …… 147

第二节　红色故事 …… 162
Section Ⅱ　Red Stories …… 162

第三节　红色景点 ……………………………………… 172
Section Ⅲ　Red Tourism Attractions ……………………… 172
专栏5:延安精神与伟大抗战精神 ……………………… 186
Special Column Ⅴ：The Yan'an Spirit and the Great Spirit of
　　　　　　　　Resisting Aggression …………………… 186

第六章　重庆:艰苦斗争　红岩精神 ……………… 188
Chapter Ⅵ　Chongqing：The Red Rock Spirit Through Hardship and Struggle ……………………………………… 188

第一节　历史回眸 ……………………………………… 189
Section Ⅰ　A Glimpse of History ………………………… 189
第二节　红色故事 ……………………………………… 193
Section Ⅱ　Red Stories …………………………………… 193
第三节　红色景点 ……………………………………… 197
Section Ⅲ　Red Tourism Attractions ……………………… 197
专栏6:红岩精神 ……………………………………… 204
Special Column Ⅵ：The Red Rock Spirit ………………… 204

第七章　西柏坡:人民胜利　国旗飘扬 …………… 205
Chapter Ⅶ　Xibaipo：The People's Triumph，the National Flag Fluttering …………………………………………… 205

第一节　历史回眸 ……………………………………… 206
Section Ⅰ　A Glimpse of History ………………………… 206
第二节　红色故事 ……………………………………… 215
Section Ⅱ　Red Stories …………………………………… 215
第三节　红色景点 ……………………………………… 219
Section Ⅲ　Red Tourism Attractions ……………………… 219
专栏7:西柏坡精神 …………………………………… 232
Special Column Ⅶ：The Xibaipo Spirit …………………… 232

参考文献 ……………………………………………… 233

第一章 上海：开天辟地 党的创立

Chapter I Shanghai: Emergence and Establishment of the Communist Party of China

1921年7月的一个夜晚,中国共产党第一次全国代表大会在上海法租界一座二层居民小楼中秘密召开。这次会后,一个以马克思列宁主义为行动指南的、完全新式的无产阶级政党诞生了,这是中国历史上开天辟地的大事变。从此,长期在黑暗中探索的中国人民有了指路明灯。谋求民族独立、人民解放和国家富强、人民幸福的斗争就有了主心骨,中国历史翻开了新的一页。

One night in July of 1921, the First National Congress of the Communist Party of China opened in secret in a small two-story residence in Shanghai's French Concession. After the congress, a completely new proletarian party to be guided by Marxism-Leninism was born. This was a groundbreaking event in China's history. Since then, the Chinese people have found the guiding light to end their long exploration in the dark, the supporting backbone in their struggle for national independence, liberation, prosperity and happiness. A new page has hence been opened in China's history.

第一节 历史回眸
Section I A Glimpse of History

近代中国的民族危机和各种探索
Various Forces Explore Ways to Rejuvenate China in Modern Times

中华民族有着五千多年连绵不断的文明历史,创造了璀璨的中华文化,为人类的文明进步作出了不可磨灭的贡献，成为世界上伟大的民族。近代以来，西方列强对中国进行了多次侵略战争，如1840年至1842年的鸦片战争，1856年至1860年的第二次鸦片战争，1894年至1895年的中日甲午战争，1900年八国联军侵略中国，强迫清政府割地、赔款，签订了一系列不平等条约，攫取了在华的种种特权。中国逐渐沦为半殖民地半封建社会，国家蒙辱、人民蒙难、文明蒙尘，中华民族遭受了前所未有的劫难。

With the longest continuous civilization of more than 5,000 years, the Chinese people have created a brilliant Chinese culture, made invaluable contributions to the progress of human civilization, and become a great nation in the world. Since 1840, Western powers had waged many wars of aggression against China. The Opium War (1840 – 1842), the Second Opium War (1856 – 1860), the Sino-Japanese War (1894 – 1895), and the invasion of the Eight-Power Alliance in 1900 had resulted in a series of unequal treaties that forced the Qing government to concede territorial rights and sovereignty and pay large amounts of indemnities. The Chinese people suffered greatly under the colonial yoke and the corrupt Qing court. China was gradually reduced to a semi-colonial, semi-feudal society and suffered greater ravages than ever before. The country endured intense humiliation, the people were subjected to great pain, and the Chinese civilization was plunged into darkness.

近代以来，实现中华民族伟大复兴成为全民族最伟大的梦想；争取民族独立、人民解放和实现国家富强、人民幸福，成为中国人民的历史任务。为拯救民族危亡，无数仁人志士奔走呐喊，进行了各种各样的探索。可是，历次反对外国侵略的战争也好，太平天国的农民起义也好，"中体西用"的洋务运动也好，试图变法图强的戊戌维新也好，起自社会下层并有着广泛群众规模的义和团运动也好，由于没有科学的理论、正确的道路和可依靠的社会力量，一次又一次地失败了。

Since 1840, national rejuvenation has been the greatest dream of the Chinese people and the Chinese nation. Striving for national independence and emancipation, as well as seeking prosperity and happiness for the people have become a historical inevitability. Countless patriotic and aspirational Chinese intellectuals have carried out various uprisings and movements in order to save the nation from peril. Be it the Taiping Rebellion, the Westernization Movement, the Wuxu Reform (Hundred Days of Reform) or the Boxer Rebellion, all failed to change the downtrodden fate of the nation and its people. These struggles, along with many other wars against foreign aggression, though socially reformative, lacked a scientific guiding theory, a correct approach and reliable social forces.

1911年10月10日爆发的辛亥革命一举推翻了统治中国两千多年的君主专制制度。1912年元旦,孙中山在南京就任中华民国临时大总统,"中华民国"成立。然而,袁世凯在帝国主义和国内反动势力的支持下窃取了临时大总统的职位,政权落入腐败的北洋军阀手中。中国半殖民地半封建的社会性质和中国人民的悲惨命运没有改变,迫切需要新的思想引领救亡运动,迫切需要新的组织凝聚革命力量。

The Chinese Revolution, which broke out on October 10, 1911, overthrew the monarchical dictatorship that had ruled China for more than 2,000 years. On January 1, 1912, the Republic of China was established in Nanjing, with Sun Yat-sen inaugurated as the provisional president. However, the fruits of the revolution were seized by the Northern Warlords led by Yuan Shikai, with the support of imperialist countries and domestic reactionary forces. The nature of China's semi-colonial and semi-feudal society and the miserable fate of the Chinese people did not change, and there was an urgent need for new ideas to lead the salvation movement and an urgent need for new organizations to unite revolutionary forces.

五四运动和马克思主义在中国的传播
The May Fourth Movement and the Spread of Marxism in China

十月革命一声炮响,给中国送来了马克思列宁主义。1917年,俄国发生了十月革命,建立了世界上第一个社会主义国家。中国先进分子从十月革命的光辉实践中找到了马克思列宁主义这一锐利的思想武器,从马克思列宁主义的科学真理中看到了解决中国问题的出路。

The salvoes of the October Revolution brought the ideas of Marxism-

Leninism to China in 1917, when the world's first socialist state was established. From the glorious practice of the October Revolution, the Chinese progressives found Marxism-Leninism, a sharp ideological weapon and solution to China's problems.

1918年,德国战败,第一次世界大战结束。1919年,英、法、美、日等国在巴黎召开"巴黎和会",中国作为战胜国之一也参加了巴黎和会。会上,中国代表提出从德国收回山东特权的要求,但这个合理的要求却被会议拒绝,列强决定把德国在山东的特权转交给日本,强迫中国代表签字。

In 1918, Germany was defeated and World War I ended. In 1919, Britain, France, the United States, Japan and other countries held the Paris Peace Conference, which China attended as one of the victorious nations. At the conference, Chinese delegates put forward a request to reclaim the sovereignty of Shandong province from Germany. However, the conference rejected China's just request and stipulated that Germany should transfer the concession to Japan and forced the Chinese representative to sign the treaty.

消息传到国内,中国人民积蓄已久的反帝爱国情绪终于像火山一样爆发了。1919年5月4日,北京大学等13所大专院校3000多人在天安门前集会,高喊"还我青岛""取消二十一条""打倒卖国贼"等口号抗议示威,震惊中外的五四运动拉开序幕。翌日,北京的大学生开始罢课,他们走上街头向群众进行爱国讲演和宣传,山东、天津、上海等地的学生也纷纷起来声援。反动的北洋政府逮捕了近千名学生,激起了全国人民更大的愤怒。

The news reached China and ignited the long-accumulated indignation of the Chinese people. On May 4, more than 3,000 students from thirteen colleges and universities, including Peking University, gathered in front of Tiananmen Square to demonstrate. The protesters shouted slogans such as "Return Qingdao to China", "Annul the Twenty-One Demands", and "Get Rid of Internal Traitors". This was the eruption of the May Fourth Movement, which stunned people in China and around the world. The next day, college students in Beijing went to the streets to give patriotic speeches to the masses. Students in Shandong, Tianjin,

Shanghai and other areas also joined in. The reactionary Northern Warlords arrested approximately a thousand students, provoking greater anger among the Chinese people.

6月5日,上海工人率先举行罢工,支持学生的爱国行为。随后,北京、唐山、汉口、长沙等地的工人也相继举行罢工,许多城市的商人举行罢市。罢课、罢工、罢市的"三罢"斗争迅速扩展到全国。与此同时,在巴黎参加和会的中国代表团收到了几千份全国各界群众要求他们拒签和约的通电。在巨大的压力面前,北洋政府不得不释放被捕学生,并撤了卖国贼曹汝霖、章宗祥、陆宗舆的官职。6月28日,中国代表拒绝在巴黎和约上签字,五四运动取得了胜利。

On June 5, Shanghai workers took the lead in staging a strike in solidarity with students. Within a few days, strikes followed in Beijing, Tangshan, Hankou, Changsha and other places. As strikes were ongoing in three different arenas—schools, workplaces, and markets—the struggle swept across the country. At the same time, the Chinese delegation to the Paris Peace Conference received thousands of telegrams from people from all walks of life across China, asking them to refuse to sign the peace treaty. As a result of public pressure, the Northern Warlord government released the students it had taken into custody, and announced the dismissal of the internal traitors Cao Rulin, Zhang Zongxiang, and Lu Zongyu. On June 28, Chinese delegates refused to sign the Paris Peace Treaty, and the May Fourth Movement ended in victory.

五四运动是近代中国革命史上具有划时代意义的事件,新民主主义革命由此开始。五四运动中,中国无产阶级开始作为独立的政治力量登上历史舞台,显示出巨大的能量。五四运动的意义不仅仅体现在外交方面。在运动发生前的几年中,以民主与科学为主要诉求的新思想、新文化在以北京大学为中心的知识界迅速传播。五四运动促进了马克思主义在中国的广泛传播,促进了马克思主义与中国工人运动的结合,为中国共产党的建立作了思想上和组织上的准备。

The May Fourth Movement was an epoch-making event in the history of the modern Chinese revolution in that it signaled the dawn of the New Democratic Revolution. In the movement, the Chinese working class, as an independent political force, entered the historical arena. The significance of the May Fourth Movement extends beyond diplomacy. In the years preceding the movement, new ideas and culture that focused on democracy and science, spread rapidly within intellectual circles, with Peking University at their center. The May Fourth Movement facilitated the propagation of Marxism in the country, promoted the integration of Marxism with the Chinese workers' movement, and laid ideological and organizational groundwork for the founding of the Communist Party of China.

中国共产党早期组织的建立
The Establishment of the Early Organizations of the Communist Party of China

五四运动后,具有初步共产主义思想的知识分子主张以马克思主义为指导,依靠工人阶级,通过革命的方式来推翻旧制度,建立新社会。中国共产党的早期组织是在工人阶级最为密集的上海首先成立的。1920年8月,陈独秀、李达、李汉俊等在上海发起成立了中国第一个共产党早期组织。10月,李大钊、邓中夏等在北京成立了共产党早期组织。1920年秋至1921年春,董必武、陈潭秋、包惠僧等在武汉,毛泽东、何叔衡等在长沙,王尽美、邓恩铭等在济南,谭平山、谭植棠等在广州,成立了共产党早期组织。在日本、法国的中国留学生和华侨中也成立了共产党早期组织。1920年8月,陈望道翻译的《共产党宣言》中文全译本出版,成为马克思主义在中国传播史上的一件大事。

After the May Fourth Movement, intellectuals with rudimentary communist ideas advocated overthrowing the old system and establishing a new society by conducting revolutions with Marxism as the guide and the working class as the leading force. The first early organization of the Communist Party of China was established in Shanghai, a core city with the greatest concentration of workers in China. It was initiated by Chen Duxiu, Li Da, Li Hanjun and others in August 1920. In October, another communist party organization was founded in Beijing by Li Dazhao, Deng Zhongxia, and others. From the autumn of 1920 to the spring of 1921, communist party organizations were formed in Wuhan by Dong Biwu, Chen Tanqiu, and Bao Huiseng, in Changsha by Mao Zedong and He Shuheng, in Jinan by Wang Jinmei and Deng Enming, and in Guangzhou by Tan Pingshan and Tan Zhitang. In Japan and France, communist party organizations composed of Chinese students and progressive overseas Chinese were also established. In August 1920, Chen Wangdao's Chinese translation of *The Communist Manifesto* was published, which became a major event in the history of the dissemination of Marxism in China.

中国共产党的成立
The Founding of the Communist Party of China (hereinafter shortened as CPC)

1921年7月23日,中国共产党第一次全国代表大会在上海法租界望志路106号(今兴业路76号)开幕。参加会议的代表有13位:上海的李达、李汉俊,北京的张国焘、刘仁静,长沙的毛泽东、何叔衡,武汉的董必武、陈潭秋,济南的王尽美、邓恩铭,广州的陈公博,旅日的周佛海;包惠僧受陈独秀派遣出席了会议。他们代表着全国各地的50多名党员。共产国际代表马林和尼克尔斯基列席了会议。中国共产党的创始人陈独秀和李大钊因事务繁忙未出席会议。

On July 23, 1921, the First National Congress of the CPC opened at No. 106 Wangzhi Road (now No. 76 Xingye Road) in the French Concession of Shanghai. There were thirteen delegates in attendance at the meeting: Li Da and Li Hanjun from Shanghai, Zhang Guotao and Liu Renjing from Beijing, Mao Zedong and He Shuheng from Changsha, Dong Biwu and Chen Tanqiu from Wuhan, Wang Jinmei and Deng Enming from Jinan, Chen Gongbo from Guangzhou, Zhou Fohai from Japan, and Bao Huiseng who was sent by Chen Duxiu. They represented more than 50 CPC members across the country. Henk Sneevliet (alias Maring) and V. A. Nikolsky attended as representatives of the Communist International (Comintern). The founders of the CPC, Chen Duxiu and Li Dazhao, did not attend the meeting because of their busy schedules.

会议进行到7月30日时,会场受到暗探的注意和法租界巡捕的搜查。为了安全,代表们离开上海,最后一天的会议转移到距离上海100公里左右的浙江省嘉兴南湖的一条画舫上继续举行。此次会议讨论通过了中国共产党的纲领,规定党的奋斗目标是:革命军队必须与无产阶级一起推翻资本家阶级的政权,承认无产阶级专政,消灭资本家私有制,最终消灭阶级差别。这次会议后,一个以马克思列宁主义为行动指南的、完全新式的无产阶级政党诞生了。在中国的政治舞台上,正式出现了一支崭新的力量——中国共产党,给中国人民带来了光明和希望。

On July 30, the meeting had to be suspended when spies and police searching for the venue in the French Concession came precariously near. To escape their attention, the meeting was quickly relocated to Jiaxing, 100 kilometers away from Shanghai, where it resumed for a final day on a pleasure boat on Nanhu Lake. The congress discussed and adopted the first program of the CPC, which consists of the following points: the revolutionary army shall join hands with the proletariat in overthrowing the bourgeois regime; and the Party shall accept the dictatorship of the proletariat until the end of class struggle, abolish capitalist private ownership, and finally eliminate class differences. After this conference, a completely new proletarian party with Marxism-Leninism as its guide to action came into being. The CPC, as a brand-new force, officially emerged on China's political stage, bringing light and hope to the Chinese people.

习近平总书记在庆祝中国共产党成立100周年大会上的重要讲话中指出:"中国产生了共产党,这是开天辟地的大事变,深刻改变了近代以后中华民族发展的方向和进程,深刻改变了中国人民和中华民族的前途和命运,深刻改变了世界发展的趋势和格局。中国共产党一经诞生,就把为中国人民谋幸福、为中华民族谋复兴确立为自己的初心使命。一百年来,中国共产党团结带领中国人民进行的一切奋斗、一切牺牲、一切创造,归结起来就是一个主题:实现中华民族伟大复兴。"

In his speech at the Ceremony Marking the Centenary of the CPC, General Secretary Xi Jinping pointed out: "The founding of a communist party in China was an epoch-making event, which profoundly changed the course of Chinese history in modern times, transformed the future of the Chinese people and nation, and altered the landscape of world development. Since the very day of its founding, the Party has made seeking happiness for the Chinese people and rejuvenation for the Chinese nation its aspiration and mission. All the struggle, sacrifice, and creation through which the Party has united and led the Chinese people over the past hundred years has been tied together by one ultimate theme—bringing about the great rejuvenation of the Chinese nation."

第二节 红色故事
Section Ⅱ Red Stories

李大钊：铁肩担道义妙手著文章
Li Dazhao: Iron Shoulders Take Duties, Smart Hands Write Articles

李大钊是中国共产党的主要创始人之一。1889年,生于河北省乐亭县大黑坨村。1913年,李大钊东渡日本,就读于东京早稻田大学,在那里接触到社会主义思想和马克思主义学说。当日本提出旨在灭亡中国的"二十一条"后,李大钊积极参加留日学生总会的爱国斗争,起草了《警告全国父老书》,呼吁全国人民团结一致,保卫锦绣河山。

Li Dazhao was one of the main founders of the CPC. He was born in Leting County, Hebei Province in 1889. In 1913, Li Dazhao traveled east to Japan to study at Waseda University in Tokyo, where he came into contact with socialist ideas and Marxist doctrines. The Japanese government made the "Twenty-one Demands", which would greatly extend Japanese control of China. Chinese students studying in Japan strongly responded, and Li Dazhao actively joined the protests. He drafted the "Letter of Warning to My Fellow Chinese", calling on the people of the whole country to unite and defend the country.

1916年初,李大钊回国,任北京大学图书馆主任兼经济学教授,并参加《新青年》杂志编辑部的工作。他积极投身新文化运动,宣传民主、科学精神,抨击旧礼教、旧道德,成为新文化运动的一员主将。他在《新青年》第二卷第一号上发表了《青春》一文,号召青年"冲决历史之桎梏,涤荡历史之积秽,新造民族之生命,挽回民族之青春"。

At the beginning of 1916, Li Dazhao returned to China and was later appointed the director of the library at Peking University and a professor of economics. He became an editor for the *New Youth*, the principal journal of the new Western-oriented literary and cultural movements. As a leading intellectual of China's New Cultural Movement, he wrote hundreds of articles to promote democracy and science, and to attack old etiquette and morality. In his article entitled "Youth", published in the first issue of the second volume of the *New Youth*, he called on young people to "Fight against the shackles of history, clean up the filth of history, create a new life for the nation, and restore the youth of the nation".

俄国十月革命的胜利令李大钊备受鼓舞,他连续发表了《法俄革命之比较观》《庶民的胜利》《布尔什维主义的胜利》等文章,从一个爱国的民主主义者转变为一个马克思主义者,进而成为我国最早的马克思主义传播者。1919年五四运动后,他更加致力于马克思主义的宣传,在《新青年》上发表《我的马克思主义观》,比较全面地介绍了马克思主义理论。李大钊推动了马克思主义在中国的广泛传播,为中国共产党的创建准备了思想条件。

Li Dazhao was greatly encouraged and inspired by the victory of the October Revolution in Russia, and he successively published articles such as "A Comparison of the French and Russian Revolutions", "The Victory of the Common People", and "The Victory of Bolshevism". He was intensely nationalistic before he embraced Marxism, and he was China's earliest self-converted communist dedicated to promoting Marxism. After the May Fourth Movement in 1919, Li Dazhao became more committed to the spread of Marxism, publishing "My View on Marxism" in the *New Youth*, which provided a comprehensive introduction to Marxist theory and had widespread influence among intellectual circles, preparing the ideological conditions for the founding of the CPC.

1920年秋,李大钊领导建立了北京的共产党早期组织和北京社会主义青年团,积极推动建立全国范围的共产党组织。中国共产党成立后,李大钊代表党中央指导北方的工作,在北方广大地区宣传马克思主义,开展工人运动,建立党的组织。1922年至1924年,他受党的委托,奔走于北京、上海、广州之间,帮助孙中山改组国民党,为第一次国共合作的实现作出重大贡献。

In the autumn of 1920, Li Dazhao started China's earliest communist and socialist groups in Beijing and actively promoted the establishment of nationwide Communist Party organizations. After the founding of the CPC, Li Dazhao, representing the CPC Central Bureau, spread Marxism in the vast areas of the north, launched the workers' movement, and established party organizations. From 1922 to 1924, he was entrusted by the CPC to travel to Beijing, Shanghai, and Guangzhou, assisting Sun Yat-sen in reorganizing the Kuomintang (hereinafter shortened as KMT) and making a significant contribution to the first KMT-CPC Cooperation.

1927年4月6日,李大钊在北京被捕入狱。在狱中,他备受酷刑,始终严守党的秘密,坚贞不屈、大义凛然。4月28日,李大钊英勇就义,时年38岁。"铁肩担道义,妙手著文章",是李大钊光辉一生的真实写照。李大钊开创的伟大事业和留下的思想遗产永远不可磨灭,他播撒的革命种子已经在中国大地上生根、开花、结果。

On April 6, 1927, Li Dazhao was arrested and imprisoned in Beijing. Although he was horribly tortured in prison, he stayed unyielding and righteous, and refused to reveal the secrets of the CPC. On April 28, Li Dazhao, steadfast in his beliefs, was executed at the age of 38. "Iron shoulders take duties and smart hands write articles" is a realistic portrayal of Li Dazhao's glorious life. The great cause pioneered by Li Dazhao and the ideological legacy he left behind will never be erased, and the revolutionary seeds he sowed have taken root, blossomed and borne fruit in the land of China.

真理的味道非常甜:陈望道翻译《共产党宣言》
The Taste of Truth Is So Sweet: Chen Wangdao's Translation of the *Communist Manifesto*

近代中国,积贫积弱。随着帝国主义的侵略,民族危机日益加深,一批先进知识分子开始转向西方寻求救国之道,陈望道便是其中之一。最初,他主张"实业救国"和"科学救国",希望到欧美留学。1915年,由于费用问题,陈望道的留学目标由欧美改为日本。他先后在早稻田大学、东洋大学、中央大学和东京夜校学习,完成了经济、法律、物理、哲学与文学的课程,毕业于中央大学法科,获法学学士学位。

In the late 19th and early 20th centuries, China was plunged into deepening crisis due to imperialist aggression, leading to widespread poverty and weakness. Faced with this dire situation, a number of progressive intellectuals, including Chen Wangdao, turned to the West in search of solutions to save the nation. At first, Chen Wangdao advocated "saving the nation through industry" and "saving the nation through science", with aspirations to study abroad in Europe or the United States. In 1915, however, he decided to study in Japan instead due to financial constraints. He studied economics, law, physics, philosophy and literature at Waseda University, Toyo University, Chuo University and Tokyo night school successively, obtaining his Bachelor of Laws at Chuo University.

1919年夏,五四运动爆发,陈望道回国投身运动。一日,陈望道接到《民国日报》经理邵力子的来信。邵力子在信中称,《星期评论》周刊主编戴季陶约请陈望道翻译《共产党宣言》,译文将在该刊连载。精通日语英语、汉语功底深厚、具有扎实的马克思主义理论基础,这三个缺一不可的条件,让陈望道成为《共产党宣言》汉译本翻译者的最佳人选。

Chen returned to China just in time for the May Fourth Movement in the summer of 1919 and committed himself to the movement. One day, he received a letter from Shao Lizi, manager of *Minguo Daily*, a newspaper dedicated to promoting the anti-Yuan Shikai campaign. In his letter, Shao said that Dai Jitao, editor-in-chief of the *Weekly Review*, asked Chen Wangdao to translate the *Communist Manifesto* into Chinese, which would be serialized in the journal. With a solid foundation in Chinese, Chen was a polyglot fluent in both Japanese and English, and had a full grasp of the basic Marxist theories. These skills made him suitable to undertake the task.

为了能专心致志地译书,陈望道的一日三餐都是陈母送到柴房。一盏昏暗的煤油灯、《英汉词典》《日汉词典》《共产党宣言》的日译本和英译本分摊在书桌上,陈望道每天字斟句酌地埋头苦译。陈母见他夜以继日地工作,整个人都瘦了一圈,就用糯米包了几个粽子,让他进补身体。母亲将粽子端至柴房时还放了一碟红糖水。过了一会儿,母亲在屋外高声问他是否还需要添些红糖时,他说:"够甜了,够甜了。"而当母亲进来收拾碗碟时,看见陈望道嘴边都是墨汁,红糖水却没有动。原来,他只顾全神贯注工作,把墨汁当作红糖水还全然不知。

In order to concentrate on translating the book, Chen had his mother deliver his meals to the firewood room where he was working. With a dim kerosene lamp, an English-Chinese Dictionary, a Japanese-Chinese Dictionary, and Japanese and English versions of the *Communist Manifesto* on his desk, Chen devoted himself to the translation task day and night. Chen's mother, seeing him working hard and slimming down, felt worried and sent him several Zongzi along with a dish of brown sugar syrup. Moments later, she asked Chen if he needed more sugar. Chen answered, "it's sweet enough." But when she walked into the room to clean up, she saw her son's lip covered with ink. It turned out that Chen unwittingly mistook his ink for the syrup used as a dip for Zongzi.

1920年4月底,陈望道带着《共产党宣言》译稿到上海,准备在《星期评论》连载,但因《星期评论》被迫停刊未能按原计划刊发。陈独秀与共产国际代表维经斯基商议,决定建立"又新印刷所",以"社会主义研究社"的名义出版此书。经李汉俊、陈独秀校稿,1920年8月,《共产党宣言》由上海社会主义研究社列为"社会主义研究小丛书"的第一种,首次刊行问世。初版1000册,封面上的书名"共产党宣言"错印成"共党产宣言",但仍然立刻被抢购一空。9月再版时改正了书名,封面马克思的肖像也从原来的红色改为蓝色。至1926年5月,该书已相继印行17版,传播之广可见一斑。

At the end of April of 1920, Chen Wangdao took his translation of the *Communist Manifesto* to Shanghai to be published in the *Weekly Review*, only to find the journal had been suspended. Chen Duxiu consulted with Vyjingsky, a representative of the Comintern, and decided to establish the "Youxin Printing House" to publish the book as the "Socialist Research Society". After being proofread by Li Hanjun and Chen Duxiu, the first *Communist Manifesto* was published in August 1920, listed by the Shanghai Socialist Research Society as the first of the "Small Series of Socialist Studies". A total of 1,000 copies were printed by the hand-operated press and sold out quickly. However, the original copies had a typographical error on the cover due to the hasty editing. The Chinese title was supposed to be "Gongchandang Xuanyan" [共产党宣言] (*Communist Manifesto*) but it was wrongly printed as "Gongdangchan Xuanyan" [共党产宣言]. This was later corrected in September 1920 with the second edition, which came with a blue cover. By May 1926, the book had been reprinted seventeen times, which demonstrated its widespread dissemination.

陈望道翻译的《共产党宣言》,是中国共产党成立前后在中国传播最早、影响最大的马克思主义著作,为中国共产党的建立和党的早期理论建设做了重要的思想准备。1936年,在陕北保安的窑洞里,毛泽东对美国记者埃德加·斯诺说:"有三本书特别深刻地铭刻在我的心中。"其中一本,便是陈望道翻译的《共产党宣言》。"真理的味道非常甜。"习近平总书记多次讲述了陈望道在翻译《共产党宣言》时"蘸着墨汁吃粽子、还说味道很甜"的故事。

Chen Wangdao's translation of the *Communist Manifesto* is the earliest and most influential Marxist work that spread in China before and after the founding of the CPC. As such it paved the way for the establishment of the CPC and the early theoretical construction of the Party. In 1936, Mao Zedong told the American journalist Edgar Snow in a cave dwelling in Bao'an, Northern Shaanxi, "Three books were especially deeply engraved upon my mind". One of them was the *Communist Manifesto* translated by Chen Wangdao. "The taste of truth is so sweet," quoting Chen's words, General Secretary Xi Jinping has repeatedly told Chen Wangdao's ink-dipping story when translating the *Communist Manifesto*.

缺席一大会议的"南陈北李"去了哪里?
Where Did the Absentees of the First National Congress "Southern Chen and Northern Li" Go?

"南陈北李"指的是中国共产党的主要创始人陈独秀和李大钊。建党时期,陈独秀在上海、广东,而李大钊则在北京从事活动。陈独秀被称为"五四运动的总司令",他发起创办了《新青年》并作为主要编辑宣传新文化和新思想。李大钊是中国共产主义运动的先驱、杰出的无产阶级革命家和中国最早的马克思主义传播者。

"Southern Chen and Northern Li" refers to Chen Duxiu and Li Dazhao, two leading founders of the CPC. In the process of founding the party, Chen Duxiu was actively working in Shanghai and Guangdong, while Li Dazhao worked in Beijing. Chen Duxiu, known as the "commander-in-chief of the May Fourth Movement", initiated the creation of the monthly magazine *New Youth* and worked as chief editor to promote new culture and new thoughts. Li Dazhao was a pioneer of the Chinese communist movement, an outstanding proletarian revolutionary and the earliest promoter of Marxism in China.

陈独秀和李大钊在传播马克思主义、发动和组织工人的过程中,积极开展建党工作。1920 年,陈独秀和李大钊相约分别在北京和上海开展活动,筹建中国共产党。然而,1921 年 7 月在上海召开的中国共产党第一次全国代表大会中,却没有两位同志的身影。作为建党的两个关键人物,为什么会缺席这个有着开天辟地历史意义的会议呢?

Chen Duxiu and Li Dazhao put a great deal of effort in establishing a leading party in the process of disseminating Marxism and mobilizing and organizing workers to carry out movements. In 1920, the two revolutionary pioneers met in Beijing and Shanghai to prepare for the establishment of the CPC. However, at the First National Congress of the CPC held in Shanghai in July 1921, they were absent. What was it that had prevented the two key figures from attending this historic meeting?

原来那时陈独秀正忙于筹款,而李大钊则忙于"讨薪"。陈独秀身为广东政府教育委员会的委员长,正在争取一大笔款项来建设一所大学,公务繁忙很难抽出时间。李大钊除了担任北京大学图书馆主任、教授外,还兼任北京国立大专院校教职员代表联席会议主席。由于北洋军阀政府财政困难,停发了北京八所高校教职员工的薪金,李大钊作为八所高校"索薪委员会"的重要成员,忙于追讨北京八所高校教职员工的工资,也无法亲自前往上海出席会议。

It turned out that Chen Duxiu was busy raising funds at that time, while Li

Dazhao was busy demanding unpaid wages. Chen Duxiu, head of the education board of the provincial government in Guangzhou, had a busy schedule vying for a large sum of money to build a university. Li Dazhao, in addition to serving as a professor and the chief librarian of Peking University, was the chairman of the joint meeting of faculty representatives of Beijing national colleges and universities. Due to the financial difficulties of the Northern Warlord government, the salaries of the faculty and staff of the eight colleges and universities in Beijing were suspended. Li Dazhao was a leading figure in the "Unpaid Wage Demanding Committee". Therefore, he could not personally go to Shanghai to attend the meeting.

尽管"南陈北李"都没有参加一大，但这无损于他们作为中国共产党主要创始人的卓越贡献。1936年，毛泽东在陕北保安的窑洞里与来访的美国记者埃德加·斯诺谈话时说："1921年5月，我到上海去出席共产党成立大会。在这个大会的组织上，起领导作用的是陈独秀和李大钊，他们两个人都是中国最有才华的知识界领袖。我在李大钊手下担任国立北京大学图书馆助理员的时候，就迅速地朝着马克思主义的方向发展。陈独秀对于我在这方面的兴趣也是很有帮助的。我第二次到上海去的时候，曾经和陈独秀讨论我读过的马克思主义书籍。陈独秀谈他自己的信仰的那些话，在我一生中可能是关键性的这个时期，给我留下了深刻的印象。"毛泽东等一大代表没有忘记"南陈北李"，全中国人民也将永远铭记他们的伟大功绩。

Although Chen Duxiu and Li Dazhao did not attend the historic meeting in person, their outstanding contributions as the main founders of the CPC were nationally recognized. In 1936, Mao Zedong told the visiting American journalist Edgar Snow in a cave dwelling in Bao'an, Northern Shaanxi, "In May of 1921, I went to Shanghai to attend the founding meeting of the Communist Party. In its organization, the leading roles were played by Chen Duxiu and Li Dazhao, both of whom were among the most brilliant intellectual leaders of China. Under Li Dazhao, as assistant Librarian at Peking National University, I had rapidly developed toward Marxism, and Chen Duxiu had been instrumental in my interests in that direction too. I had discussed with Chen, on my second visit to

Shanghai, the Marxist books that I had read, and Chen's own assertions of belief had deeply impressed me at what was probably a critical period of my life." Mao Zedong and the other deputies would never forget the contributions that "Southern Chen and Northern Li" had made, nor will all the people in China.

"此面被上海法捕房没收去了"
"This Page Has Been Confiscated by the Shanghai French Concession Police"

《共产党》月刊于1920年11月7日在上海创刊,是上海共产主义小组主办的理论刊物,由李达主编。该刊是中国共产党的第一个党刊,在中国历史上第一次喊出了"共产党万岁""社会主义万岁"的口号。刊物为16开本,每期约50页,半公开编辑出版,最高发行量达5000余份,一年后停刊,共出版发行了6期。这份杂志选定11月7日为创刊之日,是经过仔细考虑的。三年前,即1917年11月7日,正是俄国劳工农民推倒资本家和军阀,组织苏维埃共和国的成功日,也就是十月革命纪念日。选择十月革命三周年的纪念日作为《共产党》月刊的创刊日,就是希望中国革命走俄国革命的道路。

The *Communist Party*, a monthly theoretical journal edited by Li Da and sponsored by Chen Duxiu's Shanghai Communist Group, started publication in Shanghai on November 7, 1920. It was the first official journal of the CPC, and for the first time in Chinese history, the slogans "Long live the Communist Party" and "Long live socialism" were publicly proclaimed. It was 26 centimeters in length and 19 centimeters in width, and each issue consisted of about 50 pages. Though it was a semi-public journal, its highest circulation reached more than 5,000 copies for one single issue. One year later, it was discontinued, after a total of six issues were published. It can hardly be accidental that the inaugural issue of the *Communist Party* was dated November 7, coinciding with the three-year anniversary of the Russian October Revolution. It was the day when the Russian peasants successfully overthrew capitalists and warlords and established the Union of Soviet Socialist Republics. The careful choice of the anniversary date of the October Revolution expressed the editors' hope that China would follow the path of the Russian revolution.

《共产党》月刊是一份既秘密又公开的新杂志。说它秘密,是因为这份新杂志的编辑部地址保密,杂志上所有文章一律署化名,杂志的印刷、发行者也保密。说它公开,则因为这份杂志的要目广告,公开刊登在《新青年》杂志上,也就使这份新杂志广为人知。《共产党》月刊在1920年12月出版了第二期,因经费困难,直到1921年4月才出版了《共产党》月刊的第三期。第三期全文发表了第三国际第二次代表大会通过的《加入第三国际大会的条件》这个重要的历史文件,系统地论述了列宁的建党思想,指出列宁的建党思想正是治疗中国痼疾的灵丹妙药。然而,这一期《共产党》月刊一开篇就开了个大"天窗",刊物的第一页没有文章的原文,而是印了12个大号铅字"此面被上海法捕房没收去了"。这是为什么呢?

The *Communist Party* was a new journal that was both secret and public. It was secret because the addresses of the editorial office and the printing house, as well as the names of the publishers, were unrevealed. Additionally, all the articles were published under pseudonyms. It was public because its main advertisement was published in the journal *New Youth*, making it known to the public. The second issue was published in December 1920. But due to financial difficulties, the third issue did not come out until April 1921, in which the full text of the historically important document "Conditions for Joining the Comintern" was published. This document systematically expounded Lenin's thoughts on party building and pointed out that Lenin's thoughts were precisely the panacea for curing China's "chronic diseases". However, the first page of this issue printed nothing but 12 large Chinese characters stating "This page has been confiscated by the Shanghai French Concession Police". What could be the reason?

原来,第三期《共产党》月刊在出版印刷时,遭到法租界巡捕房的干扰,原计划刊登的文章《告中国的农民》被当时的法国巡捕房收走了。当原文被法国巡捕房收走后,编辑部商量决定照常开印,留一页空白开天窗,以此告知读者,这是反动势力没收该刊稿件的有力证明,也表达了刊物对此的强烈抗议。

It turned out that when the third issue of the *Communist Party* was being printed, some policemen from the French Concession appeared and confiscated the article "A Letter to the Peasants in China" that was originally planned to be published on the first page. The editorial department decided to continue the printing, leaving the first page blank so as to inform the readers of the strong proof that reactionary forces confiscated the manuscript. In this way they expressed their strong protestation.

《共产党》月刊虽然只出版了六期,但它通过对俄国共产党的发展历程、俄国社会主义制度的介绍,以及在驳斥无政府主义、机会主义的过程中,旗帜鲜明地回答了"建设什么样的党""如何建设党""半殖民地半封建的中国社会往何处去"等一系列问题。可以说,《共产党》月刊是为了完成建立中国共产党这一光荣的历史任务而创办的,它为建党所做的宣传,为将全国各地的共产主义小组组成一个统一的党作出了不可磨灭的贡献,为党的建立提供了充足的理论准备。

Although the monthly journal *Communist Party* only published six issues, it made an indelible contribution to the unification of communist groups throughout the country into a united party and provided sufficient theoretical preparation for the establishment of the CPC. It introduced the development of the Russian Communist Party, and the Socialist system in Russia. It refuted anarchism and opportunism and took a clear-cut stand in answering a series of questions such as "what kind of party should be built", "how to build the party", and "where is the semi-colonial and semi-feudal Chinese society going". It can be said that the *Communist Party* was created to accomplish the glorious historic mission of establishing the Communist Party of China.

"红船"的故事
Story of the Red Boat

1921年7月23日,中国共产党第一次全国代表大会在上海法租界望志路106号秘密召开。7月30日晚,大会第六次会议刚刚开始,法租界巡捕突然闯入,会议被迫中断。此后,一大代表李达的夫人王会悟女士提出能否转移到嘉兴,代表们以游客的身份一边游湖一边开会的建议,这个建议得到了代表们的认可。

On July 23, 1921, the First National Congress of the CPC was held secretly at No. 106 Wangzhi Road in the French Concession of Shanghai. On the evening of July 30, when the sixth meeting of the Congress had just begun, two policemen from the French Concession suddenly broke in, interrupting the meeting. Wang Huiwu, wife of delegate Li Da, suggested transferring to Jiaxing and continuing the meeting as tourists. This suggestion was readily accepted by the delegates.

1921年8月1日，部分代表与王会悟先行来到嘉兴，住在市内张家弄的鸳湖旅馆内，并委托旅馆账房在嘉兴南湖租下一艘用于开会的画舫船，而其余代表则于第二天乘坐早班火车到达嘉兴。8月2日代表们从嘉兴东门的狮子汇渡口摆渡登上湖心岛，来到烟雨楼观测地形，最终选取了烟雨楼东南方向200米处的僻静水域，一边游湖一边开会。

On August 1, 1921, some of the delegates and Wang Huiwu went to Jiaxing and stayed at the Yuanhu Hotel in Zhangjia lane. Wang entrusted the hotel to rent a pleasure boat on the Nanhu Lake. After the other delegates arrived on a morning train the next day, they went on to the island in the middle of the lake by boat and checked the surroundings around the Yanyulou building on the island. Finally, the delegates decided to continue their meeting on the pleasure boat some 200 meters southeast off the building.

会议从上午11点一直持续到下午6点，审议通过了中国共产党的第一个纲领和第一个决议，并以无记名投票的方式选举产生了党的领导机构——中央局。会议结束时，与会代表全体起立，坚定地举起右手，庄严地宣告中国共产党诞生。"共产党万岁！第三国际万岁！共产主义万岁！"中国革命的航船自此扬帆起航。这艘中共一大用过的小船，后来被称作"红船"。

The meeting lasted from 11 a.m. to 6 p.m., during which the delegates reviewed and adopted the CPC's inaugural Program and Resolution. Moreover, the party's leading body — the Central Bureau — was established through a secret ballot. At the end of the meeting, all the delegates stood up, firmly raised their right hands, and solemnly announced the birth of the CPC. "Long live the

Communist Party! Long live the Third International! Long live communism!" The ship of the Chinese revolution has since set sail. This small boat, which witnessed the First National Congress, was later referred to as the "Red Boat".

第三节　红色景点
Section Ⅲ　Red Tourism Attractions

中国共产党第一次全国代表大会纪念馆
The Memorial of the First National Congress of the CPC

中国共产党第一次全国代表大会纪念馆,简称中共一大纪念馆,位于上海市黄浦区黄陂南路。1952年9月,中国共产党第一次全国代表大会会址被改建为纪念馆。1961年3月,被国务院列为第一批全国重点文物保护单位。1997年6月成为全国爱国主义教育示范基地。2016年9月入选中国第一批20世纪建筑遗产名录。

图1-1　上海中国共产党第一次全国代表大会纪念馆
Figure 1-1　The Memorial of the First National Congress of the CPC

The Memorial of the First National Congress of the CPC is located on South Huangpi Road in the Huangpu District of Shanghai. In September 1952, the site of the First National Congress of the CPC was converted into a memorial. In March 1961, the State Council proclaimed the memorial as a National Key

Cultural Relics Protection Unit. In June 1997, it was named a National Patriotism Education Demonstration Base. In September 2016, it was included in "the First Heritage List for Architecture Built in the 20th Century".

2021年6月3日,在庆祝建党百年之际,中共一大纪念馆新馆经过600多个日日夜夜的精心建设,终于以崭新的风貌展现在世人面前。一大纪念馆和一大会址隔街相望,交相辉映。新馆展陈面积约3700平方米,包括基本陈列展厅、报告厅、观众服务中心等设施,提供了更丰富、更完备、更充足的展陈空间。新馆从馆藏12万件(套)文物和近年来从国际国内新征集的档案史料中精挑细选612件文物展品,加上各类图片、艺术展项等展品,展品总量1168件,其中包含国家一级文物30多件。

On June 3, 2021, right before the celebration of the centenary of the CPC, the newly built memorial hall was opened to public. After more than 600 days' meticulous construction, the glorious memorial hall stands across the street where the Site of the First National Congress is located. The memorial hall has an exhibition space of 3,700 square meters, including basic exhibition halls, lecture halls, visitor service centers and other facilities. On display are 612 relics carefully chosen from a collection of 120,000 housed cultural relics (sets) and some newly collected archival historical materials from China and abroad in recent years. Among them are over 30 national first-class cultural relics. The total number of exhibits is 1,168, including various pictures and art exhibits.

走进新馆,映入眼帘的首先是三幅巨大的瓷板画。其创作历时九个月,由《日出东方》《民族脊梁》《中流砥柱》三幅作品组成。以祖国雄伟壮丽的自然山川、凝练文化精神的历史景观、见证奋斗征程的革命旧址艺术性地诠释党领导人民自强不息、砥砺奋进的光辉历程。

Stepping into the hall, visitors find themselves in a large lobby and surrounded by three huge ceramic paintings named *Sunrise in the East*, *National Backbone* and *Mainstay*, whose creation took nine months. Depicting the majestic natural mountains and rivers of China, the historical landscape of condensing the cultural spirit, and the revolutionary sites that witnessed the journey of Chinese people's struggle, the paintings artistically interpreted the glorious course of the CPC in leading the Chinese people to rejuvenation with unremitting efforts and strong determination.

三幅画相互呼应,形成空间整体,将艺术画作与党史历程和精神相结合,不仅使参观者了解到我们党从"小小红船"到"巍巍巨轮"、从九死一生到蓬勃兴旺的奋斗历程,更从中感悟到我们党"不忘初心、牢记使命、永远奋斗"的精神。

The three paintings resonate each other, creating a unified space that intertwines artistic expression with the historical journey and spirit of the CPC. Not only do they allow visitors to perceive the CPC's journey from a "small red boat" to a "majestic ship" and its struggle from the brink of collapse to flourishing prosperity, but also inspire a deeper appreciation of the party's enduring spirit of "staying true to the original aspiration and the founding mission, and never cease striving".

中共一大纪念馆新馆地下一层是《伟大的开端——中国共产党创建历史陈列》基本陈列展厅。展览以"初心使命"贯穿全篇,共分为序厅、"前仆后继、救亡图存""民众觉醒、主义抉择""早期组织,星火初燃""开天辟地、日出东方""砥砺前行、光辉历程"和尾厅7个板块,综合采用文物实物、图片图表、动态视频、油画雕塑、实景还原、多媒体声像等多种展示手段,全面、系统、生动地展示了中国共产党的诞生和发展历程。从新文化运动,到五四运动、马克思主义早期传播、共产党早期组织的成立、中共一大会议及代表,乃至中共二大、第一次工人运动高潮等建党前后的珍贵文献、照片、实物,甚至不少平日难得一见的小众红色文物,都一一被挖掘展示出来。

The basement floor of the new hall is dedicated to permanent exhibits featuring the founding of the CPC. Entitled "Epoch-Making Beginnings—Exhibition of CPC's Founding", the exhibition highlights "CPC's original aspiration and mission", which is divided into seven sections including the preface hall, "Struggle for national survival", "Public awakening and rising interest in Marxism", "Early party groups mushrooming", "Emergence and rise of the CPC", "Forging ahead for a glorious course" and the final hall. Historical objects, pictures, charts, dynamic video projections, oil paintings, sculptures, scenic reproductions, multimedia, and other display media are incorporated to tell the vivid story of the birth and development of the CPC. Many precious and rarely seen historical relics are displayed, featuring the New Culture Movement, the May Fourth Movement, the early spread of Marxism, the early organizations of the Communist Party, the First National Congress of the CPC and the delegates, the Second National Congress of the CPC, and even the first wave of the Chinese Labor Movement.

中国共产党第一次全国代表大会会址
The Site of the First National Congress of the CPC

中共一大会址位于上海原法租界望志路106号(今兴业路76号),建于1920年秋。此楼坐北朝南,一楼一底,使用沿街砖木结构,是一幢典型的上海石库门风格建筑。建成后不久,即被李汉俊及其兄李书城租用为寓所。1921年7月23日,中国共产党第一次全国代表大会就在楼下一间18平方米的客厅内召开。

图1-2 中国共产党第一次全国代表大会会址
Figure 1-2 The Site of the First National Congress of the CPC

The Site of the First National Congress of the CPC is located at No. 106 Wangzhi Road (now No. 76 Xingye Road) in the former French Concession in Shanghai. Built in the autumn of 1920, the two-floor shikumen brick-and-wood building sits north and faces south. Soon after its completion, it was rented and used as an apartment by Li Hanjun, a delegate to the Congress, and his brother Li Shucheng. On July 23, 1921, the First National Congress of the CPC was held in an 18-square-meter living room downstairs.

会址还原了一大召开时的实景,客厅正中是一张长方形的西式大餐桌,桌上摆放着茶具、花瓶和紫铜烟缸。客厅内的餐桌、圆凳、茶几、椅子等家具陈设均按有关当事人的回忆照原样仿制,使观众有身临其境之感。其中陈列室内还按照历史资料开辟了一个蜡像室,形象地刻画出当年出席中共"一大"会议的15位出席者(包括2位共产国际代表)围桌而坐、热烈讨论的生动场景。栩栩如生的蜡像人物增强了陈列的直观性和历史感染力,成为参观中的新热点。

The site was restored to its 1921 appearance. In the middle of the living room is a large rectangular Western-style dining table with tea sets, vases and copper ashtrays. The furniture such as the dining table, the round stools, the coffee table, and chairs are placed where they were on the day of the historic meeting, creating a sense of immersion for the visitors. According to historical materials, a room with wax figures was opened up in the exhibition room, which vividly depicts the lively scene of 15 participants (including two representatives of the Comintern) sitting around the table and having a heated discussion. The lifelike wax figures enhance the visualization and historical appeal of the display and have become a new hot spot for visitors.

南湖革命纪念馆
Nanhu Revolutionary Memorial Hall

为纪念中国共产党第一次全国代表大会在嘉兴南湖胜利闭幕这一重大历史事件,党中央和浙江省委决定设立嘉兴南湖革命纪念馆。1959年10月1日,纪念馆正式成立。2011年6月30日,在建党90周年前夕,南湖革命纪念馆新馆正式落成。

图 1-3　嘉兴南湖革命纪念馆
Figure 1-3　Nanhu Revolutionary Memorial Hall

In order to commemorate the historic event of the successful closure of the First National Congress of the CPC, the CPC Central Committee and the Zhejiang Provincial Party Committee decided to build the Nanhu Revolutionary Memorial Hall. On October 1, 1959, the memorial hall was officially established and opened to public. The construction of a new memorial hall was officially completed just in time to mark the 90th anniversary of the founding of the CPC on June 30, 2011.

南湖革命纪念馆新馆由"一主两副"三幢建筑组成，呈"工"字造型，建筑面积19633平方米，展陈面积达7794平方米，具有陈列展览、文物库房、多媒体演示、学术报告厅等功能。

The new hall is composed of three buildings, one main building and two auxiliary buildings forming the shape of the Chinese character "Gong" [工]. With a construction area of 19,633 square meters and an exhibition area of 7,794 square meters, it includes exhibition rooms, cultural relics storage areas, multimedia presentation facilities, academic lecture halls, and more.

南湖革命纪念馆新馆展陈内容将分两大篇章：一是"开天辟地"，讲述世界资本主义的兴起和对外侵略，鸦片战争以后中国逐步沦为半殖民地半封建社会，中华民族的苦难、抗争，志士仁人救国图存的艰辛探索，主要展示中国共产党早期领导人和"一大"代表们的经历及会议概况，使广大党员、人民群众、社会各界明白中国共产党的诞生和发展壮大是中国近现代史发展的必然结果。

The exhibition of the new Nanhu Revolution Memorial Hall is divided into two major parts. The first part—"Epoch-Making Events"—mainly recounts the stories of the early leaders of the Communist Party and the delegates to the first National Congress who arduously explored ways to save the Chinese people from the suffering in the Opium War and the aggression of many Western powers when China was turned into a semi-colonial and semi-feudal society. Visiting this exhibition, members of the CPC, the general public, and people from all walks of life can understand that the inception, development and expansion of the CPC are the inevitable outcome of the evolution of China's modern and contemporary history.

二是"光辉历程",以中国共产党建党以后的重要史实为节点展示党带领全国各族人民艰苦奋斗取得的光辉成就。让参观者能迅即饱览党领导的波澜壮阔、气势磅礴的革命、建设、改革历程,深刻感受到社会主义基本政治制度、中国特色社会主义道路就是中国各族人民的正确选择,是实现民族复兴的必由之路。

The second part—"Glorious Course"—chronologically displays the glorious achievements of the CPC since its founding. Visitors can quickly comprehend the magnificent course of revolution, construction, and reform of the CPC. They can deeply understand that it was the right choice of the people of all ethnic groups in China to adopt socialism as the basic political system. It highlights the inevitable path of socialism with Chinese characteristics and underscores that this choice is the only way to realize national rejuvenation.

整个展陈以"开天辟地——中国共产党诞生"这一历史事件为核心,以党的"一大"为重点,向前延伸至中国近代史,向后延伸至中国当代史。除了照片、文字这些传统的展陈手法之外,新馆更多地运用了雕塑、场景复原、油画、三维立体影像、多媒体系统、触摸屏等新手法进行展陈,生动展示了中国革命的磅礴气势和艰苦卓绝,富有历史的震撼力。

Taking the historical event of "Epoch-Making Event—The Birth of the CPC" as the core, the entire exhibition focuses on the first National Congress, and also displays featured events in China's modern history and contemporary times. In addition to traditional exhibition techniques such as photography and text, the new halls employ other techniques and technologies including sculptures, scenes, oil paintings, three-dimensional images, multimedia systems, and touch screens, vividly demonstrating the grand momentum and the incredible hardships of the Chinese revolution, leaving visitors deeply moved by its powerful historical impact.

专栏1：伟大建党精神

Special Column Ⅰ: The Great Founding Spirit of the CPC

2021年7月1日，习近平总书记在庆祝中国共产党成立100周年大会上的重要讲话中指出："一百年前，中国共产党的先驱们创建了中国共产党，形成了坚持真理、坚守理想，践行初心、担当使命，不怕牺牲、英勇斗争，对党忠诚、不负人民的伟大建党精神，这是中国共产党的精神之源。一百年来，中国共产党弘扬伟大建党精神，在长期奋斗中构建起中国共产党人的精神谱系，锤炼出鲜明的政治品格。历史川流不息，精神代代相传。我们要继续弘扬光荣传统、赓续红色血脉，永远把伟大建党精神继承下去、发扬光大！"

On July 1, 2021, President Xi Jinping pointed out in his Speech at the Ceremony Marking the Centenary of the Communist Party of China, "A hundred years ago, the pioneers of Communism in China established the CPC and developed the great founding spirit of the Party, which is comprised of the following principles: upholding truth and ideals, staying true to our original aspiration and founding mission, fighting bravely without fear of sacrifice, and remaining loyal to the Party and faithful to the people. This spirit is the Party's source of strength. Over the past hundred years, the Party has carried forward this great founding spirit. Through its protracted struggles, it has developed a long line of inspiring principles for Chinese Communists and tempered a distinct political character. As history has kept moving forward, the spirit of the Party has been passed on from generation to generation. We will continue to promote our glorious traditions and sustain our revolutionary legacy, so that the great founding spirit of the Party will always be kept alive and carried forward."

伟大建党精神是中国共产党人精神谱系的历史源头。在新民主主义革命时期，中国共产党团结带领人民浴血奋战、百折不挠，推翻了三座大山，建立了中华人民共和国，铸就了井冈山精神、长征精神、遵义会议精神、延安精神、红岩精神、西柏坡精神等。

社会主义革命和建设时期,党团结带领人民自力更生、发愤图强,确立了社会主义基本制度,推进了社会主义建设,铸就了抗美援朝精神、红旗渠精神、大庆精神和铁人精神、雷锋精神、焦裕禄精神、"两弹一星"精神等。

The great founding spirit of the Party is the historical source of the intellectual genealogy of the Chinese Communists. In the period of the New-democratic Revolution, the Party united and led the Chinese people, through bloody battles and unyielding struggles, to the successful overthrow of imperialism, feudalism, and bureaucrat-capitalism and the historic founding of the People's Republic of China. This period witnessed the formation of the Jinggangshan Spirit, the Long March Spirit, the Spirit of Zunyi Meeting, the Yan'an Spirit, the Hongyan Spirit and the Xibaipo Spirit.

During the period of socialist revolution and construction, the Party united and led the Chinese people, through a spirit of self-reliance and a desire to build a stronger China, to establish the basic socialist system and promote socialist construction. The joint efforts forged the Spirit of the War to Resist US Aggression and Aid Korea, the Spirit of the Red Flag Canal, the Daqing Spirit (the Iron Man Spirit), the Lei Feng Spirit, the Jiao Yulu Spirit, and the Spirit of "Two Bombs and One Satellite".

改革开放和社会主义现代化建设新时期,党团结带领人民解放思想、锐意进取,开创、坚持、捍卫、发展了中国特色社会主义,铸就了特区精神、抗洪精神、抗击"非典"精神、载人航天精神、抗震救灾精神等。

中国特色社会主义新时代,党团结带领人民自信自强、守正创新,推动党和国家事业取得历史性成就、发生历史性变革,铸就了探月精神、新时代北斗精神、脱贫攻坚精神等。

In the new period of reform and opening up, as well as socialist modernization, the Party united and led the people to emancipate their minds and forgeahead, creating, upholding, defending, and developing socialism with Chinese characteristics. Their brave endeavors gave rise to the Spirit of the Special Economic Zones, the Spirit Forged in Combating Floods, the Spirit of Persistence in Combating SARS, the Spirit of the Manned Space Program, and the Spirit of Disaster Relief.

In the new era of socialism with Chinese characteristics, the Party has united and led the Chinese people, through a spirit of self-confidence, self-reliance, and innovating on the basis of what has worked in the past, to propel the cause of the Party and the country toward historic achievements and changes. The Lunar Exploration Spirit, the Beidou Spirit in the New Era, and the spirit of Poverty Alleviation are fostered in this period.

这一系列伟大精神,是中国共产党在完成不同历史任务中弘扬伟大建党精神的具体表现,共同构筑起中国共产党人的精神谱系。

This series of great spirits has concretely manifested how CPC carried forward the great founding spirit of the Party in accomplishing different historical tasks and jointly built up the spiritual genealogy of Chinese communists.

第二章 江西:革命摇篮 红都瑞金

Chapter II Jiangxi: The Cradle of the Revolution with Ruijin as the Capital

江西,这是一个充满红色记忆和红色传奇的地方。在16.69万平方公里的赣鄱大地上,散布着一个个红色的经典称号与地名:中国革命的摇篮——井冈山、军旗升起的地方——南昌、中国工人运动的策源地——安源、共和国的摇篮——瑞金……江西这片红土圣地,到处红旗漫卷、红星闪闪、红歌嘹亮,红色故事口口相传。

Jiangxi is a place full of red memories and red legends. In these 166,900 square kilometers of land, there are many red classic titles and places scattered around: the cradle of the Chinese revolution—Jinggangshan; the place where the military flag was raised—Nanchang; the birthplace of the Chinese labor movement—Anyuan; the cradle of the Republic—Ruijin… In this glorious land, Jiangxi, red flags fly, red stars glitter, red songs are sung clearly and loudly, and red stories are passed down by word of mouth from generation to generation.

第一节 历史回眸
Section Ⅰ A Glimpse of History

第一次国共合作和北伐战争
The First KMT-CPC Cooperation and the Northern Expedition

20世纪20年代初,为推翻帝国主义和北洋军阀在中国的统治,正在苦苦寻找正确革命道路的孙中山,得到了共产国际、苏俄和中国共产党的真诚帮助。他接受共产国际代表马林等人的建议,欢迎中国共产党同他合作,同意共产党以个人身份加入国民党。中国共产党方面也于1923年6月在广州召开第三次全国代表大会,集中讨论了共产党员加入国民党的问题,确立了国共合作的方针。

In the early 1920s, in order to overthrow the rule of the imperialists and the Northern Warlords in China, Sun Yat-sen, who was strenuously seeking the right revolutionary path, received valuable support from the Comintern, the Soviet Union, and the CPC. Following the suggestion from Comintern representatives, Maring and others, Sun Yat-sen extended a welcome to the CPC to cooperate with him and agreed that members of the CPC could join the KMT as individuals. The CPC held the Third National Congress in Guangzhou in June 1923, which focused on the issue of how Communist Party members could join the KMT and established the policy of cooperation between the KMT and the CPC.

1924年1月,中国国民党第一次全国代表大会在广州召开,李大钊、毛泽东等共产党员也参加了会议。大会事实上确立了联俄、联共、扶助农工的三大政策,第一次国共合作正式形成。国共合作实现后,国共两党以广东为革命基地,于1926年7月开始了以推翻军阀黑暗统治、打破帝国主义国家对中国的政治军事控制,使中国人民摆脱苦难为目的的北伐战争。

In January 1924, the First National Congress of the Chinese KMT was held in Guangzhou. Communist Party members, such as Li Dazhao, Mao Zedong, and others, attended the meeting, at which the Three Great Policies—alliance with Russia, cooperation with the CPC, and assistance to peasants and workers—were laid down. The First KMT-CPC Cooperation was formally initiated. After that, the two parties, choosing Guangdong as the revolutionary base, started the Northern Expedition in July 1926 with the aim of overthrowing the dark reign of the warlords, breaking the political and military control of imperialist countries over China, and freeing the Chinese people from suffering.

国共合作的破裂和四一二反革命政变
The End of KMT-CPC Cooperation and the April 12th Counterrevolutionary Coup

北伐战争得到了全国人民的热烈拥护和支持,出师不到十个月就消灭了军阀吴佩孚、孙传芳的主力部队,占领了长江以南的大部分地区,沉重打击了封建军阀和帝国主义在中国的统治。特别是叶挺领导的、以共产党员为主力的第四军独立团冲锋在前,英勇无比,为第四军赢得了"铁军"称号。

Warmly supported by the people of the whole country, the Northern Expedition wiped out the main forces of the warlords Wu Peifu and Sun Chuanfang, and occupied most of the areas of south Yangtze River within ten months. It dealt a heavy blow to the rule of the feudal warlords and imperialists in China. In particular, the Independent Regiment of the Fourth Army, led by Ye Ting and mainly composed of the members of the CPC, charged ahead with great courage. This earned them the title of "Iron Army".

但是,随着形势的发展,国民党右派敌视共产党,破坏国共合作的面目日益暴露出来。1927年4月12日,蒋介石在上海发动反革命政变,300多名共产党员和革命群众被杀,500多人被捕,5000多人失踪。随后,江苏、浙江、安徽、福建、广东、广西等省都发生了屠杀共产党人和革命群众的惨案。4月18日,蒋介石在南京另行成立"国民政府"。7月15日,以汪精卫为首的武汉国民政府也背叛了革命,大规模逮捕杀害共产党人。至此,国共合作彻底破裂,大革命宣告失败,中国出现了白色恐怖的局面。

However, as the situation developed, the hostility of the right wing of the KMT to the CPC and their idea of undermining the KMT-CPC cooperation was increasingly exposed. On April 12, 1927, Chiang Kai-shek launched the counter-revolutionary coup in Shanghai, leaving more than 300 communists and revolutionaries killed, over 500 arrested, and approximately 5,000 missing. Subsequently, massacres of communists and revolutionaries took place in Jiangsu, Zhejiang, Anhui, Fujian, Guangdong, Guangxi and other provinces. On April 18, Chiang Kai-shek established a separate "Nationalist Government" in

Nanjing. On July 15, the Wuhan Nationalist Government headed by Wang Jingwei also betrayed the revolution, arresting and killing the communists extensively. Thus KMT-CPC cooperation entirely broke down. The Great Revolution ended in failure, leading to the onset of White terror in China.

南昌起义
Nanchang Uprising

面对国民党的白色恐怖,中国共产党人为挽救革命进行了英勇顽强的斗争。1927年8月1日,周恩来、贺龙、叶挺、朱德、刘伯承等发动并领导了南昌起义。经过4个多小时的激战,起义军打败了国民党的军队,占领了南昌。随后,起义军根据中央的计划撤离南昌,向广东进军,准备重建广东革命根据地。这一计划由于受到敌人的围攻而失败。南昌起义打响了武装反抗国民党反动派的第一枪。南昌城头的枪声,像划破夜空的一道闪电,标志着中国共产党独立领导革命、创建人民军队和武装夺取政权的开端。

Facing the White terror of the KMT, the Chinese communists fought valiantly and tenaciously to save the revolution. On August 1, 1927, Zhou Enlai, He Long, Ye Ting, Zhu De, Liu Bocheng and others launched and led the Nanchang Uprising. After more than four hours of fierce fighting, the insurrectionary army defeated the army of KMT and occupied Nanchang. According to the plan of the central government, the insurrectionary army subsequently evacuated from Nanchang and marched towards Guangdong, preparing to rebuild the Guangdong revolutionary base. However, this plan failed due to the siege of the enemy. The Nanchang Uprising fired the first shot of armed resistance against the KMT reactionaries. The gunshot in Nanchang City, like a bolt of lightning piercing the night sky, marked the beginning of the CPC's independent leadership of the revolution, the creation of the people's army, and the beginning of the armed seizure of power.

八七会议
The August 7th Meeting

1927年8月7日,中共中央在湖北汉口俄租界三教街41号(今鄱阳街139号)召开紧急会议,即八七会议。会议纠正了陈独秀的右倾机会主义错误,确立了开展土地革命和武装反抗国民党反动派的方针,决定在湖南、湖北、江西、广东四省举行秋收起义。出席这次会议的毛泽东在发言中强调:"以后要非常注意军事。须知政权是由枪杆子中取得的。"八七会议是一个转折点,为中国革命指明了新的方向,在中国共产党的历史上有重要意义。

On August 7, 1927, the Central Committee of the CPC held an emergency meeting at No. 41, Sanjiao Street (now No. 139, Poyang Street) in the Russian Concession in Hankou, Hubei province, namely the August 7th Meeting. The meeting corrected Chen Duxiu's right opportunism mistakes, established the policy of carrying out the agrarian revolution and armed resistance against the KMT reactionaries, and decided to start the Autumn Harvest Uprising in Hunan, Hubei, Jiangxi and Guangdong provinces. Mao Zedong, who attended the meeting, emphasized in his speech: "In the future, we must pay great attention to military affairs. We must know that political power lies in the barrel of a gun." The August 7th Meeting was a turning point, which indicated a new direction for the Chinese revolution and was of great significance in the history of the CPC.

秋收起义与井冈山会师
The Autumn Harvest Uprising and Jinggangshan Reunion

八七会议后,1927年9月9日,毛泽东领导了湘赣边界秋收起义,将参加秋收起义的5000余人组建为"工农革命军第一师",第一次公开打出"工农革命军"的旗帜。9月29日,毛泽东领导起义军在江西省永新县三湾村进行了著名的三湾改编,将党的支部建在连上,确立了党对军队的领导。10月,毛泽东带领起义军在湖南、江西两省边界罗霄山脉中段的井冈山建立了第一个农村革命根据地。1928年4月下旬,朱德、陈毅率领南昌起义保留下来的部队和湘南起义的部队来到井冈山,与毛泽东领导的工农革命军会师,成立工农革命军第四军(后改称"工农红军第四军"),朱德任军长,毛泽东任党代表。从此,他们领导的军队被称为"朱毛红军"。毛泽东、朱德在连续打退湘赣两省国民党军队的进攻中,总结出"敌进我退,敌驻我扰,敌疲我打,敌退我追"的游击战术。井冈山会师壮大了井冈山的革命武装力量,对巩固扩大全国第一个农村革命根据地,推动全国革命事业的发展,具有深远的意义。

On September 9, 1927, Mao Zedong led the Autumn Harvest Uprising on the Hunan-Jiangxi border and organized more than 5,000 people for participation in the Autumn Harvest Uprising into the "First Division of the Workers' and Peasants' Revolutionary Army". On September 29, Mao Zedong led the insurrectionary army to start the famous Sanwan Reorganization in Sanwan Village, Yongxin County, Jiangxi province. Party branches started to be organized at the company level, establishing the Party's leadership over the military. Later in October, the first rural revolutionary base, under the leadership of Mao Zedong, was established in Jinggangshan, which is in the middle section of the Luoxiao Mountains on the border of Hunan and Jiangxi provinces. In late April 1928, Zhu De and Chen Yi led the remaining troops from the Nanchang Uprising and the Hunan Uprising to Jinggangshan, where they united with the workers' and peasants' revolutionary army led by Mao Zedong and formed the Fourth Army of the Workers' and Peasants' Revolutionary Army (later renamed as the Fourth Army of the Workers' and Peasants' Red Army), with Zhu De as the army commander and Mao Zedong as the party representative. From then on, the army they led was called the "Red Army of Zhu Mao". While persistently warding off the attacks of the KMT army in Hunan and Jiangxi provinces, Mao Zedong and Zhu De devised the guerrilla tactics of "When the enemy advances, we retreat; when the enemy camps, we harass; when the enemy tires, we fight; and when the enemy retreats, we pursue." The Jinggangshan Reunion strengthened the revolutionary armed forces in Jinggangshan and had far-reaching significance in consolidating and expanding the country's first rural revolutionary base and in promoting the development of the national revolutionary cause.

中华苏维埃共和国的成立
The Founding of the Chinese Soviet Republic

随着斗争的发展,党创建了江西中央革命根据地和湘鄂西、海陆丰、鄂豫皖、琼崖、闽浙赣、湘鄂赣、湘赣、左右江、川陕、陕甘、湘鄂川黔等十余处根据地,得到广大农民的热烈支持和拥护。农民以参加红军为荣,红军规模增加到30万人。毛泽东、朱德领导的红军在连续粉碎敌人的"围剿"中,形成了"避敌主力、诱敌深入、集中优势兵力、各个击破"的战略战术思想。

As the struggle went on, the CPC created the Jiangxi Central Revolutionary Base and more than ten other bases including West Hunan and Hubei; Hailufeng; Hubei, Henan, and Anhui; Qiongya; Fujian, Zhejiang and Jiangxi; Hunan, Hubei and Jiangxi; Hunan and Jiangxi; Zuoyoujiang; Sichuan and Shaanxi; Shaanxi and Gansu; Hunan, Hubei, Sichuan and Guizhou. These revolution bases received strong support from a vast number of peasants who took pride in joining in the Red Army. Therefore, the size of the Red Army increased rapidly to 300,000 people. Mao Zedong and Zhu De led the Red Army in continuously repelling the enemy's encirclement and suppression campaigns, during which they developed a strategic and tactical approach of "avoiding the enemy's main force, luring the enemy in deep, concentrating superior forces, and defeating in detail".

1931年11月7日,就在俄国十月革命14周年纪念日的同一天,中华苏维埃第一次全国代表大会在江西瑞金召开,宣布成立中华苏维埃共和国临时中央政府,定都瑞金;选举毛泽东为中央执行委员会主席和中央执行委员会人民委员会主席,朱德为中央革命军事委员会主席。中华苏维埃共和国是中国历史上第一个全国性的工农民主政权,它的成立谱写了中国共产党领导的革命根据地建设和红色政权建设的新篇章。

On November 7, 1931, the same day as the 14th anniversary of the October Revolution in Russia, the First National Congress of the Chinese Soviet was held in Ruijin, Jiangxi province, which announced the establishment of the Provisional Central Government of the Chinese Soviet Republic and made Ruijin the capital. Mao Zedong was elected as the Chairman of the Central Executive Committee and Chairman of the People's Committee of the Central Executive Committee. Zhu De was elected as the chairman of the Central Revolutionary Military Commission. The Chinese Soviet Republic was the first nationwide democratic regime of workers and peasants in Chinese history. Its establishment composed a new chapter in the construction of revolutionary bases and the construction of the red regime under the leadership of the CPC.

第二节 红色故事
Section II Red Stories

一盏马灯照亮"红带兵"起义之路
A Lantern Illuminates the Uprising Road of the "Soldiers Wearing Red Ties"

"八一大天亮,老百姓早起床,昨夜晚机枪,其格格其格格响啊,它是为哪桩?原来是共产党武装起义,原来是红带兵解决了国民党!"南昌起义胜利后,有这样一首脍炙人口的歌谣《八一起义歌》在民间广为流传。歌谣中所提到的"红带兵"究竟是怎么一回事呢?

"It was dawn on August 1st. The civilians got up early. Last night, the machine guns were rattling. What was it for? It turned out to be an armed uprising of the CPC, and it turned out that the soldiers wearing red ties defeated the KMT!" After the victory of the Nanchang Uprising, a well-known ballad named "Song of the August 1st Uprising" was widely circulated among the people. What exactly does the ballad mean by "soldiers wearing red ties"?

众所周知,每一支军队都会有他们独有的标识,这些标识包括军服、军徽、肩章、军旗以及武器装备等,为的就是到战场上进行交战时敌我识别以及日常的正规化管理。1927年,参加南昌起义的部队主要有贺龙率领的国民革命军第20军、叶挺率领的第11军第24师以及朱德率领的第三军军官教育团部分学生和南昌公安局的两个保安队,再加上蔡廷锴的第10师以及在起义后赶到南昌的第4军第25师。当时这些参加起义的部队大部分名义上还为国民革命军,和敌军一样的穿着国民革命军军服。

It is well-known that for the purpose of distinguishing friends from foes when fighting on the battlefield and regularizing daily management, each army has its unique identifiers including military uniforms, military emblems, epaulets, military flags, and weapons and equipment. In 1927, the troops participating in the Nanchang Uprising were mainly from the 20th Army of the National Revolutionary Army led by He Long; the 24th Division of the 11th Army led by Ye Ting; students of the Officer Education Corps of the Third Army and two security teams of the Nanchang Public Security Bureau led by Zhu De; the 10th Division led by Cai Tingkai; and the 25th Division of the Fourth Army that rushed to Nanchang after the uprising. At that time, most of the troops participating in the uprising were still nominally the National Revolutionary Army, wearing the same uniforms as the enemy troops.

由于南昌起义是在秘密的情况下举行的,为保证战斗能顺利打响,起义时间确定在夜间进行。如何保证起义战士们在夜间也能准确辨认敌我？佩戴既醒目又秘密的标识就显得极为重要。

The Nanchang Uprising was conducted in secrecy, and in order to ensure a smooth initiation of the battle, the Party decided to begin the uprising at night. How to ensure that the soldiers could accurately distinguish their own troops from the enemy at night? It became extremely important to wear identifiers that were both distinguishable and secretive.

于是,胸前佩戴红色领带、左臂扎白毛巾、马灯和水壶上贴上红十字成为起义时战士们辨别敌我的关键。选择红、白两色作为标识颜色,是因为这两种颜色在夜间特别醒目;而选择这几样标识物品,则因为它们都便于携带、便于隐藏、便于佩戴。除此之外,起义军标识还拥有深刻的寓意:红色领带代表着与旧时代的决裂,象征一支红色的军队;马灯是夜间照明工具,预示着南昌起义即将照亮中国革命的新方向。也正因为起义军都佩戴着红领带,当时的南昌老百姓都亲切地称呼他们为"红带兵"。时至今日,《八一起义歌》仍在全国被传唱。

Therefore, wearing a red tie, putting on a white towel on the left arm, and sticking the red cross on the barn lantern and water bottle became the key for the soldiers to distinguish friends from foes during the uprising. The reason to choose red and white as the colors of the identifiers was that they were particularly eye-catching at night; these items were easy to carry, hide, and wear. In addition, the identifiers used by the uprising army also had a profound meaning: the red tie represented a break with the old times, which symbolized a red army; and the barn lantern was a lighting tool, which indicated that the Nanchang Uprising was about to illuminate the new direction of the Chinese revolution. It was because the army wore red ties that the people of Nanchang at that time affectionately called them "Hong Dai Bing" (soldiers wearing red ties). Today, the "Song of the August 1st Uprising" is still widely sung all over the country.

八角楼的灯光
The Light of the Octagon Building

八角楼位于江西井冈山茅坪村,是毛泽东1927年10月至1929年1月期间经常居住和办公的地方,因为屋顶有一个八角形的天窗,故称为"八角楼"。在八角楼,毛泽东当年借着清油灯一根灯芯的微弱灯光,写下《中国的红色政权为什么能够存在?》《井冈山的斗争》两篇重要著作。

The Octagon Building, where Mao Zedong often lived and worked from October 1927 to January 1929, is located in Maoping Village, Jinggangshan, Jiangxi province. With an octagonal skylight on the roof of the building, it is therefore called the "Octagonal Building". In this building, Mao Zedong wrote two significant works in the faint light of an oil lamp: "Why Does China's Red Regime Exist?" and "The Struggle of Jinggangshan".

这两篇著作第一次提出了实行工农武装割据、建立革命红色政权的思想,成为"农村包围城市、武装夺取政权"这条中国革命道路的理论发端,指引中国革命万里征程。这两篇著作的背后,是毛泽东"上山"的心路历程。对毛泽东来说,"上山"这条路是被迫的,是艰难的,也是积极努力的探索。

These two works, for the first time, proposed an idea of implementing the armed separation of workers and peasants and of establishing a revolutionary red regime. The idea became the theoretical foundation of the Chinese revolutionary approach of "encircling cities from the countryside and seizing political power by armed force", guiding the thousand-mile journey of the Chinese revolution. Behind these two works lies Mao Zedong's mental journey of "Going up the mountain". For Mao Zedong, this forced and challenging path was also a scene of active exploration.

1927年9月9日,毛泽东以前敌委员会书记的身份在湖南发动了秋收起义,但由于敌我力量悬殊,起义后按上级要求攻打长沙的计划严重受挫。秋收起义失败后,毛泽东把部队撤到湖南浏阳文家市。摆在毛泽东面前的严峻问题是:把剩下的人带到哪里去? 中国革命向何处去?

On September 9, 1927, Mao Zedong, as the secretary of the Front Committee, launched the Autumn Harvest Uprising in Hunan. However, due to the disparity between their strength and that of the enemy, the attack to Changsha was a terrible defeat. After the failure of the Autumn Harvest Uprising, Mao Zedong withdrew his troops to Wenjia City, Liuyang, Hunan. At that time, Mao Zedong was confronted with two pressing questions: Where should he lead the remaining troops, and what direction should the Chinese revolution take?

毛泽东带着队伍,走上崎岖的山路,来到了井冈山,开始创建井冈山革命根据地。但上山这条路走得很突然,许多人思想一时转不过来。弱小的红军经常面临敌军频繁的军事"会剿"和严密的经济封锁,井冈山斗争遇到了极大困难。不少人感到革命前途渺茫,南昌起义失败了,秋收起义失败了,广州起义也失败了……井冈山能待下去吗?"红旗到底打得多久"的疑问不断出现。

Mao Zedong, together with the troops, walked up the rugged mountain road to Jinggangshan and began to establish the Jinggangshan Revolutionary Base. At that time, however, many people could not understand the sudden decision of going up the mountain. The weak Red Army often faced frequent military suppression campaigns and strict economic blockade by the enemy. Consequently,

第二章 江西：革命摇篮 红都瑞金

the struggle in Jinggangshan encountered great difficulties. The future of the revolution looked bleak as the Nanchang Uprising had failed, the Autumn Harvest Uprising had failed, and the Guangzhou Uprising had also failed... Can Jinggangshan survive? The question of "how long can the Red Army last?" kept emerging.

为从理论上阐明中国革命发展的道路，毛泽东观察形势、总结经验，深入研究思考红色政权理论。山沟沟里的夜晚，八角楼上亮起了一盏灯，毛泽东坐在油灯前通宵达旦奋笔疾书。

In order to theoretically elucidate the developmental path of the Chinese revolution, Mao Zedong observed the situation, summed up experiences, and studied and thought about the theory of the red regime in depth. Every night in the valley, a lamp was lit in the octagonal building. Mao Zedong sat in front of the oil lamp, worked hard, and wrote all night.

1928年10月，毛泽东为中共湘赣边界第二次代表大会起草了会议决议，《中国的红色政权为什么能够存在？》是决议的一部分。毛泽东总结一年来创建井冈山革命根据地的实践经验，透彻地分析了中国国内的政治形势，从五个方面回答了红色政权能够长期存在并发展的原因。1930年1月，毛泽东在总结井冈山革命斗争经验的基础上撰写了《星星之火，可以燎原》，明确提出中国革命必须走"农村包围城市、武装夺取政权"道路，并充满诗意地豪迈指出，中国革命高潮快要到来。

In October 1928, Mao Zedong drafted a conference resolution for the Second Congress of the Hunan-Jiangxi Boundary of the Communist Party of China. "Why Does China's Red Regime Exist?" was part of the resolution. Mao Zedong summed up the practical experience of establishing the Jinggangshan Revolutionary Base in the past year, thoroughly analyzed the domestic political situation in China, and provided the reasons for the long-term existence and development of the red regime from five aspects. In January 1930, Mao Zedong wrote "A Single Spark Can Start a Prairie Fire" based on his experience of Jinggangshan's revolutionary struggle. It clearly stated that the Chinese revolution must follow the path of "encircling cities from the countryside and seizing political power by armed force". Mao Zedong also pointed out poetically and boldly that the upsurge of the Chinese revolution was about to come.

朱德的扁担
Zhu De's Pole

1928年11月中旬,由于湘赣两省国民党军的严密封锁,井冈山根据地同国民党统治区几乎断绝了一切贸易往来,根据地军民生活十分困难,食盐、棉布、药材以及粮食奇缺。红军官兵一日三餐大多是糙米饭、南瓜汤,有时还吃野菜。严冬已到,战士们仍然穿着单衣。

In mid-November 1928, due to the tight lockdown of the KMT army in Hunan and Jiangxi provinces, the trade between the Jinggangshan revolutionary base and the KMT-ruled areas was almost cut off. As salt, cotton cloth, medicines, and food were in short supply, the military and civilians in the base area led a very tough life. Three meals of the Red Army soldiers were mostly brown rice, pumpkin soup, and sometimes wild herbs. Soldiers wore thin clothes even in harsh winter.

为解决根据地军民的粮食问题,红四军司令部发起"挑谷上坳"运动。从井冈山上到山下宁冈的茅坪,上下足有五六十里路,山又高,路又陡,着实难走。那年,朱德已经四十多岁了,但他总是跟着大家一道去挑粮,而且每次都是挑得满满的。大家看到朱军长夜里计划作战大事,白天还要参加劳动,生怕累坏了他,就把他的扁担藏了起来。哪知道朱军长却另找来了一根扁担,在扁担的正中,写上了"朱德的扁担"五个大字。

In order to solve the food problem in the base area, headquarters of the Fourth Front Red Army initiated a movement to carry grain uphill from the foot of the mountain. The fifty-to-sixty-mile mountain road from Maoping, Ninggang at the foot of the mountain to the base area on the top of Jinggangshan Mountain was steep and extremely difficult to get through. Zhu De, who was over forty years old that year, also joined the team to carry grains. At night, Zhu De made battle plans, while in the daytime, he carried grains with a pole and climbed the mountain along with the soldiers. Afraid that he'd become worn out, the soldiers hid Zhu De's pole. Unexpectedly, Commander Zhu went and found another pole, on which he wrote the words "Zhu De De Bian Dan"［朱德的扁担］(Zhu De's Pole).

从此,朱德的扁担再没有人"偷"了。井冈山军民为了永远纪念朱德这种身先士卒、艰苦奋斗的精神,专门编了一首歌赞颂他:"朱德挑谷上坳,粮食绝对可靠,大家齐心协力,粉碎敌人'围剿'。"

Since then, no one "stole" Zhu De's pole again. In order to commemorate Zhu De's pioneering and hard-working spirit, soldiers and civilians of Jinggangshan composed a song to laud him: "When Zhu De carries grain uphill, the food will be absolutely ensured; when everyone works together, the enemy's encirclement and suppression campaigns will be smashed."

八子参军
Eight Sons Joining the Army

杨荣显是瑞金下肖区七堡乡第三村的农民,有八个儿子,分别取名为一生保,二生保,三生保……八生保。红军来之前,杨荣显一家穷得上无片瓦、下无寸地,身穿破衣裳,家无过夜粮。苏维埃政权建立后,杨荣显一家分得了田地、山林,几个儿子也娶上了媳妇,日子过得一天比一天好。但是,国民党反动派多次对苏区发动军事"围剿",企图消灭红军,消灭苏区。特别是第五次"围剿",蒋介石派出50万大军向中央苏区逼近,妄图一举歼灭中央红军。中央苏区的红军人数仅有敌人的五分之一,"扩红"成了当时的重要任务。

Yang Rongxian, a peasant from the third village of Qibao Township, Xiaxiao District, Ruijin, had eight sons named Yi (one) Shengbao, Er (two) Shengbao, San (three) Shengbao... all the way up to Ba (eight) Shengbao. Before the arrival of the Red Army, Yang's family was so poor that they didn't have a roof over their head or a patch of ground to call their own. They wore torn clothes and suffered from food shortages. Not until the establishment of the Soviet regime was Yang's family allotted their distribution of farmland. With life improving day by day, his sons could also get married thereafter. However, in an attempt to eliminate the Red Army and the Soviet area, the KMT reactionaries continued launching several military encirclement and suppression campaigns against the Soviet area. Particularly in the Fifth Encirclement and Suppression Campaign, Chiang Kai-shek mobilized an army of 500,000 to approach the Central Soviet Area, trying to wipe out the Red Army in one fell swoop. Since the size of the Red Army in the Central Soviet Area was only one-fifth of that of its opponents, expanding its military strength became an essential task.

杨荣显响应号召,将八个儿子全部带到了报名处。第一次,杨荣显有五个儿子被部队要下了,另外三个因年龄不够,只能带回家。结果,在激烈的战斗中,他的五个儿子全部战死沙场。在第五次反"围剿"最为激烈的时候,杨荣显又把剩下的三个儿子六生保、七生保和八生保一起送上了前线。"扩红"干部请杨老留下一个儿子照顾家庭。他却说:"不要紧,要上都上。"不久,六生保在广昌战役中不幸牺牲。后来,在宁都黄陂战场,七生保、八生保也壮烈牺牲。

Yang Rongxian responded to the call and brought all eight sons to the registration office. At first, five of Yang's sons were recruited by the army; the other three had to be brought home because they were not old enough. Unfortunately, the five brothers died one after another on the battlefield in the ruthless battles. During the fiercest period of the Fifth Campaign against Encirclement and Suppression, Yang Rongxian sent his remaining three sons (Liu Shengbao, Qi Shengbao and Ba Shengbao) to the front line. The party member in charge of recruiting soldiers persuaded the old man to keep one son at home to look after the family, but Yang said, "It doesn't matter. I want them all to go provide support." Soon, Liu Shengbao died in the Battle of Guangchang. Later, Qi Shengbao and Ba Shengbao also died heroically on the battlefield of Huangpi, Ningdu.

杨荣显一家八子参军的壮举,只是瑞金人民全力支援革命的一个缩影。而当时这样的人更是有千千万万。正是千千万万的苏区群众,用淳朴和热情,表达对革命事业的满腔挚爱。

The feat of Yang Rongxian's eight sons joining the army is just a microcosm of Ruijin people's full support for the revolution. There were tens of thousands of people in the Soviet area like Yang's family, expressing their love and support for the revolutionary cause with simplicity and enthusiasm.

红井的故事:吃水不忘挖井人
The Story of the Red Well: Don't Forget the Well-Digger When You Drink from the Well

在瑞金城外的沙洲坝,有一口中央苏区时期,毛泽东亲自带领干部群众开挖的水井,当地人亲切地称它是"红井"。这口井直径85厘米,深约5米,井壁用鹅卵石砌成。红井至今还能使用,打上来的水清凉甘甜。但是在20世纪三十年代,沙洲坝人能喝上一口这样的井水,是件难事。那时,沙洲坝不仅无水灌田,就连群众喝水也非常困难。1933年4月,中华苏维埃共和国临时中央政府搬到沙洲坝办公后,毛主席偶然发现了这个问题。

In Shazhouba, just outside of Ruijin, there is a well that was dug under the leadership of Mao Zedong during the Central Soviet Area period. The local people affectionately called it "Red Well". The well, with a wall made of pebble, is 85 centimeters in diameter and about 5 meters deep. The Red Well remains functional today and the water it provides is cool and sweet. However, back in the 1930s, drinking such quality well water was of great difficulty for Shazhouba's people. At that time, Shazhouba was lack in water to irrigate the farmland. Also, it was very hard for its people to get clean and drinkable water. In April 1933, after the office of the Provisional Central Government of the Chinese Soviet Republic relocated to Shazhouba, Chairman Mao came across this problem unintentionally.

一天,毛主席看见一个老乡挑着浑浊的水往家里走,就问:"老乡,这水挑来做什么用呀?"老乡回答说:"吃呀!"毛主席疑惑地问:"水这么脏,能吃吗?"老乡苦笑着说:"没法子,再脏的水也得吃呀!"毛主席又问:"是从哪里挑的?"老乡回答:"从塘里挑的。"毛主席请老乡带他去看看。走了一阵,只见一个不大的水塘,杂草丛生,池水污浊。全村人洗衣、洗菜、吃水全在这里。毛主席关切地问："能不能到别处挑水吃？"老乡摇摇头，说："我们沙洲坝就是缺水呀！挑担水要走好几里路。"毛主席皱了皱眉头，若有所思地走了。

One day, seeing a villager carrying muddy water to his house, Chairman Mao greeted him, "Fellow villager, what is this water used for?" The villager replied, "For drinking!" Chairman Mao asked with puzzlement, "It's so muddy. Is it drinkable?" The man said with a wry smile, "We don't have a choice. We need water no matter how dirty it is!" Chairman Mao then asked, "Where is it from?" The man replied, "It's from a pond." Chairman Mao asked the villager to show him where the pond was. After walking for a while, they saw a small pond with muddy water and overgrown weeds. People in the village did their laundry as well as cleaned their vegetables there. Chairman Mao asked with concern, "Can you get water anywhere else?" The man shook his head and said, "Shazhouba is short of water! We walk many miles to carry water." Chairman Mao frowned and walked away thoughtfully.

毛主席找来村里人一起商量挖水井的事。当井位确定后，毛主席挽起衣袖，卷起裤腿，带头挖了起来。于是，大伙挖的挖，铲的铲，干得热火朝天。在挖井的日子里，毛主席和临时中央政府的其他领导人，一有空就到工地参加劳动。经过十几天的奋战，水井挖成了，沙洲坝的人民终于喝上了清澈甘甜的井水。群众激动地说："我们从来没有喝过这么甜的水，毛主席真是我们的大恩人哪！"新中国成立以后，沙洲坝人民在井旁立了一块石碑，上面刻着："吃水不忘挖井人，时刻想念毛主席！"

The next day, Chairman Mao invited the villagers to discuss the idea of digging a well. When the location of the well was determined, Chairman Mao, rolling up his sleeves and the legs of the trousers, took the lead in digging. Everyone worked together, digging and shoveling in full swing. During the daytime, Chairman Mao and other leaders of the central government went to the construction site to help whenever they were free. After ten days of hard work, the job was done and people of Shazhouba finally had clear and sweet well water to drink. The villagers said excitedly, "We have never had such sweet water.

Chairman Mao is really our great benefactor!" After the founding of new China, the people of Shazhouba erected a stone tablet with an inscription beside the well: "Chi Shui Bu Wang Wa Jing Ren, Shi Ke Xiang Nian Mao Zhu Xi."［吃水不忘挖井人,时刻想念毛主席］(Don't forget the well-digger when you drink from the well, and always remember Chairman Mao!)

方志敏与《可爱的中国》
Fang Zhimin and "Lovely China"

方志敏是早期中国革命的领导人之一,1899年生于江西省弋阳县一个世代务农之家,1924年3月加入中国共产党。他是赣东北革命根据地和红军第十军的主要创建人。他"两条半枪闹革命"开创的革命根据地,被毛泽东评价为"方志敏式"的农村革命根据地。

Fang Zhimin was one of the leaders of the early Chinese revolution. He was born into a family that had been farming for generations in Yiyang County, Jiangxi province in 1899. Fang Zhimin joined the CPC in March 1924, and became the main founder of the revolutionary base in northeastern Jiangxi and the 10th Army of the Red Army. The revolutionary base was created by adopting his unique idea, "two and a half guns make revolution"①, and was later evaluated by Mao Zedong as a "Fang Zhimin style" rural revolutionary base.

中央红军开始长征以后,方志敏担任了中国工农红军北上抗日先遣队随军政治委员会主席。1935年1月,组成北上抗日先遣队的红十军团在通过怀玉山封锁线时陷入敌人的重围之中,部队被敌人截成了两节。方志明率领的800余人冲出了包围圈,却发现大部队没有跟上来。作为主要领导的方志敏提出要去寻找被围的部队。另一位负责人说:"你是主要领导,还是让我去吧!"方志敏说:"不行!我没有理由留在这里,我要把战士们带出来!"

After the Central Red Army started the Long March, Fang Zhimin served as

---

① In 1926, Fang Zhimin led a peasant uprising in Qigong town in northeastern Jiangxi. Though poorly equipped, the peasants occupied the local police station and captured three guns, one of which was broken with only a half gun-barrel. Hence the legend has it that Fang Zhimin began the revolution with two and a half guns.

the chairman of the Political Committee of the Northbound Anti-Japanese Advance Team of the Chinese Workers' and Peasants' Red Army. In January 1935, the 10th Red Army, which formed the main force of the Advance Team, came under siege when it was passing the Huaiyu Mountain blockade. The troops were cut into two sections by the enemy. More than 800 soldiers led by Fang Zhimin broke through the encirclement, only to find that most of the troops did not follow. Fang Zhimin, the main leader, proposed to search for the encircled troops. Another officer in charge said: "As you are the key leader, it would be better if I go!" However, Fang Zhimin responded: "No! There is no reason for me to stay put. I must bring our soldiers out!"

1935年1月24日，由于叛徒出卖，方志敏在皖浙赣交界处的陇首村不幸被捕。国民党反动派抓住了方志敏，千方百计想劝降方志敏。劝降失败后，他们开始残酷地折磨方志敏，然而方志敏忍受着巨大的疼痛，毫不动摇。1935年8月6日，方志敏在南昌被国民党反动派杀害，年仅35岁。

On January 24, 1935, due to betrayal, Fang Zhimin was unfortunately arrested in Longshou Village at the junction of Anhui, Zhejiang and Jiangxi province. The KMT reactionaries seized Fang Zhimin and made every attempt to persuade him to surrender. After the failure in persuasion, they began to torture Fang Zhimin brutally. Though suffering enormous pain, Fang Zhimin remained unbroken. On August 6, 1935, he was killed by the KMT reactionaries in Nanchang and died heroically at the age of 35.

在极为艰苦的条件下，方志敏饱含激情和对党的忠诚，在敌人的牢房里写下了《可爱的中国》《清贫》等作品。在《可爱的中国》中，方志敏将祖国称作"美丽的母亲，可爱的母亲"，在文末，他写出了中国革命的光明前景："中国一定有个可赞美的光明前途……到那时，到处都是日新月异的进步，欢歌将代替了悲叹，笑脸将代替了哭脸，富裕将代替了贫穷，健康将代替了疾苦，智慧将代替了愚昧，友爱将代替了仇杀，生之快乐将代替了死之悲哀，明媚的花园，将代替了凄凉的荒地！"

Even under extremely difficult conditions, Fang Zhimin was still full of passion and loyalty to the party. He wrote his masterpieces in the enemy's cell: "Lovely China", "Poverty" and other works. In "Lovely China", Fang Zhimin referred to the motherland as "a beautiful mother, a lovely mother". At the end of the article, he wrote about the bright future of the Chinese revolution: "China will definitely have an admirable bright future…Until then, there will be rapid progress everywhere. Singing will replace lamentation. Smiling faces will replace crying faces. Wealth will replace poverty. Health will replace suffering. Wisdom will replace ignorance. Friendship will replace vendetta. The joy of life will replace the sorrow of death and the bright garden will replace the desolate wasteland!"

十八杆红缨枪
Eighteen Red Tassel Spears

今天的超田村崇下小组,在苏区时属"瑞京"县黄安区(今云石山乡属地)的超田乡。这里居住着欧阳家族。

Today's Dongxia of Chaotian Village originally belonged to Chaotian Township, Huang'an District of "Ruijing" County (now the territory of Yunshishan Township) in the Soviet area. The Ouyang family has lived in Dongxia of Chaotian Village for decades.

1929年初夏,崇下组村民欧阳克淇带着二十余个青壮年到福建泉州贩盐,途经瑞金与长汀交界的九里岭时,遭遇山匪抢劫。危急关头,两名红军骑兵救了他们。离别时,红军排长程昂华从腰间拔出两把扎着红缨的铁家伙,递给欧阳克淇:"这两把没来得及上把的红缨梭镖,送给你们路上防身吧。"

In the early summer of 1929, Ouyang Keqi, a villager from Dongxia, went with 20 young adults to sell salt in Quanzhou, Fujian. When passing through Jiuliling, the border between Ruijin and Changting, they were robbed by bandits. At that critical juncture, two cavalrymen from the Red Army rescued them. When parting, Cheng Anghua, the platoon leader, drew out two iron darts with red tassels from his waist and handed them to Ouyang Keqi. "These are two red tassel darts without a handle yet. I give them to you for self-defense on the road," said

Cheng.

红军的所作所为打动了他们。他们决定学习红军,替穷人撑腰。领头人欧阳克淇提议成立一支红缨枪队,全系上红绸带,从此跟着红军走。说干就干,他们请铁匠打了十六把梭镖,加上程排长送的两把,正好是十八把,配上坚硬的木棍,系上红绸带,红缨枪队成立了。此后,崇下村红缨枪队一有空闲便操练武艺。全村二十多户人家没有事的,也聚集在场上看后生操练,连几个幼童也拿着长短不一的木棍,一招一式地跟着练了起来。

Greatly touched by what the Red Army did, the group of young villagers decided to learn from them and support the poor. The leader, Ouyang Keqi, proposed to form a red tassel spear team with red ribbons tied on all spears and follow the Red Army from then on. As soon as they decided, they asked the blacksmith to make 16 new spears with hard wooden sticks and red ribbons. Hence, they had 18 spears, together with the two sent by the platoon leader. Since the Red Tassel Spear Team was established, they practiced martial arts whenever they had free time. Another 20 households in the village who were not busy also gathered in the field to watch the training. Even a few young children held wooden sticks of different lengths and followed them to practice.

1930年初,欧阳克淇带着村民到兴国贩货,遭敌军抢劫和关押。逃脱后又遇红军与敌军作战,见到了曾救过他们的红军战士罗一民。此时,程昂华排长已升任营长,罗一民也当上了排长。他们来到东韶红军营地,看到很多穷苦兄弟报名参加红军,通过交谈和接触,更深刻地了解了红军是一支为穷人打天下的革命队伍。

At the beginning of 1930, Ouyang Keqi and villagers were robbed and imprisoned by the enemy when selling goods in Xingguo. After escaping, they encountered the Red Army again and met Luo Yimin, a Red Army soldier who had rescued them before. At this time, platoon leader Cheng Anghua had been promoted to battalion commander, and Luo Yimin had become the platoon leader. They came to the Red Army camp in Dongshao and saw many poor fellows signing up for the Red Army. Through conversation and contact, they had a deeper understanding of the Red Army as a revolutionary armed force that fought for the poor.

"我们也想当红军,你们接收吗?"欧阳克淇一行十八人找到程昂华营长,得到允许后,被编入彭德怀领导的红三军团。不但参加了"一苏大"的阅兵,还加入了长征的队伍。

The 18 men led by Ouyang Keqi found the battalion commander Cheng and said, "We also want to become members of the Red Army. Will you accept us?" After obtaining permission, they were incorporated into the Third Red Army Corps led by Peng Dehuai. Later, they not only participated in the military parade of the "First National Congress of the Chinese Workers, Peasants and Soldiers' Soviets", but also joined the troops of the Long March.

后来,欧阳可椿在长汀松毛岭战役中右脚中弹,长征出发后无法跟队,被抬回家医治,从而幸存;欧阳可森随军长征,千辛万苦到达陕北。除他们两人以外,其余16位因长征途中异常惨烈的战火,全部血洒湘江之滨。

Afterwards, one of the members, Ouyang Kechun, was shot in the right foot at the Battle of Songmaoling in Changting. Since he was unable to follow the team to the Long March, he was carried home for medical treatment, and this led to his survival. Another member, Ouyang Kesen, joined the Long March and arrived in northern Shaanxi after innumerable hardships. Except for these two members, the remaining 16 all perished in the extremely violent combat of the Long March.

第三节　红色景点
Section Ⅲ　Red Tourism Attractions

南昌八一起义纪念馆
Nanchang August 1st Uprising Memorial Hall

南昌八一起义纪念馆坐落在江西省南昌市西湖区中山路380号,占地面积5903平方米,是为纪念南昌起义而设立的专题纪念馆。1956年,南昌八一起义纪念馆筹备处成立,1959年10月正式对外开放,1961年被国务院指定为全国首批重点文物保护单位(所辖五处革命旧址——总指挥部旧址、贺龙指挥部旧址、叶挺指挥部旧址、朱德军官教育团旧址和朱德旧居)。

图 2 - 1　南昌八一起义纪念馆
Figure 2 - 1　Nanchang August 1st Uprising Memorial Hall

Nanchang August 1st Uprising Memorial Hall, located at No. 380, Zhongshan Road, Xihu District, Nanchang City, Jiangxi province, covers an area of 5,903 square meters. It is a memorial hall specially established to commemorate the Nanchang Uprising. In 1956, the preparatory office of the Nanchang August 1st Uprising Memorial Hall was established. The Memorial Hall officially opened to the public in October 1959. In 1961, it was announced as one of the first National Key Cultural Relics Protection Units by the State Council (There are five former revolutionary sites under its jurisdiction: the former site of the General Headquarters, the former site of He Long's Headquarters, the former site of Ye Ting's Headquarters, the former site of Zhu De's Officer Education Corps, and the former residence of Zhu De).

南昌起义总指挥部旧址位于南昌中山路和胜利路交叉处的洗马池,是一座灰色的五层大楼,原为"江西大旅社",是当时南昌城内首屈一指的旅社,共有96个客房。1927年7月下旬,贺龙领导的起义部队到达南昌,包下这个旅社,在喜庆厅召开会议,成立了以周恩来为书记的中共前敌委员会。

"江西大旅行社"成了南昌八一起义的总指挥部。1957年,在八一起义总指挥部旧址上兴建了"南昌八一起义纪念馆",纪念馆大门上悬挂着陈毅元帅手书的"南昌八一起义纪念馆"匾额。

The former site of the Nanchang Uprising General Headquarters is at Ximachi, which is located at the intersection of Zhongshan Road and Shengli Road in Nanchang. It is a five-story gray building with a total of 96 rooms, formerly known as "Jiangxi Grand Travel Agency". The travel agency was second to none in Nanchang at that time. In late July 1927, when the troops led by He Long arrived in Nanchang, they booked out the entire hotel, held a meeting in Xiqing assembly hall, and established the Front Committee of the Communist Party of China, with Zhou Enlai as the secretary. Then the "Jiangxi Grand Travel Agency" became the headquarters of the Nanchang August 1st Uprising. In 1957, the Nanchang August 1st Uprising Memorial Hall was built on the former site of the General Headquarters. On the gate of the memorial hall, there hangs the plaque of "Nan Chang Ba Yi Qi Yi Ji Nian Guan"[南昌八一起义纪念馆] (Nanchang August 1st Uprising Memorial Hall) written by Marshal Chen Yi.

南昌八一起义纪念馆采用的现代化的高科技展示手段,全面、生动地展现了周恩来、贺龙、叶挺、朱德、刘伯承等老一辈无产阶级革命家领导南昌起义、同国民党反动派浴血奋战的情景。时任中共中央总书记江泽民为南昌八一起义纪念馆题字:军旗升起的地方。

Using modern high-tech display methods, the Nanchang August 1st Uprising Memorial Hall fully and vividly shows scenes of the older generation of proletarian revolutionaries, such as Zhou Enlai, He Long, Ye Ting, Zhu De, Liu Bocheng, leading the Nanchang Uprising and fighting fiercely with the KMT reactionaries. Jiang Zemin, then General Secretary of the CPC Central Committee, wrote an inscription: Jun Qi Sheng Qi De Di Fang[军旗升起的地方](The Place Where the Military Flag Was Raised) for the Nanchang August 1st Uprising Memorial Hall.

南昌新四军军部旧址
The Former Site of the New Fourth Army in Nanchang

南昌新四军军部旧址坐落于江西省南昌市西湖区象山南路119号,建于1915年,原为北洋军阀张勋的公馆,内有两栋砖木结构楼房和一栋平房,属中西合璧的古建筑。1938年1月6日至4月4日,新四军军部在此正式对外办公,组织指挥南方八省红军游击队下山改编为新四军,开赴抗日前线,南昌因此成为"新四军的摇篮和军旗升起的地方"。

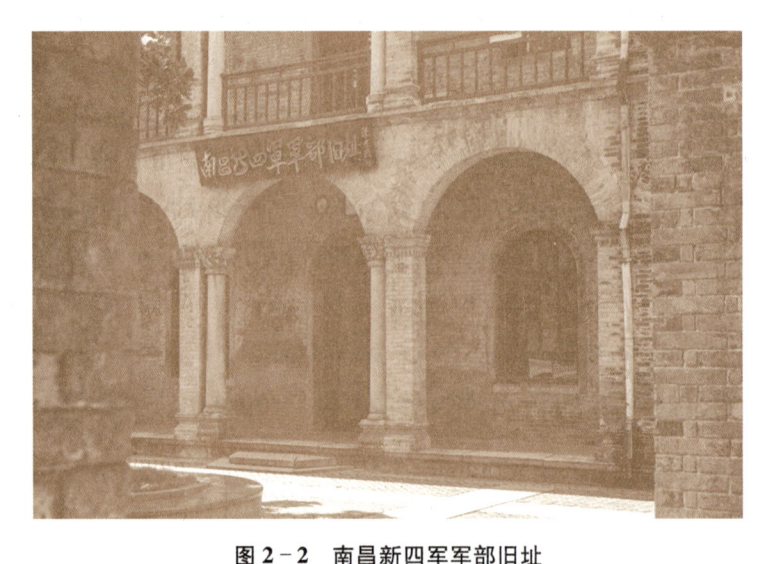

图 2-2 南昌新四军军部旧址
Figure 2-2 The Former Site of the New Fourth Army in Nanchang

The Former Site of the New Fourth Army in Nanchang is located at No. 119, South Xiangshan Road, Xihu District, Nanchang City, Jiangxi province. It was built in 1915 and was originally the residence of Zhang Xun, a Northern warlord. There are two buildings made of brick and wood and one bungalow inside. It is an ancient building featured with both Chinese and Western architectural style. From January 6 to April 4, 1938, the headquarters of the New Fourth Army officially opened its office here. It led the Red Army guerrillas from eight southern provinces down the mountain, reorganized them into the New Fourth Army, and then headed to the Anti-Japanese front line. Nanchang, therefore, became "the cradle of the New Fourth Army and the place where the military flag was raised".

南昌新四军军部旧址因其历史价值重大而被定为省级文物保护单位、省级爱国主义教育基地。目前旧址内设有4个展览：一是新四军军部旧址复原展，展出新四军领导人叶挺、项英、曾山、黄道、周子昆、邓子恢、陈丕显、赖传珠办公和居住的房间及他们的生平图片展。二是《铁的新四军》大型展览，分为四个展厅：铁流滚滚出深山、群英聚集南昌城、大江南北抗敌寇、铁军精神万代传，全面、系统地展现了新四军从1937年成立至1947年改编为华东野战军十年间的光辉历程和英雄业绩。三是《新四军木刻展》，展出创作于抗战时期保存至今的新四军木刻作品60幅。四是张勋公馆建筑艺术作品长廊展。

Owing to its great historical value, the Former Site of the New Fourth Army in Nanchang has been designated as a Historical and Cultural Site Protected at the Provincial Level and a Provincial Patriotism Education Base. Now the site houses four exhibitions: the first is a restoration exhibition of the former site of the New Fourth Army, showcasing the offices, rooms, and photos of the life and work of the leaders of the New Fourth Army, including Ye Ting, Xiang Ying, Zeng Shan, Huang Dao, Zhou Zikun, Deng Zihui, Chen Pixian and Lai Chuanzhu. The second is a large-scale exhibition named "The Iron New Fourth Army", divided into four exhibition halls: the Iron Army Soldiers Emerging from Deep Mountains, the Gathering of Heroes in Nanchang City, Resisting Enemies by the People All over the Country, and the Spirit of the Iron Army Passed Through Generations. These four exhibition halls comprehensively and systematically show the glorious history and heroic achievements of the New Fourth Army in the past ten years, from its establishment in 1937 until 1947 when it was adapted to the East China Field Army. The third is the "New Fourth Army Woodcut Exhibition", which displays 60 woodcut works created by the New Fourth Army during the Anti-Japanese Aggression War. The fourth is the Zhang Xun Mansion Architectural Art Exhibition.

茨坪毛泽东同志旧居
The Former Residence of Comrade Mao Zedong in Ciping

茨坪毛泽东旧居（中共井冈山前敌委员会旧址），坐落在茨坪中心的东山脚下,面临风姿秀丽的挹翠湖,是一栋土木结构的民房,面积798平方米。1927年10月至1929年1月,毛泽东常在这房内居住、工作。在此屋的厅堂里,毛泽东多次召开重要会议,研究部署根据地的各项工作。1928年11月6日,毛泽东在这里主持召开中共湘赣边界特委扩大会议,根据中央的指示,重新组织了井冈山根据地内党的最高领导机关——井冈山前委。此后,前委机关也在此屋办公。

图 2-3 茨坪毛泽东同志旧居
Figure 2-3 The Former Residence of Comrade Mao Zedong in Ciping

The former residence of Mao Zedong in Ciping (originally the former site of Jinggangshan Front Committee of the CPC) is located at the foot of the East Mountain in the center of Ciping, facing the beautiful Yicui Lake. It is made of wood and brick and covers an area of 798 square meters. From October 1927 to January 1929, Mao Zedong often lived and worked here. In the living room, Mao Zedong held many important meetings to investigate and deploy work for the base. On November 6, 1928, according to the Party's Central Committee's instructions, Mao Zedong presided over an enlarged meeting of the CPC's Hunan-Jiangxi Border Special Committee and reorganized the Jinggangshan Front Committee, the highest leading organ of the party in Jinggangshan base. Since then, the Front Committee has also worked in this house.

红军第四军军部旧址
The Former Site of the Fourth Red Army

红军第四军军部旧址位于茨坪店上村,毗邻毛泽东同志旧居。朱德、陈毅率领南昌起义保留下来的部分队伍,经过在湘、粤、赣三省边界的艰苦转战,于1928年4月下旬来到井冈山,和毛泽东领导的秋收起义队伍胜利会师,组建中国红军第四军,朱德任军长,毛泽东任党代表,陈毅任军政治部主任,王尔琢任军参谋长。开始,红四军军部先后设在原宁冈县的砻市和茅坪村的洋桥湖,同年夏,军部迁来井冈山茨坪村李神龙家办公。此后,军部领导便经常在这里召开军事会议,研究和部署作战计划,成为巩固和发展井冈山革命根据地的军事指挥中心。

图 2-4 茨坪红军第四军军部旧址
Figure 2-4 The Former Site of the Fourth Red Army in Ciping

The Former Site of the Fourth Red Army is located in Dianshang Village, Ciping and adjacent to the former residence of Comrade Mao Zedong. In late April 1928, after strenuous battles along the borders of Hunan, Guangdong and Jiangxi provinces, Zhu De and Chen Yi led some of the remaining troops from the Nanchang Uprising and came to Jinggangshan. They joined forces with the troops from the Autumn Harvest Uprising led by Mao Zedong. The Fourth Chinese Red Army was then formed, with Zhu De serving as the commander, Mao Zedong the party representative, Chen Yi the director of the military and political department, and Wang Erzhuo the chief of staff. At first, the Fourth Red Army's military headquarters were successively established at Long City in Ninggang County and Yangqiao Lake in Maoping Village. In the summer of the same year, the military headquarters moved to Li Shenlong's house in Ciping Village, Jinggangshan. Since then, military leaders often held meetings there to study and deploy operational plans. This place became the military command center for consolidating and developing the Jinggangshan Revolutionary Base.

朱德、陈毅同志主要负责军部的日常工作,他们常在军部居住,此屋中间的厅堂是军委召开干部会议的场所,右间是朱德同志的住房,左间是陈毅同志的住房。住房内陈设简朴,桌上除批阅文稿的笔墨外,就只有晚间照明用的一盏一根灯芯的青油灯,床上垫的是稻草,铺上土布床单,盖的也只是一床旧的军用线毯。

Zhu De and Chen Yi, mainly responsible for the daily work of the military headquarters, often lived in the house of the headquarters. The hall in the middle of this house was the place where the Military Commission held meetings. On the right of the hall was Zhu De's bedroom, and on the left was Chen Yi's bedroom. The interior of the house was simply furnished. Apart from the pen and ink, there was only an oil lamp on the table for lighting at night. The bed was covered with bits of straw, a home-made sheet, and an old thin line blanket.

黄洋界保卫战旧址
The Former Site of the Huangyangjie Defense

黄洋界位于井冈山茨坪的西北面,海拔1343米,因为这里经常浓雾弥漫,好似汪洋大海一望无垠,故又名汪洋界。黄洋界哨口是井冈山根据地五大哨口之一,扼守从湖南酃县(今炎陵县)、江西宁冈方向来犯之敌。1928年夏,红军在这里修筑了三个工事和一个瞭望哨。右边的两个工事用以阻击江西宁冈方向来的敌人;左边的一个工事用以阻击湖南方向来的敌人;山顶上的瞭望哨便于监视敌人。还在原来一家客栈的遗址上建造了一栋红军营房,布兵驻守。

Huangyangjie is located in the northwest of Ciping, Jinggangshan, with an altitude of 1,343 meters. Often filled with thick fog, it looks like an endless ocean, hence the name Wangyangjie, which literally means "a vast body of water". Huangyangjie is one of the five sentry posts in the Jinggangshan base, preparing against enemies from Ling County (now Yanling County), Hunan and Ninggang, Jiangxi. In the summer of 1928, the Red Army built three fortifications and a lookout here. The two fortifications on the right were used to block the enemy from the direction of Ninggang, Jiangxi, while the one on the left was to block the enemy from the direction of Hunan. The lookout on top of the mountain was used to monitor enemy movement. Additionally, a Red Army barrack was built on the former site of an inn, where troops were stationed.

图 2-5 井冈山黄洋界保卫战胜利纪念碑
Figure 2-5 The Monument of Victory in the Battle of Defense at Huangyangjie in Jinggangshan

1928年的七八月间,湘赣两省敌军调集重兵对井冈山根据地发动第二次"会剿"。反"会剿"之初,因湖南省委的错误指示,红军主力盲目出兵湘南,造成根据地内部兵力空虚。8月30日,敌军以4个团的兵力进攻井冈山,红军以2个连的兵力凭险抵抗,打退敌人多次进攻,取得了黄洋界保卫战的胜利。率领主力红军从湘南回师井冈山的毛泽东在途中听到黄洋界保卫战胜利的消息,欣然写下了《西江月·井冈山》这首著名的词。

西江月·井冈山

山下旌旗在望,山头鼓角相闻。
敌军围困万千重,我自岿然不动。
早已森严壁垒,更加众志成城,
黄洋界上炮声隆,报道敌军宵遁。

Figure 2-6 The Former Site of Huangyangjie Defense in Jinggangshan

In July and August of 1928, enemy forces in Hunan and Jiangxi provinces mobilized a large number of troops and launched the second suppression campaign against the Jinggangshan base. At the beginning, due to wrong instructions from the Hunan Provincial Party Committee, the main force of the Red Army blindly dispatched troops to southern Hunan, resulting in a weak defense in the base area. On August 30, the enemy troops attacked Jinggangshan with four regiments. The Red Army's two companies, resisted and repulsed the enemy's repeated attacks, achieving victory in the Huangyangjie Defense. Hearing news of the victory, Mao Zedong, who led the main force of the Red Army back to Jinggangshan from southern Hunan, gladly wrote the famous poem "Jinggangshan".

Tune: The Moon over the West River
Jinggangshan

(Translated by Xu Yuanchong)

Flags and banners insight below,
Drum-beats mingle atop with bugle-blast.
Surrounded ring on ring by the foe,
Aloft we still stand fast.
Our ranks as firm as rock,
Our wills form a new wall.
The cannon roared at Huangyang Block,
The foe fled at night-fall.

为纪念黄洋界保卫战的胜利,1965年,当地政府修造了黄洋界保卫战胜利纪念碑,碑上刻着朱德的题字"黄洋界保卫战胜利纪念碑",背面是毛泽东的手迹"星星之火,可以燎原"。1977年增建一横碑,上面刻着毛泽东的词《西江月·井冈山》全文。

In 1965, the Monument of Victory in the Battle of Defense at Huangyangjie was built to commemorate the victory. The front of the monument was inscribed with Zhu De's handwriting, "Huang Yang Jie Bao Wei Zhan Sheng Li Ji Nian Bei"[黄洋界保卫战胜利纪念碑](Monument of Victory in the Battle of Defense at Huangyangjie). On the back, there are eight characters in Mao Zedong's handwriting, "Xing Xing Zhi Huo, Ke Yi Liao Yuan"[星星之火,可以燎原](A Single Spark Can Start a Prairie Fire). In 1977, a horizontal stele was added with the full text of Mao Zedong's poem "Jinggangshan, Tune: The Moon over the West River".

井冈山革命博物馆
Jinggangshan Revolutionary Museum

井冈山革命博物馆是为了纪念中国共产党创建的第一个农村革命根据地——井冈山革命根据地而建立的。它是我国第一个地方性革命史类博物馆,也是首批83家国家一级博物馆之一。井冈山革命博物馆旧馆于1958年经国家文物局批准兴建,1959年10月,中华人民共和国成立10周年之际竣工并对外开放。1965年5月毛主席重上井冈山时,亲自审定博物馆的基本陈列内容大纲。

Jinggangshan Revolutionary Museum was established to commemorate the Jinggangshan Revolutionary Base, the first rural revolutionary base founded by the CPC. It is the first local museum of revolutionary history in China and is listed among the first batch of 83 national first-class museums. With the approval of the National Cultural Heritage Administration, the former Jinggangshan Revolutionary Museum was built in 1958. In October 1959, on the 10th anniversary of the founding of the People's Republic of China, it was completed and opened to the public. When Chairman Mao returned to Jinggangshan in May 1965, he reviewed and approved the outline of the exhibition contents of the museum in person.

图 2-7　井冈山革命博物馆
Figure 2-7　Jinggangshan Revolutionary Museum

2004年，中宣部将井冈山革命博物馆的新馆建设列为全国爱国主义教育示范基地"一号工程"。2005年9月29日，井冈山革命博物馆新馆开工建设，2007年10月27日，井冈山革命根据地创建80周年之际竣工，中共中央政治局常委李长春亲自为"一号工程"——井冈山革命博物馆的落成剪彩。

In 2004, the Publicity Department of the CPC Central Committee listed the construction of the new Jinggangshan Revolutionary Museum as the "No. 1 Project" of the National Demonstration Base for Patriotism Education. On September 29, 2005, the construction of the new Jinggangshan Revolutionary Museum started. It was completed on October 27, 2007, on the occasion of the 80th anniversary of the founding of the Jinggangshan Revolutionary Base. Li Changchun, a member of the Standing Committee of the Political Bureau of the CPC Central Committee, attended the ceremony to cut the ribbon, marking the completion of this No. 1 Project.

新建的井冈山革命博物馆坐落在茨坪红军南路，占地面积1.782公顷，依山面水，与茨坪革命旧址群隔湖相望。主体建筑为四层，一层为停车场、报告厅，二层为文物库房及办公用房，三、四层为展厅，总建筑面积20030平方米，其中展厅面积8436平方米，共展出文物800余件，照片2000多张。馆内珍藏着一大批珍贵的历史文物:当年毛泽东撰写《中国红色政权为什么能够存在?》《井冈山的斗争》时用过的油灯、砚台,以及朱德在井冈山挑粮用过的扁担等;毛泽东、朱德和其他老红军重上井冈山的影视资料等;党和国家领导人毛泽东、朱德、邓小平、江泽民、胡锦涛、习近平等视察井冈山的照片和题词;社会各界著名人士的书画墨宝真迹。

The newly built Jinggangshan Revolutionary Museum is located on South Hongjun Road, Ciping, covering an area of 1.782 hectares. It sits by the mountain and faces the water, overlooking the former Ciping Revolutionary Sites across the lake. The main building has four floors. The first floor is the parking lot and the lecture hall. The second floor is the cultural relics warehouse and offices. The third and fourth floors are the exhibition halls. The total construction area covers 20,030 square meters, including 8,436 square meters of exhibition halls, where over 800 cultural relics and more than 2,000 photos are on display. The museum houses a large number of precious historical relics, such as the oil lamps and inkstones used by Mao Zedong when he wrote "Why Does China's Red Regime Exist?" and "The Struggle in Jinggangshan". It contains the pole used by Zhu De to carry grains in Jinggangshan, the film and video documents of Mao Zedong, Zhu De and other Red Army veterans returning to visit Jinggangshan, and the photos and inscriptions of Party and national leaders, including Mao Zedong, Zhu De, Deng Xiaoping, Jiang Zemin, Hu Jintao, and Xi Jinping, during their visit to Jinggangshan. Lastly, it displays paintings and calligraphy of the elites from all walks of life.

第一次全国苏维埃代表大会会址
The Site of the First National Congress of the Chinese Soviet

第一次全国苏维埃代表大会会址原是谢氏宗祠,已有几百年的历史,是中华苏维埃共和国临时中央政府的诞生地和1931年11月至1933年4月的驻地。

The Site of the First National Congress of the Soviet is originally the ancestral temple of the Xie family, which has a history of hundreds of years. It is

图 2-8 瑞金第一次全国苏维埃代表大会会址
Figure 2-8　The Site of the First National Congress of the Chinese Soviet in Ruijin

the birthplace of the Provisional Central Government of the Chinese Soviet Republic and its residence from November 1931 to April 1933.

1931年11月7日,中华苏维埃第一次全国代表大会在这里隆重召开。来自闽西、赣东北、湘赣、湘鄂西、琼崖、中央苏区等根据地红军部队以及在国民党统治区的全国总工会、全国海员总工会的610名代表出席了大会。大会历时14天,通过了《中华苏维埃共和国宪法大纲》,颁布了《劳动法》《土地法》以及关于经济政策、红军政策、少数民族政策等决议案;大会选举产生了毛泽东、项英、张国焘、周恩来、朱德等63人组成的中央执行委员会,作为大会闭幕后的最高政权机关。大会最后发表了《中华苏维埃共和国临时中央政府对外宣言》,向全世界庄严宣告:中华苏维埃共和国临时中央政府正式成立,定都瑞金。

On November 7, 1931, the first National Congress of the Chinese Soviet was held here. Six hundred and ten representatives attended the conference, including representatives from the Red Army troops in the base areas of western Fujian, northeastern Jiangxi, Hunan-Jiangxi, western Hunan-Hubei, Qiongya, and the Central Soviet Area, as well as representatives from the All-China Federation of Trade Unions and the National Union of Seamen in KMT-ruled areas. The conference, lasting 14 days, passed the "Outline of the Constitution of the

Chinese Soviet Republic" and promulgated the "Labor Law", the "Land Law", as well as the resolutions on economic policy, Red Army policy, and policies for the minorities and others. The Central Executive Committee, composed of 63 people including Mao Zedong, Xiang Ying, Zhang Guotao, Zhou Enlai, Zhu De, and others, was elected and functioned as the highest organ of political power. At the end of the conference, the "International Declaration of the Provisional Central Government of the Chinese Soviet Republic" was issued, solemnly announcing to the world that the Provisional Central Government of the Chinese Soviet Republic was officially established, with Ruijin selected as its capital.

瑞金中央革命根据地纪念馆/中央革命根据地历史博物馆
The Memorial Hall of the Ruijin Central Revolutionary Base / The Museum of History of the Central Revolutionary Base

瑞金中央革命根据地纪念馆又名中央革命根据地历史博物馆,位于江西省瑞金市城西,是为纪念土地革命战争时期中国共产党及其领袖毛泽东、朱德、周恩来等老一辈无产阶级革命家直接领导创建中央革命根据地和红一方面军,缔造中华苏维埃共和国的历史而建立的革命类纪念馆。1958年正式开馆,2004年进行改扩建,2007年竣工并免费对外开放。

图2-9 瑞金中央革命根据地纪念馆/历史博物馆
Figure 2-9 The Memorial Hall of the Ruijin Central Revolutionary Base / The Museum of History of the Central Revolutionary Base

The Memorial Hall of the Ruijin Central Revolutionary Base, also known as the Museum of History of the Central Revolutionary Base, is located in Ruijin City, Jiangxi province. It is built to commemorate the history of the establishment of the Central Revolutionary Base, the first front Red Army, and the Chinese Soviet Republic led by CPC leaders Mao Zedong, Zhu De, Zhou Enlai and other older generation of proletarian revolutionaries during the Agrarian Revolutionary War. Officially opened in 1958, it was renovated and expanded in 2004. In 2007, after completion of the expansion, it reopened to the public for free.

该馆占地面积40000多平方米,建筑面积10100平方米,馆藏文物1万多件,其中一级藏品148件,二级藏品365件,三级藏品621件,管辖瑞金革命旧居旧址126处,其中全国重点文物保护单位36处,省级文物保护单位22处,县(市)级文物保护单位25处。是全国爱国主义教育示范基地、国家一级博物馆、全国中小学生研学实践教育基地、全国红色旅游经典景区等。

The museum covers an area of over 40,000 square meters, with a construction area of 10,100 square meters. It has a collection of more than 10,000 cultural relics, including 148 first-class collections, 365 second-class collections, and 621 third-class collections. There are 126 former sites and residences of the Ruijin Revolution, among which 36 are National Key Cultural Relics Protection Units, 22 are Cultural Relics Protected at the Provincial Level, and 25 are Cultural Relics Protected at the County Level. This museum has also been listed as a National Demonstration Base for Patriotism Education, a national first-class museum, a National Research and Practice Education Base for K-12 School Students, and a National Classic Scenic Spot of Red Tourism.

该馆以《人民共和国从这里走来》陈列馆为主展区,采用了动画、场景、多媒体、幻影成像等先进的展陈手段,再现了中国共产党领导苏区军民进行反"围剿"斗争,创建巩固革命根据地,建立中华苏维埃共和国临时中央政府的艰难历程以及进行治国安邦伟大实践,积极开展武装斗争、土地革命和根据地建设所取得的辉煌成就,展现了中华苏维埃共和国历史演变的全过程,诠释了中华苏维埃共和国与中华人民共和国传承关系。

The main exhibition area is the hall named "The People's Republic Comes from Here". Adopting various advanced exhibition methods, such as animation, scenes, multimedia, and phantom imaging, the exhibition reproduces the difficult process of the CPC leading the soldiers and civilians in the Soviet area to fight against the enemy's encirclement and suppression campaign, to create and consolidate revolutionary bases, and to establish the Provisional Central Government of the Chinese Soviet Republic. It also highlights the CPC's significant achievements in armed struggle, agrarian revolution and base construction. In addition, the exhibition represents the whole process of the historical evolution of the Chinese Soviet Republic and interprets the inherent relationship between the Chinese Soviet Republic and the People's Republic of China.

专栏 2：井冈山精神与苏区精神

Special Column Ⅱ: The Jinggangshan Spirit and the Spirit of the Soviet Areas

井冈山精神

The Jinggangshan Spirit

2016年2月1日至3日,习近平总书记在江西看望慰问广大干部群众时指出:井冈山是中国革命的摇篮。井冈山时期留给我们最为宝贵的财富,就是跨越时空的井冈山精神。习近平总书记指出"井冈山精神,最重要的方面就是坚定信念、艰苦奋斗,实事求是、敢闯新路,依靠群众、勇于胜利",强调"今天,我们要结合新的时代条件,坚持坚定执着追理想、实事求是闯新路、艰苦奋斗攻难关、依靠群众求胜利,让井冈山精神放射出新的时代光芒"。

From February 1 to 3, 2016, Xi Jinping, General Secretary of the CPC Central Committee, visited Jiangxi and met with local cadres and the public. During his visit, he emphasized that Jinggangshan is the cradle of the Chinese revolution. The Jinggangshan Spirit which spans time and space is the most precious treasure left to us from the Jinggangshan period. General Secretary Xi Jinping also stated that "the essence of the Jinggangshan spirit lies in firm conviction, integrity and diligence, seeking truth from facts, daring to forge new paths, relying on the masses, and the courage to strive for victory." He highlighted that "Today, in the context of the new era, we must pursue ideals with determination and perseverance, break new ground with a fact-based approach, strive hard to overcome difficulties, and rely on the masses for victory, letting the Jinggangshan Spirit shine in the new era."

苏区精神
The Spirit of the Soviet Areas

2011年11月,习近平同志在纪念中央革命根据地创建暨中华苏维埃共和国成立80周年座谈会的讲话中指出:"在革命根据地的创建和发展中,在建立红色政权、探索革命道路的实践中,无数革命先辈用鲜血和生命铸就了以坚定信念、求真务实、一心为民、清正廉洁、艰苦奋斗、争创一流、无私奉献等为主要内涵的苏区精神。"苏区精神是土地革命战争时期以毛泽东同志为主要代表的中国共产党人把马克思主义普遍原理与中国革命具体实际相结合、在艰辛探索中国革命正确道路的伟大实践中培育形成的伟大革命精神。

In November 2011, Comrade Xi Jinping pointed out in his speech at a symposium commemorating the founding of the Central Revolutionary Base and the 80th anniversary of the founding of the Chinese Soviet Republic: "In the construction and development of the revolutionary bases, in the practice of establishing the red regime and exploring the revolutionary path, countless revolutionary forbearers have forged the spirit of the Soviet Areas with their blood and lives. It features a firm conviction, a realistic and pragmatic approach, wholehearted service to the people, integrity and diligence, pursuit of excellence, and selfless devotion." The Spirit of the Soviet Areas is a profound revolutionary ethos, formed by Chinese Communists—with Comrade Mao Zedong as the principal representative—during the Agrarian Revolutionary War. It was cultivated through arduous exploration to find the correct path for the Chinese revolution, by integrating the universal principles of Marxism with the specific realities of the Chinese revolution.

第三章　长征:伟大壮举　革命奇迹

Chapter Ⅲ　The Long March: An Unprecedented Feat and a Revolutionary Miracle

长征是人类历史上的伟大壮举。习近平总书记在纪念红军长征胜利80周年大会上的讲话中指出:"长征历时之长、规模之大、行程之远、环境之险恶、战斗之惨烈,在中国历史上是绝无仅有的,在世界战争史乃至人类文明史上也是极为罕见的。"长征途中,红军将士同敌人进行了600余次战役战斗,跨越近百条江河,攀越40余座高山险峰。红军将士以坚定的理想信念和一往无前的革命英雄主义精神,创造了气吞山河的人间奇迹。

The Long March (1934 – 1936) is an unprecedented achievement in human history. In the speech at the Ceremony Commemorating the 80th Anniversary of the Victory of the Long March, General Secretary Xi Jinping underscored that "the sheer duration, scale, distance, severity, and ferocity of the Long March were not only unparalleled in Chinese history, but almost totally unheard of in the history of war and human civilization." During the Long March, the Red Army soldiers engaged the enemy over 600 times, crossed almost 100 rivers, and scaled over 40 treacherous peaks. Steadfastly upholding their ideals and beliefs, the Red Army demonstrated revolutionary heroism and created a monumental human miracle.

第一节　历史回眸
Section I　A Glimpse of History

九一八事变的爆发与抗日救亡运动的兴起
The Outbreak of September 18th Incident and the Rise of the Resistance War Against Japanese Aggression

日本对中国领土垂涎已久。从19世纪后期开始,日本多次发动侵华战争,并且武装占领了台湾。但是,日本对这一切并不满足。1927年6月,日本首相田中义一主持召开"东方会议",确立了"把满洲从中国本土分裂出来,置于日本势力之下"的侵略方针。

China has long been a coveted territory for Japan. Since the late 19th century, Japan launched several aggressive wars against China and forcibly occupied Taiwan with its armed forces. However, Japan was not satisfied with all this. In June 1927, Japanese Prime Minister Tanaka Giichi held the Eastern Conference, which led to the aggressive policy of "separating Manchuria from the mainland of China and placing it under Japanese control".

1931年9月18日夜,日本关东军炸毁南满铁路柳条湖段轨道,反而说是中国军队破坏铁路,想袭击日本军队,随即炮击中国东北军的驻地北大营,进攻沈阳,制造了九一八事变。

On the night of September 18, 1931, the Japanese Kwantung Army blew up a section of the Nanman Railway track near Liutiaohu and then falsely accused the Chinese army of the explosion. Using this as a pretext, the Japanese bombarded the Northeast Army's North Camp and attacked Shenyang, triggering the September 18th Incident.

九一八事变发生时,国民党政府正竭尽全力"围剿"红军。蒋介石命令东北军首领张学良:"沈阳日军行动,可作为地方事件,望力避冲突,以免事态扩大。"由于中国军队不抵抗,日军一夜之间就占领了沈阳,仅用4个多月的时间就轻而易举地占领了中国东北三省。为稳固统治,日本侵略者在东北三省成立了所谓的"满洲国",让早已退位的清朝末代皇帝溥仪来当傀儡皇帝,实际上,权力则完全被日本所掌握。

While the Japanese were staging the September 18th Incident, the KMT regime was going all out to encircle and suppress the Red Army. Chiang Kai-shek (leader of the KMT) warned Zhang Xueliang, general of the Northeast Army, of the Japanese who may use the incident in Shenyang as part of its move to occupy the northeast. Given this, he ordered that General Zhang should do everything he could to avoid conflicts and prevent the situation from getting worse. Unfortunately, the Japanese army occupied Shenyang overnight, encountering almost no resistance from the Chinese military forces. Within a short period of four months, the Japanese army had overrun three northeastern provinces. To consolidate its control in these provinces, the Japanese declared a new state of Manchukuo and made Puyi, the last emperor of the Qing Dynasty, its emperor. Pu had abdicated the throne long ago and was the "puppet emperor" of the new nation, which was under the absolute control of the stationed Japanese army.

日本的侵略激起了中国人民的激烈反抗。九一八事变爆发后的第二天,中国共产党立即发表宣言,谴责日本帝国主义的侵略,揭露蒋介石的不抵抗政策,发出"在满洲更应该加紧地组织群众的反帝运动,发动群众斗争,来反抗日本帝国主义的侵略,组织兵变与游击战争,直接给日本帝国主义以严重的打击"的号召。此后,东北各地的抗日武装斗争迅速发展,抗日义勇军在极其恶劣的斗争环境和自然环境下与日本侵略者展开了英勇斗争。

The Chinese people resisted Japanese aggression, fighting gallantly against the invaders. The day right after the September 18th Incident, the CPC immediately issued a manifesto condemning Japanese imperialism and aggression, as well as Chiang Kai-shek's non-resistance order. It called for people in Manchuria to deal a heavy blow directly to Japanese imperialism and step up an even greater anti-imperialist movement to fight against Japanese invaders by launching mutinies and guerrilla warfare. Since then, the counter-Japanese armed forces across the northeast intensified their attacks in various ways. Meanwhile, the counter-Japanese volunteer army fought heroically against the Japanese invaders in the harshest natural environment.

蒋介石的"攘外必先安内"与红军第五次反"围剿"的失败
Chiang Kai-shek's Policy of Attending to Internal Unrest Before Resisting Foreign Invasion & the Failure of the Red Army's Fifth Campaign Against Encirclement and Suppression

九一八事变后,蒋介石的不抵抗政策激起了全国人民的愤怒,他们纷纷要求国民政府停止内战,一致对外。面对社会舆论的强大压力,蒋介石提出"攘外必先安内"的政策,继续推行向日本帝国主义妥协、对红军"围剿"的反动方针。

After the September 18th Incident, Chiang Kai-shek's non-resistance order angered every Chinese across the country. They demanded the Nationalist Government stop the civil war and work unanimously to fight against the invaders. Facing tremendous pressure from the public, Chiang Kai-shek adopted a policy advocating eliminating communist armies before forming a frontline defense against invasion, making compromises with the Japanese, and insisting on launching the Encirclement and Suppression Campaign to get rid of the Red Army.

1933年9月至1934年夏,蒋介石调集庞大兵力,对中央苏区进行第五次"围剿"。由于中共中央领导人博古(秦邦宪)和共产国际派来的军事顾问李德的"左"倾冒险主义错误,红军屡战失利,苏区日渐缩小。1934年10月初,国民党军向中央苏区的中心区域进攻,迅速占领了兴国、宁都一线。中央红军在苏区内打破国民党军的"围剿"已无可能,于是被迫退出中央苏区,踏上了战略转移的征程,开始了世界历史上前所未有的二万五千里长征壮举。

From September 1933 to the summer of 1934, Chiang Kai-shek raised massive amounts of troops and launched the Fifth Encirclement and Suppression Campaign against the Central Soviet Area. Due to the "Leftist" adventurism held by Bo Gu (Qin Bangxian), the then leader of the CPC Central Committee, and Li De (Otto Braun), the military adviser appointed by the Comintern, the Red Army suffered constant defeats and lost its grip on parts of the Soviet Area. In early October 1934, the KMT army attacked the center of the Soviet Area and occupied the frontlines in the counties of Xingguo and Ningdu. As it seemed impossible to break the Encirclement and Suppression Campaign of the KMT forces in the Soviet Area, the Central Red Army had to retreat and embarked on the 25,000-li Long March. It was a strategic shift for the Red Army and an unprecedented long journey in world history.

艰苦卓绝的长征
The Arduous Long March

长征的道路十分艰难。红军爬雪山、过草地,没有粮食就挖野菜、啃树皮,遇到了很多难以想象的困难。在国民党军队的围攻下,红军多次陷入被动挨打的局面。1935年1月,红军攻克遵义,在这里举行了著名的遵义会议,及时纠正了第五次反"围剿"和长征以来中央在军事指挥上的"左"倾冒险主义和转移中的逃跑主义错误,事实上确立了毛泽东在党中央和红军的领导地位。此后,红军变被动为主动,打了很多胜仗:四渡赤水、巧渡金沙江、强渡大渡河、飞夺泸定桥……冲破了国民党军队的围追堵截。

The Long March was more than just a difficult journey. The Red Army encountered countless hardships, climbing over snow-capped mountains, trekking across vast grasslands, and eating wild greens and tree barks to stave off hunger. The Red Army, besieged by the KMT's forces, found it difficult to launch active attacks. In January 1935, the Red Army forces took over the city of Zunyi, where they held the monumental Zunyi Meeting. During the conference, the CPC Central Committee acted promptly to stop the "Leftist" adventurism and flightism since the KMT's Fifth Campaign against Encirclement and Suppression and the Long March. At this meeting, Mao Zedong was confirmed as the de facto leader of the Central Committee and the Red Army. Since then, the Red Army turned the tide, shifting from passivity to active strategies and winning many battles. During the Long March, the Red Army forces fought tooth and nail in countless battles, such as making four crossings at the Chishui River, ingeniously crossing the Jinsha River, fighting their way across the Dadu River, and seizing the Luding Bridge, and others, and ultimately thwarted large-scale encirclement, pursuit, obstruction and interception by KMT troops.

三大主力红军会师
The Forces of the Three Front Red Armies Amalgamate

1935年10月19日,中央红军到达陕北吴起镇,与刘志丹领导的陕北红军胜利会师。至此,中央红军主力行程二万五千里,纵横11个省的长征胜利结束。毛泽东写下了《七律·长征》,艺术地表现了红军将士不怕牺牲、英勇斗争的精神风范和革命的乐观主义精神。

七律·长征
红军不怕远征难,万水千山只等闲。
五岭逶迤腾细浪,乌蒙磅礴走泥丸。
金沙水拍云崖暖,大渡桥横铁索寒。
更喜岷山千里雪,三军过后尽开颜。

On October 19, 1935, the Central Red Army arrived at Wuqi Town in northern Shaanxi Province and joined forces with the Red Army troops led by Liu Zhidan there. Up to this point, the Central Red Army main forces had successfully completed the long journey of the 25,000-li March across eleven provinces. In Mao Zedong's famous poem, "the Long March", he artistically revealed the heroism and optimism of the Red Army soldiers, who were not fearful of death for the revolution.

The Long March
(**Translated by Xu Yuanchong**)

Of the trying Long March the Red Army makes light;
Thousands of rivers and mountains are barriers slight.
The five serpentine ridges outspread like rippling rills;

The pompous Wumeng peaks tower but like mole-hills.
Against warm cloudy cliffs beat waves of Golden Sand;
With cold iron-chain bridge River Dadu is spanned.
Glad to see the Min Range snow-clad for miles and miles,
Our warriors who have crossed it break into broad smiles.

1936年10月9日,红一、红四方面军在甘肃省会宁县会师;22日,红二方面军到达甘肃隆德将台堡(今属宁夏西吉),同红一方面军会合。至此,红军三大主力胜利会师,长征宣告胜利结束。长征的胜利,粉碎了国民党反动派阻止中国革命的企图,是中国革命转危为安的关键。毛泽东曾评价说:"长征是历史记录上的第一次,长征是宣言书,长征是宣传队,长征是播种机。……长征是以我们胜利、敌人失败的结果而告结束。"长征的胜利宣告了中国共产党和红军肩负着民族希望实现了北上抗日的战略转移,实现了中国共产党和中国革命事业从挫折走向胜利的伟大转折。此后,中国共产党以延安为中心,不断开创中国革命的新局面。

On October 9, 1936, the First and Fourth Front Red Armies joined forces in Huining County, Gansu Province. On October 22, the Second Front Red Army joined forces with the First Front Red Army after arriving at Jiangtaibao Town in Longde County, Gansu Province (now in Xiji County, Ningxia Province). The successful meeting of the three main Red Army forces indicated the end of the Long March and its triumph over the reactionary KMT's efforts to obstruct the Chinese Revolution, proving to be a pivotal moment in ensuring its success. As Mao Zedong once commented, "The Long March is the first of its kind in the annals of history; it is a manifesto, a propaganda force, a seeding machine... The Long March came to an end with our victory and the enemy's defeat." The victory of the Long March marked the successful strategic retreat of the CPC and Red Army to northern China, where they carried national hope for resistance against Japanese aggression. It also marked a critical turning point for the CPC and the Chinese revolution, putting them on the path to victory. Most significantly, from then on, the CPC would be based in Yan'an City, the wartime stronghold of the Chinese communists, and continue to open up new horizons for the Chinese revolution.

第二节　红色故事
Section Ⅱ　Red Stories

彝海结盟：刘伯承与小叶丹的故事
Yihai Lake Alliance：Liu Bocheng Drank a "Chicken-blood Oath" with the Leader of the Yi Minority，Xiaoyedan

1935年5月，中央红军要想跳出国民党军重兵包围圈，必须尽快渡过天险大渡河。当时，从中央红军所在的泸沽到大渡河，中间隔着大凉山地区，有两条路可走：一条是大路，从泸沽东面翻越小相岭，经越西县城到大树堡，由此渡过大渡河；另一条是小路，从泸沽北面到冕宁县城，经拖乌彝族聚居区到达大渡河边的安顺场。但是，在当时，人们把经彝族区的小路视为"畏途"，军队，尤其是汉人军队要通过这一地区是很不容易的。

In May 1935, the Central Red Army was encircled by the KMT forces and needed to cross the treacherous Dadu River in Sichuan Province. The troops were stationed at Lugu Town, but to get to the Dadu River, they had to pass through the Daliangshan area, in what is today the Yi People's Autonomous Prefecture. They had two routes to cross the river. The main route required soldiers to climb over the Xiaoxiangling mountains from the east of Lugu, pass through Yuexi county town, and reach Dashubao Town to cross the river. The alternative was a shortcut, which would take the Red Army from north of Lugu through various locations, including Mianning County's county seat and Tuowu area of the Yi people, before reaching Anshunchang Town near the Dadu River. However, it was known as a "dreadful passage" due to its difficulty, even for Han armies who ventured through it.

为正确宣传并执行党的民族政策，朱德发布了《中国工农红军布告》，宣传红军宗旨，揭露反动派的黑暗统治，号召彝汉人民团结起来，打倒军阀。5月19日，中央红军派出以刘伯承为司令员、聂荣臻为政治委员、萧华为群众工作队长的先遣军，准备借道彝民区，抢先渡过大渡河。

Zhu De, commander-in-chief of the Chinese Workers' and Peasants' Red Army, issued the "Proclamation of the Chinese Workers' and Peasants' Red Army" to promote and implement the CPC's policies toward ethnic groups. Spreading the message of the Red Army and its purpose while exposing the dark side of the ruling KMT regime, it appealed to both the Yi people and Han people to work together to overthrow the warlords. On May 19, the Central Red Army took measures to ensure crossing the Dadu River ahead of the KMT armies, by dispatching an advance force. The force was led by Liu Bocheng, with Nie Rongzhen serving as the political commissar and Xiao Hua as the leader of the masses. But they had to traverse through the Yi territory.

由刘伯承、聂荣臻率领的先遣部队于5月21日到达大桥镇，找好了向导和翻译后，于22日进入彝区。彝民听说军队来了，就将山涧上的独木桥拆毁，把溪水里的石墩搬开隐藏在山林里，不时挥舞着土枪、长矛，间或施放冷箭、冷枪袭击。跟在主力后面约百米远的工兵连，也遭到彝民堵截。红军坚持执行党的民族政策，严格遵守"不准开枪"的纪律，于是部队停止前进。

On May 21, the advance force led by Liu Bocheng and Nie Rongzhen reached Daqiao Town, where they found a guide and translator, before they entered the Yi territory the next day. When the Yi people heard of their coming, they tried to stop them in different ways, such as demolishing the single-plank bridge over the stream, hiding river rocks in the woods, and launching ambushes with spears or home-made guns. Positioned approximately a hundred meters behind the main body of the team, the engineer company faced similar resistance. Despite these challenges, the Red Army soldiers adhered strictly to the no-shooting order and refrained from advancing further.

萧华通过翻译耐心地向彝民解说红军的政策，可彝民仍舞刀弄枪不许红军通过。正在混乱之际，几个人骑着骡马急驰而来，翻译认出为首的一个彝人是当地彝民首领小叶丹的四叔。

Xiao Hua found a local guide who knew both the Han and Yi language and asked him to pass the message of the Red Army on to the Yi people. But the locals still refused to let them pass through and threatened them with knives and guns. At this juncture, they saw several people approaching them speedily on horses. The guide told Xiao the man in the lead was the uncle of the Xiaoyedan, the local chieftain of the Yi people.

萧华对小叶丹的四叔说明红军与国民党军不同,是替受压迫的人打天下的,进入彝民区不是打彝胞,而是借路北上。根据彝人重义气的特点,萧华又告知他,刘司令愿与彝民首领结为兄弟。很快,红军就得到回话,小叶丹愿与红军结盟。刘伯承得知这个消息后非常高兴,决定亲自前往结盟仪式。

Xiao Hua explained to Xiaoyedan's uncle that the Red Army was not the same as the KMT, but quite the contrary, they fought for the oppressed. The Red Army did not intend to invoke any war with the locals and instead they just needed passage through the area to head to the north. Well aware that the Yi people value righteousness of brotherhood, Xiao Hua suggested to the uncle that Commander Liu would like to become sworn brothers with the chieftain of the Yi people. Shortly after that, the Red Army received a positive reply from Xiaoyedan, who agreed to an alliance. Hearing this, Liu Bocheng was filled with joy and decided to attend the alliance ceremony himself.

结盟地点定在彝海子边。彝海,原名"鱼海子",海拔2000多米,是个高山淡水湖。四周山峦环抱,林木葱葱。就在这个山清水秀的地方,举行了举世闻名的"彝海结盟"。刘伯承以诚恳的态度重申红军来意,表示将来红军打败反动派以后,一定帮助彝族人民消除一切外来的欺压,建设自己美好的生活。

The alliance ceremony was scheduled to occur at Yihaizi Lake, also known as Yihai, which derived its name from "Yuhaizi". Situated at an elevation of 2,000 meters, this freshwater lake is encompassed by majestic mountains and lush forests. It was at this very location that the Yihai Lake Alliance was to take place. Liu Bocheng emphasized the Red Army's commitment to aiding the Yi people in breaking free from external oppression and creating a prosperous future of their own after defeating the reactionary forces.

结盟仪式按照彝族的风俗进行。按照彝族礼仪,人们杀了一只大红公鸡,却没有找到酒。刘伯承说只要兄弟有诚意,就以水代酒。面对着蔚蓝的天空和清澈的湖水,刘伯承和小叶丹来到海子边庄重跪下,面前摆着两碗滴过鸡血的水碗。

The ceremony, performed according to the Yi people's rituals, needed a rooster, which they killed, and some liquor, which unfortunately they couldn't find. Liu Bocheng suggested that water should work just fine as long as the bonds of brotherhood remained. So under the blue sky, near the crystal clear Yihai Lake, Liu Bocheng and Xiaoyedan knelt sincerely before two bowls of water mixed with chicken blood.

刘伯承高高端起了碗,大声宣告誓言:"上有天,下有地,我刘伯承与小叶丹今天在海子边结义为兄弟,如有反复,天诛地灭。"说罢,把鸡血水一饮而尽。小叶丹也端起碗起誓道:"我小叶丹今日与刘司令员结为兄弟,愿同生死,如不守约,同此鸡一样死。"说罢,也一饮而尽。

Liu Bocheng raised his bowl and swore solemnly, "Today, with heaven above and earth below, I, Liu Bocheng, and Xiaoyedan became brothers at Haizi (Yihai Lake). If any of us breaks the bonds, we shall be stricken with death by heaven and earth." With the words, he drank up the chicken-blood water. Likewise, Xiaoyedan raised his bowl and swore, "Today, I, Xiaoyedan, became a blood brother of Commander Liu. If I broke the promise of living and dying together, I should perish like this rooster." At this, he drank up the chicken-blood water.

当天晚上,刘伯承请小叶丹叔侄到红军宿营地大桥镇共赴晚宴。饭后,刘伯承把一面写着"中国夷(彝)民红军沽鸡(果基)支队"的红旗赠给小叶丹,并任命小叶丹为支队长,他的弟弟古基尔拉为副支队长,并当场写下任命状,还向他讲解了革命道理。小叶丹表示要铭记在心,之后还动员了一批彝族青年参加红军。之后,小叶丹亲自带路,引导红军进入彝民区,直到走出果基家支地盘,才与刘伯承依依惜别。红军后续部队边沿着"彝海结盟"这条友谊之路,胜利地通过了敌人认为无法通过的彝区,迅速抢渡大渡河,跳出国民党军的包围圈。

On the same night, Liu Bocheng invited Xiaoyedan and his uncle for a meal in Daqiao Town, where the Red Army was based. After the meal, he presented Xiaoyedan with a red flag that read "Chinese Yi People's Red Army Guji (Guoji) Division." He then appointed Xiaoyedan as the captain and his younger brother Gujierla as the deputy leader. Writing out the commission on the spot, Liu Bocheng explained to them very carefully the fundamental guidelines of the revolution. XiaoYedan pledged to remember all the principles and even mobilized some local Yi youths to join the Red Army. After this meeting, Xiaoyedan helped the Red Army find their way into the Yi people's territory and pass through the GuojiJiazhi area, where he had to part with Liu Bocheng's forces. Other Red Army troops later caught up, following the same path, where the two parties formed an ally near the Yihai Lake, Mianning County. Following this route, the Red Army managed to pass through Yi territory, which seemed impossible in the eyes of the KMT. Most critically, they crossed the Dadu River preemptively and breached the encirclement of the KMT forces.

红军走后,国民党追究小叶丹罪责,捉拿小叶丹,强逼果基家交出1.2万两白银和120头羊。小叶丹宁肯倾家荡产,也不愿交出彝家红军旗。他将旗帜随身携带,叮嘱妻子倮伍伍加嫫:"万一我死了,你一定要保护好红军旗,红军一定会回来,到时把旗交给刘伯承!"

After the Red Army left, the KMT accused Xiaoyedan of the trouble. They arrested him and forced him to hand over 12,000 taels (tahil) of silver and 120 sheep. Xiaoyedan refused to compromise, saying he would never hand over the Yi's flag of the Red Army even if he became so broke. He always carried the flag with him and kept it safe. Furthermore, he made it clear to his wife, Luowuwujiamo, "In case I die, you must protect the flag and return it to Liu Bocheng when the Red Army returns."

1942年,小叶丹死于一次伏击。倮伍伍加嫫是一位深明大义、坚韧勇敢的彝家妇女。她在丈夫遇难后的艰难岁月里,以极大的勇气和智慧保存了红军军旗。1950年，解放军解放冕宁，俅伍伍加嫫取出贴身存放的彝家红军旗，献给驻冕宁的解放军。后来，这面旗被中国人民革命军事博物馆永久收藏。它记载了红军和彝民的深厚情谊，是共产党和红军民族政策伟大胜利的见证。共产党也信守着当初向彝族同胞许下的民族自治承诺。1952年，凉山成立彝族自治区，1955年，改成自治州。

After Xiaoyedan died in an ambush in 1942, his wife, Luowuwujiamo, a righteous Yi woman with tremendous tenacity and courage, went through difficult hardships yet was able to keep the Yi people's flag of the Red Army. In 1950, after the People's Liberation Army (hereinafter shortened as PLA) liberated Mianning County, Luowuwujiamo returned the flag to the PLA based in Mianning. Subsequently, this flag found its place as a permanent exhibit at the Military Museum of the Chinese People's Revolution. Serving as a symbol of the lasting connection between the Red Army and the Yi people, it embodies the successful implementation of the CPC and Red Army's policies toward minority communities. The flag also signifies the CPC's steadfast commitment to the autonomy of the Yi people. In 1952, the CPC's government established the Liangshan Yi Autonomous Region, which later evolved into an autonomous prefecture in 1955.

半碗青稞面
Half a Bowl of Barley Flour

在杳无人烟的草地上，红军战士只有可怜的一点青稞面做干粮。周恩来副主席和战士们一样，绝不多吃一口青稞面，还教育战士们，为了能走出草地，北上抗日，一定要格外珍惜粮食。战士们听了他的话，都把仅有的青稞面装在粮袋里，拴在腰上。

Walking on the uninhabited grasslands, the Red Army soldiers didn't have much food except for a meager amount of barley flour. Vice-Chairman Zhou Enlai was as frugal as the soldiers, never eating more than enough. He kept telling the soldiers that they must save every little bit of food until one day they could get out of the grasslands and fight against the Japanese in the north. Knowing the importance of saving food, soldiers would always try to save up any barley flour they could find. They put it in their sacks and even tied it around their waists.

青稞面越来越少了,战士们只能用一点青稞面掺在野菜里煮汤喝。战士吴开生的青稞面吃完了,饿了两天。周副主席知道后,就让警卫员把自己省下的青稞面给吴开生两碗。他看着吴开生蜡黄的脸,语重心长地说:"这是革命呀!"吴开生流着眼泪,说:"我只要有一口气,就要跟你走出草地,革命到底!"

As barley flour ran low, all that the soldiers could do was serve it with wild greens in water. Wu Kaisheng, a soldier, was on an empty stomach for two days, as he had eaten up all his barley flour. When Vice-Chairman Zhou discovered this, he had his guard bring two bowls of barley flour to Wu from the portion he had saved. Looking at the pale-faced soldier, Zhou said, "This is for the revolution!" When Wu heard this, tears welled up in his eyes. He said to the Vice-chairman, "As long as I am breathing, I will walk out of the grasslands with you; I will fight for the revolution till the end of my days!"

这天晚上又是狂风暴雨,用被单搭起的"帐篷"自然挡不住风雨的袭击。战士们都淋成了落汤鸡。周副主席命令战士们都到他作为办公室的帐篷里去休息。大家怕影响他工作,都不肯去。他冒着大雨亲自来了,说:"你们不去,我心不安。"周副主席的话像火烤暖了战士们的心。这样走了几天,草原仍然无边无际。青稞面吃完了,野菜吃光了,军马也杀掉吃了。战士们只好烧皮带吃,甚至把随身带的纸张咽下去充饥,红军陷入了极大的困境。

One night, the grasslands saw another thunderstorm. The Red Army soldiers used their bedsheets to shelter themselves from heavy rain. But this didn't work at all, so they were wet all over. At this moment, Vice-Chairman Zhou ordered them to find shelter in his tent, where he handled office work. But they wouldn't go because they didn't want to interrupt him. To their surprise, Zhou came to them himself against the heavy rain and insisted that they should take shelter in his tent, saying, "I would be very concerned if you didn't go." His kind words warmed their hearts. The troops had been marching in such bad weather for days, but the grasslands still seemed hopelessly immense. Soon they ran out of barley flour and even wild herbs. To help fill their stomachs, they had to kill army horses and even boil their leather belts. Sometimes, they swallowed paper they could find to appease their hunger. The Red Army forces, trapped in these intensive hardships, underwent the most difficult moments.

周副主席命令把仅存的半碗青稞面全部分给大家泡水喝。"那您吃什么呢？"警卫员急了。周副主席说道："有同志们活着，就有我。只要多留一个战士的生命，就给革命事业增加一份力量，拿出来分掉！"这掺上一点青稞面的热水，分到战士们的手中。战士们流泪了，这不足半碗的青稞面，是周副主席的心意和生命啊！战士们又上路了，在茫茫的草地上，行进着摧不垮的钢铁红军。

Vice-Chairman Zhou brought out half a bowl of barley flour, the only portion he had left, and ordered everyone to eat it with water. "But what will you eat?" asked his guard. Vice-Chairman Zhou said: "If you all survive, I will survive. If I could help one more soldier who will contribute to the revolutionary cause, I will offer what I have!" The soldiers got a share of the barley flour mixed with hot water, all with tears in their eyes. Even though it was just half a bowl of barley flour, they understood the sacrifice the Vice-chairman had paid and the expectations he had of them. With this half-bowl of barley flour, the unbreakable Red Army troops continued to march on in the wilderness.

半截皮带
Half a Belt

在艰难的长征途中，红军战士每天面临的不仅仅是敌人的飞机大炮和围追堵截，也不只是极度恶劣的自然条件，还有缺衣少食的重重困难。在漫无边际的草地里，没有足够的粮食，不得不吃野菜。1936年7月，红四方面军31军93师274团八连和兄弟部队开始第三次穿越草地。刚进入草地没多久，战士们就陷入了断粮的困境，只好挖野菜、嚼草根、啃树皮，后来，连野菜也找不到了，只好解下自己的牛皮腰带煮着吃。

Throughout the arduous journey, the treacherous situations the Red Army soldiers underwent were not just air attacks from KMT planes, assaults from Nationalist brigades, and harsh natural conditions but also the chronic shortages of food and clothes. There were just endless fields, going far to the horizon on the grasslands. When the Red Army troops were low on food, they relied on wild herbs. In July 1936, the Eighth Company of the 274th Regiment of the 93rd Division of the 31st Army of the Fourth Front Red Army and other fellow troops began to trek through the grasslands for the third time. Since the Red Army troops entered the grasslands, food had started running low. Soldiers had to eat wild greens, grass roots, and even tree bark. But whenever even these were hard to come by, they had to boil their leather belts to fill their stomachs.

周广才是位年仅14岁的战士。他所在的班原来有14名战士,牺牲了七个,另外七名战士都只有靠吃皮带维持生命。当班里其他6名战友的皮带都吃完后,周广才不得不把自己的皮带拿出来。看着心爱的皮带被切成一根根皮带丝漂在稀溜溜的汤水里,周广才难过得掉下了眼泪。当吃完皮带第一个眼的时候,周广才眼里噙着泪水,说道:"同志们,我们把它留下作个纪念吧,带着它到陕北,去找党中央,去见毛主席!"战友们都知道,周广才的这条皮带是他在1934年任合场战斗中缴获的战利品。大家见状,没有把这根皮带吃掉,而是怀着对革命胜利的憧憬,忍饥挨饿,将这剩下的半截皮带保留了下来。在随后的长征途中,周广才的其他六位战友相继牺牲,只有他随红四方面军胜利到达了延安。为了缅怀牺牲的战友,他用铁筷子在皮带背面烙上了"长征记"三个字,并用红绸子包裹起来。1975年,周广才把珍藏了几十年的半截皮带捐赠给中国革命博物馆。

Zhou Guangcai, a 14-year-old soldier, marched with a squad of fourteen soldiers, among which seven lost their lives en route. As they were out of food, the remaining soldiers had to boil their leather belts to eat. When they ate up belts of the other six soldiers, Zhou Guangcai felt pressured to use his belt for food. Watching his belt cut off into shreds, Zhou felt upset, tears welling up in his eyes. After eating a half piece of the belt, he begged to keep the other half as a souvenir of the Long March and suggested they take it with them to the revolutionary base of the CPC Central Committee in the northern Shaanxi Province, where they would meet Chairman Mao. They all knew that this belt was a trophy of the Red Army in the battle of Renhechang in 1934. Hearing this, the other soldiers decided not to eat the remaining belt, even if it meant they had to endure starvation, but they would do it for the cause of the revolution. Unfortunately, these six soldiers died later during the Long March, and only Zhou made it to Yan'an City with the Fourth Front Red Army. To remember those who sacrificed their lives, Zhou Guangcai engraved in the belt with a hot iron chopstick three Chinese characters: Chang Zheng Ji (长征记), meaning "Something to Remember the Long March". He then wrapped it up with red silks and kept it in good condition until 1975, when Zhou donated the half-belt, preserved under his watch for decades, to the National Museum of China.

苗族战士"云贵川"
The Miao Soldier "Yun-Gui-Chuan"

1935年9月13日,红军走过草地后,于9月17日到达腊子口。而甘肃军阀(时任第14师师长)鲁大昌(1889—1962)把守住了腊子口山后的天险要道。这样一个有敌人重兵把守的天险之地,红军却必须不惜一切代价攻破它。腊子口打不开,我军往南不好回,往北又出不去,无论军事上、政治上,都会处于进退失据的境地。

On September 13, 1935, the Red Army troops, just out of the grasslands, headed toward Lazikou Pass in southern Gansu Province and arrived there on September 17. The narrow mountain pass was heavily guarded by Lu Dachang (1889–1962), a local warlord (then commander of the 14th Division of the Nationalist regime). The order came through that the Red Army must take Lazikou Pass at all costs. A failure in this mission would result in the Red Army troops being compelled to retreat through the southern grasslands, leaving them trapped at the Pass and unable to proceed northward.

鲁大昌安排两个营的兵力在腊子口层层构筑工事,还部署了三个团的兵力纵深把守住腊子口山后的天险要道,企图阻断红军北上之路。当地民谣说:"人过腊子口,像过老虎口",敌人在此构筑的工事更无异于给腊子口这个虎口装上了利齿,想一口吞噬红军。

To keep the Red Army forces from heading north, Lu Dachang had two battalions build fortifications at Lazikou Pass and deployed three regiments to guard the passages in the mountains. A folk song, saying, "To pass Lazikou is like entering the tiger's lair," reveals how impregnable the position is for the Red Army troops. And with the fortification built there, conquering Lazikou Pass seemed even more difficult.

腊子口地势十分险要,一座大山似乎是被谁用一把巨斧从中劈开,峭壁在头上直上云天,两边岩石相距只有50、60米宽,腊子河湍急地在脚下流过,穿过两山间一道长约百多米的狭窄的走廊。就在两山之间的河面上,有一道木桥,是这里的唯一通道。

The Lazikou Pass breeds danger, given its location. It is as if someone split the mountain into halves with a gigantic ax, leaving a chasm, more than fifty or sixty meters in width, flanked by cliffs on both sides, rising almost perpendicular for a thousand feet. At the foot of the pass was a river, gushing through a narrow 100-meter-long corridor. Across the chasm, between the cliffs, and over the rushing river, there is one wooden bridge, the only passage here.

红四团作为先头部队,在团长黄开湘(1901—1935)、政委杨成武(1914—2004)的带领下,向腊子口发起了攻击。然而,敌人在这里修筑了坚固的工事,依仗着武器的精良,依托大山的阻挡,给红军的前进造成了极大困难。红四团的多次冲锋都没有成功。

The vanguard army of the Red Fourth Regiment, led by regimental commander Huang Kaixiang (1901 – 1935) and political commissar Yang Chengwu (1914 – 2004), launched the first attack on Lazikou Pass, yet encountered huge setbacks. The better armed enemy built fortifications all over the mountain, which severely hampered the Red Army's operation. A succession of attacks failed.

在那个关键时刻,一名入伍不久,外号叫"云贵川"的贵州苗族战士站了出来。在腊子口战役中这个小战士毛遂自荐,说他能爬上去。小伙子从小就生活在大山里,曾在悬崖绝壁上采药,练就了一身攀岩走壁的好本领,这样的山崖对他来说并非难事。于是天黑后,团长黄开湘率一支部队来到那道绝壁之下。

The troops were planning on another attack on Lazikou, but they needed someone who could climb to the top of the mountain pass. A Miao soldier from Guizhou, nicknamed "Yun-Gui-Chuan", stood out. He told the commanders that rock climbing on cliffs was an easy job for him as he used to collect herbs on the cliffs as a child. Therefore, after nightfall, commander Huang Kaixiang led a group of soldiers to the foot of the cliff to be conquered.

"你给我一根长杆,上面系住钩子,我就可以利用悬崖峭壁的石嘴缝隙爬上去。如果我爬上去了,不要说一个班、一个排,一个营的战士都能爬上去。"这位苗族小伙不负众望,真的爬上了山崖,"云贵川"第一个撕开了长征天险腊子口。他爬到山顶后,甩下用绑带结成的长绳,让一连的战士爬到山顶,在天亮前到达了攻击位置。红军从天而降出现在敌人阵地的侧面,并向山下的部队发出总攻信号,决定红军生死存亡的腊子口战役由此拉开。最后这个小战士腰间绑着手榴弹又一次从山的后方迂回到前方直接跳到敌人最猛的碉堡中,与敌人同归于尽。

He told them, "I need a long pole with a hook attached to it, with which I can climb up through the crevices on the rocks of the cliffs. If I could make it, all troops, be it a squad, a platoon, or a battalion, would make it." What the Miao fellow promised came true. He managed to get to the top of the cliff, becoming the first person to sabotage the enemy's plan at Lazikou Pass. Standing atop the cliff, he threw the long ropes, made of straps, down the cliff to soldiers waiting underneath. With his help, the troops made it to the top of the mountain, taking up the attack position before dawn. In this way, the company could flank the enemy on one side. Soon came the order to start the general attack on Lazikou, triggering a life-and-death battle of the Red Army. In his last operation, "Yun-Gui-Chuan" took a detour to the front of the enemy from the back of the mountain and then threw himself into the enemy's bunker with a grenade tied around his waist. He died but triumphed gloriously in bringing down the enemy.

腊子口战役虽然胜利结束了,可这位小战士却永远地留在了这里。据记载,这个小战士在腊子口战役中牺牲时只有 17 岁,甚至连姓名都没有留下。由于他是在贵州入伍的苗族战士,走过了云南、贵州、四川三个省,于是,大家都叫他"云贵川"。

Although the battle of Lazikou Pass was over, this young soldier remained there forever. According to historical records, he was only 17 years old when he died. No one knew his true name, but it was known that he belonged to the Miao minority and joined the army in Guizhou province. He journeyed with the Red Army through the provinces of Yunnan, Guizhou, and Sichuan, earning him the nickname "Yun-Gui-Chuan".

第三节 红色景点
Section Ⅲ Red Tourism Attractions

大渡河上的铁索桥:泸定桥
Luding Bridge: The Iron Chain Bridge over the Dadu River

泸定桥旅游区位于四川省甘孜州泸定县泸桥镇,横跨大渡河,东接县城。泸定桥又称大渡河铁索桥,始建于清康熙四十四年(1705),建成于康熙四十五年(1706 年)。康熙御笔题写"泸定桥",桥东立康熙《御制泸定桥碑记》,记载了修桥的原因、桥的规模及维修办法等。此桥为铁索悬桥。桥长 103 米,宽 3 米,桥两端各有 20 米高的桥台,桥台内固定铁桩,13 根铁链固定在两岸桥台的落井铁桩里,其中 9 根作底链,上铺木板,4 根分两侧作扶手。铁链共有 12164 个铁环相扣,全桥铁件重 40 余吨。两岸桥头堡为木结构古建筑。

图 3-1　泸定桥
Figure 3-1　Luding Bridge

The Luding Bridge Scenic Area is situated in Luqiao Town, Luding County, Garze Tibetan Autonomous Prefecture, Sichuan Province. It is traversed by the Dadu River, which connects the town to the eastern part of the county. The Luding Bridge, also known as the Dadu River Chain Bridge, began construction in the 44th year of the reign of Emperor Kangxi in the Qing Dynasty (1705 AD) and was completed in the 45th year of Emperor Kangxi (1706 AD). At the entrance hangs the inscription of the characters for "Lu Ding Qiao" [泸定桥] (Luding Bridge) in the calligraphy of the Emperor Kangxi. On the east of the bridge stands the "Royal Stele for Luding Bridge" with an inscription by the emperor. The stele documents the details of the bridge, including reasons for construction, scale, and maintenance. The bridge, 103 meters in length and 3 meters in width, is an iron suspension bridge over the Dadu River. Each end of the bridge rests on a 20-meter-high abutment with iron piles fixed inside. Thirteen iron chains are fixed in the wells of the bridge abutments on both sides, of which nine are used as bottom chains and four as handrails on both sides (equally two on each side). There are altogether 12,164 interlocking metal rings, and the metal parts of the whole bridge weigh more than 40 tons. The bridgeheads on both ends present a style of antique Chinese wooden structure.

自清代以来,泸定桥为四川入藏的咽喉要道和军事要津。1863 年,太平天国起义中骁勇善战的翼王石达开在此抢渡大渡河失利,全军覆没。1935 年 5 月 29 日,中国工农红军第一方面军第二师以 22 位勇士为突击队,在此消灭守敌,飞夺泸定桥,摆脱了蒋介石的追兵,泸定桥因而成为中国近代史上的一座丰碑,闻名世界。

Since the Qing Dynasty, the Luding Bridge has been the most critical military fortress for people to enter the Tibetan area from Sichuan Province. In 1863, Shi Dakai, known as the Wing King and one of the most brilliant generals of the Taiping Rebellion Campaign, suffered a devastating defeat trying to cross the Dadu River, with his entire Taiping army eliminated. On May 29, 1935, the Red Army headquarters decided to organize a commando unit with 22 gallant soldiers from the Second Division of the First Front Red Army to cross the river by force. After grueling struggles, they eventually seized Luding Bridge and stopped the KMT's forces that were hotly pursuing them. The Luding Bridge battle is the most famous moment in the Long March and a defining legend of modern China.

泸定桥建筑风貌独特,为世界和我国所独有。泸定桥参观浏览点由三部分组成:一是泸定桥。二是泸定桥革命文物博物馆,馆内以照片、资料、实物展出红军强渡大渡河、飞夺泸定桥等情况,以及当时红军领导的题词,著名书法家、画家的书法、名画。三是"红军飞夺泸定桥纪念碑"及其公园,邓小平题写的碑名,聂荣臻撰写的碑文。纪念碑及其公园设计新颖,把纪念意义、地方风情、艺术博览和旅游观光融为一体。

The Luding Bridge boasts a unique architectural style, found exclusively in China and well-recognized globally. Touring the Luding Bridge involves visiting three scenes: the Luding Bridge; the Luding Bridge Revolutionary Relics Museum, which displays photos, documentary literature, physical objects, inscriptions of the Red Army leaders, and the calligraphical works and paintings of famous artists, showcasing how the Red Army forcefully crossed the Dadu River and swiftly seized the Luding Bridge; and the Red Army Seizing the Luding Bridge Memorial Monument, which displays the inscription of the monument's name written by Deng Xiaoping and the epigraph by Nie Rongzhen. It stands in a park, distinctively designed, incorporating the meaning of commemoration with local customs, art collections, and tourism.

泸定桥是土地革命战争遗址,1961年3月4日,国务院首批公布泸定桥为全国重点文物保护单位。

Luding Bridge is a relic of the Agrarian Revolutionary War. On March 4,

1961, the State Council announced the Luding Bridge as one of the first batches of the National Key Cultural Relics Protection Units.

长征翻越的第一座雪山：夹金山
Mt. Jiajin: the First Snow-Capped Mountain During the Long March

"走到夹金山，伸手能摸天。"横跨在四川省雅安市宝兴县与阿坝藏族羌族自治州小金县之间的夹金山，是毛泽东、周恩来、朱德率领中央红军长征途中翻越的第一座大雪山。

图 3-2 红军长征翻越夹金山纪念馆
Figure 3-2 Red Army Long March Crossing Mt. Jiajin Memorial Hall

As a folk rhyme says, "If you enter Mt. Jiajin, you will reach the sky." Mt. Jiajin spans somewhere between the Baoxing County of Ya'an City in Sichuan Province and Xiaojin County in Aba Tibetan and Qiang Autonomous Prefecture. The mountain is the first snow-capped summit crossed by the Red Army, under the leadership of Mao Zedong, Zhou Enlai, and Zhu De, during the Long March.

夹金山，以高山湖泊、红军遗迹、民族风情独树一帜，有大雪山、大熊猫半野生放养保护区，使自然生态与之巧妙组合构成了一幅动态的天然山水画卷，是向世界推出的一条大熊猫生态旅游精品线。

Mt. Jiajin is unique for its alpine lakes and ethnic customs where the Red Army left their footprints. There is Snowy Mountain, and a semi-wild panda reserve, presenting a picturesque view amidst the natural landscapes. Here, booming tourism has developed around the pandas in this natural environment, a site which is becoming famous globally.

会宁红军会师旧址
Huining Red Army Joint Forces Site

在丝绸古路上,坐落着一个历史重镇——会宁,在1936年,这座千年古镇再次在历史上留下了浓墨重彩的一笔:红军长征胜利会师!这标志着长征的胜利结束。会宁这座小镇也因此成为"国家第一批百名爱国主义教育基地"之一,"国家安全教育基地",入选全国红色旅游经典景区名录。景区包含了会师楼、会师塔、红军会师联欢会会址、会宁红军长征胜利纪念馆、红军总司令部旧址、红军长征将帅碑林、红一方面军指挥部旧址、红军政治部驻地旧址、红军演讲台旧址、红二方面军指挥部旧址、红四方面军指挥部旧址等景点。

图 3-3　会宁红军会师旧址
Figure 3-3　Huining Red Army Joint Forces Site

Along the Silk Road is situated a historical town—Huining. In 1936, this thousand-year-old town once again celebrated a significant victory—the joining of the Red Army forces during the Long March, marking the end of the Long March.

Because of this historic feat, Huining Town has become one of the first batch of National Patriotism Education Base, the Base for National Safety Education, and one of the National Classic Red Tourist Scenic Areas. The Scenic Area includes the Joint Forces Gate Tower, the Joint Forces Tower, the Red Army Joint Forces Celebration Site, the Huining Red Army Long March Victory Memorial Hall, the Red Army Headquarters Site, the Red Army's Long March Generals' Memorials, the First Front Red Army Headquarters Site, the Red Army Political Department Site, the Red Army's Podium Site, the Second Front Red Army Headquarters Site, and the Fourth Front Red Army Headquarters Site.

会师楼
Joint Forces Gate Tower

会师楼及城墙建于明朝洪武六年,原为古城西城门,也称"西津门",建成后历经多次损毁、补修。新中国成立后,分别在 1986 年、2006 年在原址上进行了两次维修。城墙高 10 米,城门为拱形,是明代建筑风格。城楼高 7 米,是二层木质建筑。城楼龙脊兽瓦、飞檐翘角,城墙古朴典雅、巍峨壮观。为纪念 1936 年红军主力在会宁胜利会师,1952 年,"西津门"更名为"会师门",城楼命名为"会师楼"。

图 3-4 会宁红军会师楼
Figure 3-4 Huining Red Army Joint Forces Gate Tower

The Joint Forces Gate Tower, together with its walls, was built in the sixth year of the Hongwu Emperor of the Ming Dynasty. It was the original West Gate of the ancient town, also known as "Xijin Gate". Since its completion, it has been under repair many times for damage. Since the founding of New China, it has undergone repairs and maintenance twice, once in 1986 and again in 2006. The walls are 10 meters high, featuring an arched gate, and bear the architectural style of the Ming Dynasty. The gate tower is a seven-meter-high two-story wooden structure with tiles featuring patterns of dragons and lions, particular brackets, and angled cornices. The gate's wall looks simple, elegant, and majestic. To commemorate the successful joining of three major Red Army forces in Huining in 1936, "Xijin Gate" was changed to "Joint Forces Gate" in 1952, and the gate tower as "Joint Forces Gate Tower".

会师塔
Joint Forces Tower

会师塔始建于 1986 年。塔高 28.78 米,一至十层为三塔合抱,第十一层又合为一塔。三塔合抱象征红军三大主力在会宁会师。塔高 11 层,则寓意着红军长征时途经了 11 个省、自治区。会师塔正面镌刻着邓小平题写的"中国工农红军第一、二、四方面军会师纪念塔"这 18 个白底红字的大字。

图 3-5 会宁红军会师塔
Figure 3-5 Huining Red Army Joint Forces Tower

The Joint Forces Tower was built in 1986, reaching a height of 28.78 meters. The first ten floors are comprised of three towers joined in a triangular fashion, with the final eleventh floor emerging in the center as a singular tower, symbolizing the joint forces of the three major Red Army forces. The eleven stories represent the eleven provinces and autonomous regions that the Red Army passed through during the Long March. There is an inscription of 18 Chinese characters written in red by Deng Xiaoping and engraved upon a white background, posted in front of the tower. It reads: "The Memorial Tower of the First, Second, and Fourth Front forces of the Chinese Workers' and Peasants' Red Army".

会宁红军长征纪念馆
Huining Red Army Long March Memorial Hall

会宁红军长征纪念馆始建于2006年,于当年10月份开馆。馆内有藏品千余件,珍贵文物百余件。会宁红军长征纪念馆是一座专题性纪念馆,主要展现了红军会宁师、长征胜利结束这一伟大诗篇。在有关长征的纪念馆中,该馆是规模最大、全面展示红军长征的纪念馆,入选全国爱国主义教育示范基地。

图 3-6 会宁红军长征纪念馆
Figure 3-6 Huining Red Army Long March Memorial Hall

The construction of the Huining Red Army Long March Memorial Hall began in 2006, and it was opened to the public in October of the same year. There are more than 1,000 collections, including over 100 invaluable relics on display. The Huining Red Army Long March Memorial Hall is a theme-based museum that mainly focuses on the victorious joining forces of the Red Army that marks the end of the Long March. It stands as the largest memorial hall of its kind, showcasing the resounding triumph of the Long March in its entirety, and currently serves as a National Demonstration Base for Patriotism Education.

六盘山红军长征纪念馆
Liupanshan Red Army Long March Memorial Hall

六盘山红军长征纪念馆于2005年9月落成,位于宁夏固原六盘山上。六盘山有广义和狭义之分。广义的六盘山是指六盘山脉,是中国最年轻的山脉之一。狭义的六盘山指六盘山脉第二高峰六盘山,海拔2928米。据说山路曲折险峻,须经六重盘道方能登顶,故名六盘山。这里是红军长征途中翻越的最后一座高山,毛主席在这里留下了传世名篇《清平乐·六盘山》。

图 3-7 六盘山红军长征纪念馆
Figure 3-7 Liupanshan Red Army Long March Memorial Hall

The Liupanshan Red Army Long March Memorial Hall, completed in September 2005, sits on the Liupan Mountain in Guyuan City of the Ningxia Hui Autonomous Region. Liupanshan refers to Liupan Mountains, one of the youngest mountain ranges in China; it also refers to Mt. Liupan, the second-highest peak of the Liupan Mountains, standing at an altitude of 2,928 meters. One has to take six twisting mountain roads to reach the top, hence the name of the Mt. Liupan (six twisting mountains literally). The Liupan Mountains were the last ranges that the Red Army had to conquer during the Long March. Given its strategic significance, Chairman Mao wrote a famous poem, "The Liupan Mountains", to praise the heroic deeds of the Red Army forces.

六盘山红军长征纪念馆占地面积广,是国家4A级景区。主要包括纪念碑、纪念馆、纪念广场、吟诗台、红军小道等景点构成。是全国首批百个经典红色旅游景区之一,也是"全国爱国主义教育示范基地""全国国防教育示范基地""全国廉政教育基地"。

The Liupanshan Red Army Long March Memorial Hall, covering a large area, a National 4A-level Scenic Spot, consists of a memorial monument, a memorial hall, a memorial square, a stage for poetry, a Red Army trail, and other scenes. It is one of the country's first batches of the 100 Classic Red Tourist Attractions. At the same time, the spot serves as a National Patriotism Education Demonstration Base, a National Defense Education Demonstration Base, and a National Corruption Prevention Education Base.

纪念碑修建在纪念馆顶部平台,是全国首例馆上有碑,碑下是馆的结构。整体为钢架结构,东西两侧玻璃幕墙上分别嵌着毛主席的长征途中创作的著名诗篇《七律·长征》和《清平乐·六盘山》手写体。

The Memorial Monument is built on top of the Memorial Hall. It is the first in the country with this structure. The entire structure is steel-framed, with glass walls on its east and west sides, embedded with two hand-calligraphed poems, "The Long March" and "The Liupan Mountains" by Chairman Mao.

纪念馆占地面积2159平方米,由红军长征纪念亭扩建而成。纪念馆有四个展厅,每个展厅均以毛泽东长征途中创作的诗词名句命名,分别是"红军不怕远征难""红旗漫卷西风""三军过后尽开颜""不到长城非好汉"。展出400余张图片,近300件实物,以及油画创作、雕塑、场景复原、多媒体展示等类型,主要展示红军长征过程,尤其是红军长征翻越六盘山的历史。

The memorial hall, expanded from the old Red Army Long March Memorial Pavilion, covers an area of 2,159 square meters. Inside the building there are four exhibition halls, each of which takes its name from a famous poem or line by Mao Zedong, who wrote them during the Long March. The exhibitions display more than 400 pictures, nearly 300 physical objects, and some collections such as oil paintings and sculptures. The hall also presents some replicated scenes reflecting crucial moments of the Red Army forces and multimedia rooms showcasing those critical events of the Red Army during the Long March, in particular, the historical moments of the Red Army climbing over the Liupan Mountains.

纪念广场长71米,宽81米,寓意着"七一建党""八一建军"。广场入口处是六根文化柱和两组浮雕。文化柱高10.7米,纪念红军10月7日翻越六盘山。文化柱上分别展示了井冈山、瑞金、遵义、将台堡、延安以及开国大典时天安门的恢宏景象。广场后方则是由三面红军军旗组成的影壁,上面有江泽民题词的"长征精神永放光芒"八个大字。

The 71-meter-long, 81-meter-wide Memorial Square indicates the founding of the CPC on July 1 and the establishment of the Chinese PLA on August 1. At the entrance of the Square stand six stone columns and two reliefs. The 10.7-meter-high stone columns, designed to commemorate the Red Army forces climbing over the Liupan Mountains during the Long March on October 7, showcase some significant events happening in different places, including the Jinggangshan City, Ruijin City, Zunyi City, Jiangtaibao County, Yan'an City, and Tiananmen Square featuring the founding ceremony of the People's Republic of China. At the back of the Square stands a screen wall composed of three Red Army flags with the inscriptions of eight characters written by then President Jiang Zemin, which reads "长征精神永放光芒" (changzheng jingshen yongfang guangmang, meaning "The Spirit of the Long March Shines Throughout Human History").

红军小道利用六盘山的山水景致,将诸如血战湘江、强渡乌江、遵义会议、攻占娄山关、爬雪山、过草地、决战腊子口等18个长征途中的重要场景,从山脚到山顶,按照时间顺序布置成了微缩景观。红军小道长约 2.5 公里,一路展现了红军两万五千里长征的画卷。

The Red Army Trail, built upon the Liupan Mountains and aligned with its natural landscapes, features 18 phenomenal scenes during the Long March, which include Crossing the Xiangjiang River, Crossing the Wujiang River, Holding the Zunyi Meeting, Taking the Loushanguan Pass, Climbing Over Snow-Capped Mountains, Crossing the Grasslands, and Conquering the Lazikou Pass. These scenes, starting from the foot of the mountain and then up to the mountain top in chronological order of the Long March events, present a miniature landscape. The 2.5-kilometer-long Red Army Trail mirrors the journey of the Red Army's 2,5000-Li Long March.

专栏 3：长征精神

Special Column Ⅲ: The Long March Spirit

伟大的长征铸就了伟大的长征精神。2016 年 10 月 21 日，习近平总书记在纪念红军长征胜利 80 周年大会的重要讲话中指出："长征是一次理想信念的伟大远征。伟大长征精神，把全国人民和中华民族的根本利益看得高于一切，坚定革命的理想和信念，坚信正义事业必然胜利的精神；就是为了救国救民，不怕任何艰难险阻，不惜付出一切牺牲的精神；就是坚持独立自主、实事求是，一切从实际出发的精神；就是顾全大局、严守纪律、紧密团结的精神；就是紧紧依靠人民群众，同人民群众生死相依、患难与共、艰苦奋斗的精神。"

The remarkable Long March forged the great Long March Spirit. On October 21, 2016, in the important speech at the commemoration of the 80th anniversary of the victory of the Red Army's Long March, General Secretary Xi Jinping noted that, "the Long March was a great journey built on ideals and beliefs. The Spirit of the Long March was about regarding the fundamental interests of the Chinese people and nation as paramount, holding fast to revolutionary ideals and convictions, and firmly believing that just causes will prevail. It is the spirit of sacrificing everything to save the country and the people, regardless of the difficulties and obstacles. It was about remaining committed to independence and self-reliance, seeking truth from fact, and grounding all we do in reality. It was about seeing the bigger picture, upholding strict discipline, and maintaining strong unity. And it was about relying closely on the people, sharing their fate, and standing together through tough times, and working hard alongside them."

第四章　遵义：历史转折　出奇制胜

Chapter Ⅳ　Zunyi: A Surprising and Victorious Turn in History

"遵义"之名,出自《尚书》"无偏无陂,遵王之义",意思是要遵循贤哲先王的教导,行为要端正,做事不偏颇。1935年1月,遵义迎来了一支人民自己的军队——中国工农红军。由中国共产党领导的这支军队,当时因军事领导的错误濒临绝境,来到遵义后,红军改换了掌舵人,中国革命的航船由此转危为安。在贵州的崇山峻岭中,红军创造了"四渡赤水"等人类战争史上一连串出奇制胜的经典战役。遵义这座转折之城,为中国革命带来福祉,为中国革命转运。

The name "Zunyi" comes from the *Book of Historical Documents*: "without deflection, without unevenness, pursue ('zun') the royal righteousness ('yi')", which means to follow the teachings of the sages and the previous kings that one should act in an impartial and unbiased manner. In January 1935, Zunyi ushered in an army of the people's own—The Chinese Workers' and Peasants' Red Army. The army led by the CPC was then in a severe predicament due to mistakes of its military leadership. After arriving in Zunyi, the Red Army changed helmsman, and the ship of the Chinese revolution turned from danger to safety. In the high mountains and lofty hills of Guizhou, the Red Army fought a series of classic battles in the history of human warfare, such as the "The Four Crossings of the Chishui River". Zunyi, a city of a historic turning point, proved to be a blessed city for the Chinese revolution and witnessed a positive shift of outlook for the Chinese revolution.

第一节 历史回眸
Section I A Glimpse of History

中央红军开始长征
The Central Red Army Began the Long March

井冈山革命根据地建立后,中国共产党领导的革命根据地广泛建立,并得到广大农民的支持和拥护,根据地不断扩大。红军和根据地的迅速发展使国民党统治集团感到震惊。1930年至1932年,蒋介石调集重兵向根据地和红军发动了四次大规模"围剿",企图破坏根据地,消灭共产党。共产党领导的红军在根据地人民的支持下,一次又一次地粉碎了敌人的"围剿"。红军在反"围剿"的斗争中,形成了"避敌主力,诱敌深入,集中兵力,各个歼灭""打得赢就打,打不赢就走"的战略战术思想,解决了红军以劣势兵力和落后装备战胜强大敌人的问题。

After the establishment of the Jinggangshan revolutionary base area, the revolutionary bases under the leadership of the CPC were widely established and expanded. These base areas received the support and recognition of a vast number of peasants. The rapid development of the Red Army and the base areas shocked the ruling clique of the KMT. From 1930 to 1932, Chiang Kai-shek mobilized a large number of troops to launch four large-scale encirclement and suppression campaigns against the rerolutionary base areas and the Red Army, attempting to destroy the base areas and eliminate the Communist Party. With the support of the people in the base areas, the CPC-led Red Army shattered the enemy's encirclement and suppression time and again. In the campaigns against encirclement and suppression, the Red Army had formed valuable strategic and tactical thoughts, such as "avoiding the enemy's main force, luring the enemy in deep, concentrating superior forces, and defeating in detail" and "if I can win, I will fight; if I cannot win, I will run away". These strategic and tactical thoughts laid the foundation for the Red Army, which had inferior troops and relatively backward military equipment, to be able to defeat the powerful enemy.

1933年下半年,蒋介石发动对革命根据地的第五次"围剿",调集100万军队向各地红军进攻,其中50万军队于9月下旬开始向中央革命根据地发动进攻。由于以王明为代表的"左"倾教条主义的错误,红军第五次反"围剿"失败。1934年10月,中央红军主力8.6万多人被迫撤离中央革命根据地,开始战略转移,踏上漫漫征程。

In the second half of 1933, Chiang Kai-shek launched a fifth campaign of encirclement and suppression against the revolutionary base areas. He assembled one million troops for an assault on the Red Army in various areas. 500,000 KMT troops began their attack on the central revolutionary bases in late September. Due to the mistakes of the "Left" leaning dogmatism represented by Wang Ming, the Red Army's Fifth Campaign against KMT Encirclement and Suppression ended in failure. In October 1934, the main force of the Central Red Army, with more than 86,000 people, was forced to evacuate from the central revolutionary base areas, begin a strategic shift, and embark on a long journey.

湘江战役
The Battle of Xiangjiang River

蒋介石调集了16个师、77个团的庞大兵力进行"追剿",布置了四道封锁线对红军围追堵截。中央红军接连突破敌人三道封锁线后,于1934年11月下旬进入广西湘江地区。11月27日至12月1日,中央红军在湘江上游的兴安县、全州县、灌阳县,与数倍自己的国民党军苦战五昼夜,最终强渡湘江,突破了国民党军的第四道封锁线,粉碎了蒋介石围歼中央红军于湘江以东的企图。湘江战役是红军长征的壮烈一战,是事关中国革命生死存亡的重要历史事件。此次战役后,中央红军由长征出发时的8.6万多人锐减至3万多人,红军的鲜血染红了湘江。当地百姓为纪念牺牲的红军战士,流传下"三年不饮湘江水,十年不食湘江鱼"的说法。

Chiang Kai-shek mobilized a strong force of 16 divisions and 77 regiments to "pursue" the Red Army, for which four blockade lines were set up to encircle, pursue, obstruct and intercept the Red Army. After breaking through the enemy's three blockades one after another, the Central Red Army entered the Xiangjiang area of Guangxi in late November 1934. From November 27 to December 1, the Central Red Army fought arduously for five days and nights with a KMT army several times the size of Red Army. These battles occurred in Xing'an County, Quanzhou County and Guanyang County in the upper reaches of the Xiangjiang River, and the Central Red Army finally crossed the Xiangjiang River by force, breaking through the fourth blockade of the KMT army. This battle shattered Chiang Kai-shek's attempt to encircle and destroy the Central Red Army to the east of the Xiangjiang River. The Battle of Xiangjiang was a heroic and critical battle in the Red Army's Long March, and it was an important historical event concerning the life and death of the Chinese revolution. After the battle, the Central Red Army troops dropped sharply from more than 86,000 at the time of departure to little more than 30,000, and the blood of the Red Army soldiers stained the Xiangjiang River. In order to commemorate the fallen Red Army soldiers, there was a saying circulating among the local people that "you don't drink Xiangjiang water for three years, and you don't eat Xiangjiang fish for ten years".

湘江战役后,党内对中央红军的前进方向一直存在激烈争论。1934年12月18日,中央政治局在贵州黎平举行会议,根据毛泽东的建议,通过决议,放弃到湘西北同红二、红六军团会合的计划,改向贵州北部进军。

After the Battle of Xiangjiang River, there was a heated debate within the Party over the direction of the Central Red Army. On December 18, 1934, the Political Bureau of the Party Central Committee held a meeting in Liping, Guizhou. Following Mao Zedong's suggestion, the Party passed a resolution which abandoned the plan for the Central Red Army to join the Second and Sixth Red Army Legions in the northwest of Hunan, and instead decided that the army would march to the north of Guizhou.

遵义会议
The Zunyi Meeting

在遵义会议前,红军遭受了第五次反"围剿"的失败和长征初期的一系列损失。特别是在湘江战役中遭受重大损失后,广大干部战士对王明军事路线的怀疑和不满达到顶点,一些执行王明军事路线的党和红军的高级干部重新认识到以毛泽东为代表的正确军事路线。

Before the Zunyi Meeting, the Red Army suffered the failure of the fifth counter-encirclement and suppression campaign and a series of losses in the early stages of the Long March. Especially after suffering heavy losses in the Battle of Xiangjiang, the suspicion of and the dissatisfaction with Wang Ming's military line among the majority of Red Army cadres and soldiers reached a climax, and some senior Party and Red Army cadres who had implemented Wang Ming's military line re-recognized the correct military line represented by Mao Zedong.

1935年1月7日,红军攻克遵义。1月15日至17日,党中央在遵义城琵琶桥东侧87号(现遵义市红花岗区子尹路96号)黔军第二十五军第二师师长柏辉章的公馆里召开了政治局扩大会议,即遵义会议。出席会议的有政治局委员和候补委员毛泽东、周恩来、朱德、陈云、张闻天(洛甫)、秦邦宪(博古)、刘少奇、王稼祥、邓发、何克全(凯丰),中央秘书长邓小平,红军总部和各军团负责人刘伯承、李富春、聂荣臻、彭德怀、杨尚昆、李卓然、林彪,共产国际派来的军事顾问李德,翻译伍修权。

On January 7, 1935, the Red Army captured Zunyi. From January 15 to 17, the CPC Central Committee held an enlarged meeting of the Political Bureau in the residence of Bai Huizhang, the commander of the Second Division of the 25th KMT Army or the Guizhou Army, at No. 87 east of Pipa Bridge in Zunyi City (now No. 96, Ziyin Road, Honghuagang District, Zunyi City). The meeting was known as the Zunyi Meeting. The meeting was attended by Political Bureau members and alternate members, including Mao Zedong, Zhou Enlai, Zhu De, Chen Yun, Zhang Wentian (Luo Fu), Qin Bangxian (Bo Gu), Liu Shaoqi, Wang Jiaxiang, Deng Fa, He Kequan (Kai Feng), Secretary-General of the Central Committee Deng Xiaoping, Chief of the Red Army Headquarters and Red Army Legions Liu Bocheng, Li Fuchun, Nie Rongzhen, Peng Dehuai, Yang Shangkun, Li Zhuoran, Lin Biao, the Comintern-sent military advisor Li De, and the translator Wu Xiuquan.

会议的主要议题是总结第五次反"围剿"和长征以来的经验教训。根据绝大多数同志的意见和要求,改组了中央书记处和中央革命军事委员会,毛泽东被选为政治局常委,取消了博古和李德的最高军事指挥权。推选张闻天代替博古在中央负总责,毛泽东、周恩来负责军事。随后,又成立由毛泽东、周恩来、王稼祥组成的三人军事指挥小组。从此结束了王明"左"倾冒险主义的统治,事实上确立了毛泽东在党中央和红军的领导地位。

The main topic of the meeting was to review the experience and lessons since the Fifth Campaign against KMT Encirclement and Suppression and since the departure of the Long March. According to the suggestions and demands of the majority of comrades, the Central Secretariat and the Central Revolutionary Military Commission were reorganized. Mao Zedong was elected as a member of the Standing Committee of the Political Bureau, and Bo Gu and Li De were dismissed from the highest military command. Zhang Wentian was elected to replace Bo Gu to be in charge of the central government, while Mao Zedong and Zhou Enlai took charge of the military. Subsequently, Mao Zedong, Zhou Enlai, and Wang Jiaxing would exercise command over the entire army. From then on, the rule of Wang Ming's "Leftist" adventurism was ended, while Mao Zedong's leadership in the Party Central Committee and the Red Army was established.

遵义会议是中国共产党第一次独立自主地运用马克思列宁主义基本原理解决自己的路线、方针和政策方面问题的会议。遵义会议在极端危急的关头挽救了党,挽救了红军,挽救了中国革命,成为党的历史上一个生死攸关的转折点。

The Zunyi Meeting was the first meeting in which the CPC independently applied the basic principles of Marxism-Leninism to solve the problems concerning its own line, principles and policies. The Zunyi Meeting saved the Party, the Red Army, and the Chinese revolution at a moment of greatest peril, and became a pivotal moment in the history of the Party.

第二节 红色故事
Section II Red Stories

困牛山壮举
The Feat of the Kunniushan Mountain

1934年8月,奉中革军委命令,任弼时、萧克、王震率红六军团作为红军长征先遣部队从湘赣革命根据地出发西征。10月7日,红六军团在石阡甘溪遭遇桂军的伏击,部队被截为三段,随后陷入湘桂黔三省敌军24个团的围追堵截。为了掩护军团主力去黔东根据地与贺龙领导的红三军会合,第18师52团800余人在师长龙云和团长田海清率领下负责阻敌断后,在完成任务后追赶主力军团时,被增援的敌军截断了去路。为了拖住敌军,保证主力顺利南撤,52团改道把敌人引向困牛山,也使自己所剩400余人再次陷入敌军合围之中。

In August 1934, under the order of the Central Revolutionary Military Commission, Ren Bishi, Xiao Ke, and Wang Zhen led the Sixth Red Army Legion to set off from the Hunan-Jiangxi Revolutionary Base as the advance force of the Red Army's Long March. On October 7, the Sixth Red Army was ambushed by the KMT Guangxi Army in Ganxi, Shiqian. The Sixth Red Army was broken into three sections, and subsequently fell under siege by 24 regiments of the enemy forces of Hunan, Guangxi, and Guizhou provinces. In order to cover the main force of the army so that they could make for the eastern Guizhou base area to join forces with the Third Red Army led by He Long, more than 800 Red Army soldiers from the 52nd Regiment of the 18th Division, led by the division commander Long Yun and the regiment commander Tian Haiqing, undertook the task of blocking the enemy. After completing the task, they were intercepted by enemy reinforcements when they tried to catch up with the main force. In order to hold back the enemy and ensure the smooth retreat of the main force to the south, the 52nd Regiment diverted the enemy to the Kunniushan Mountain, which also caused the remaining 400 members of the regiment to fall into the enemy's encirclement again.

10月16日,困牛山战斗打响。困牛山三面临河、四面峡谷,地势险要。尽管四周高山均被敌军占据,但红军临危不惧,与数十倍于己的敌人激烈交战。师长龙云和团长田海清兵分两路,在田海清率领的200余人的掩护下,龙云率200余人突出重围。田海清在掩护突围中,不幸中弹牺牲。

On October 16, the Battle of Kunniushan Mountain started. The Kunniushan Mountain, with dangerous terrain, was surrounded by rivers on three sides and valleys on all sides. Although the surrounding mountains were all occupied by enemy troops, the Red Army soldiers were not intimidated in the face of this danger, and they fought hard with enemy troops tens of times of their own number. The division commander Long Yun and the regiment commander Tian Haiqing split the troops into two forces. While more than 200 soldiers led by Long Yun succeeded in breaking out of the siege, it required covering fire from an equal number of soldiers led by Tian Haiqing. Tian Haiqing was unfortunately shot and died in that battle.

敌军见红军战士不打老百姓,便裹胁着百姓,将包围圈不断缩小,最后阻击敌人的100余名红军战士面对步步逼近的敌军和被胁迫挡在敌前的老百姓,边打边退,直到退到虎井沟悬崖边,为了不做俘虏、不误伤百姓,纷纷砸毁枪支,毅然纵身跳下70多米的悬崖,战士的平均年龄还不到20岁。当地群众被红军壮举打动,待敌军撤退后沿着山崖寻找生还红军,在百姓的救助下,仅有极少数红军战士得以幸存。

The enemy saw that the Red Army soldiers were not attacking the civilians, so they threatened and used the civilians to keep shrinking the encirclement. Some 100 remaining Red Army soldiers had to face the approaching enemy army and the civilians who were forced to stand in front of the enemy. The Red Army soldiers retreated while fighting until they reached the edge of the cliff of the Hujinggou Valley. In order not to be taken captive or accidentally injure the civilians, they smashed their guns, and resolutely jumped off the tall cliff one after another. The average age of the soldiers was less than 20 years old. The local people were deeply moved by the Red Army's heroic feat. After the enemy retreated, they searched for the Red Army survivors along the cliff. Despite the efforts and help of the people, only a few Red Army soldiers survived.

困牛山战斗中,百余名红军战士用鲜血和生命谱写了"宁死不做俘虏、宁死不伤百姓"的壮举,诠释了红军信仰坚定、赤诚为民、勇于牺牲的精神。困牛山战斗为红六军团主力顺利突围赢得了有利时机。1934年10月24日,任弼时、萧克、王震率领的红六军团结束了历时79天的西征,与贺龙、关向应、夏曦率领的红三军在铜仁印江县木黄胜利会师,迎来了长征中的第一次会师。

In the battle at the Kunniushan Mountain, more than a hundred Red Army soldiers used their blood and lives to tell a heroic and moving story of "better to die than to be a captive, rather to die than to hurt the civilians". This battle epitomized the Red Army's firm belief, devotion to the people, and spirit of self-sacrifice. The battle at the Kunniushan Mountain won a favorable opportunity window for the main force of the Sixth Red Army to break out of the siege. On October 24, 1934, the Sixth Red Army led by Ren Bishi, Xiao Ke, and Wang Zhen ended the 79-day westward expedition, and finally joined up with the Third Red Army led by He Long, Guan Xiangying and Xia Xi in Muhuang, Yinjiang County, Tongren, marking the first successful junction between Red Army forces in the Long March.

强渡乌江之模范连
The Model Company of Crossing the Wujiang River

1934年12月31日下午,中央红军总部抵达猴场。当天下午至次日凌晨,中共中央再次召开政治局会议,讨论是否执行黎平会议的决定,史称"猴场会议"。会议再次肯定了毛泽东渡江北上的正确主张,命令红军立即强渡乌江、挺进黔北。乌江两岸绝壁高耸,天然落差2000余米,谷深水急。敌军妄图凭借天险阻挡红军北渡,毁掉了所有船只,甚至连一块木板都未留下,并在乌江北岸修筑了防御工事,红军只能就地取材扎筏渡江。

On December 31, 1934, the Central Red Army reached Houchang,

第四章 遵义:历史转折 出奇制胜

Weng'an. From the afternoon of that day until the morning of the next day, the Party Central Committee held another meeting of the Political Bureau, historically known as the "Houchang Meeting", to discuss the decisions previously made at the Liping Meeting. The Houchang Meeting reaffirmed Comrade Mao Zedong's correct proposition of crossing the river and heading north, and directed the Red Army to immediately cross the Wujiang River by force and advance into northern Guizhou. With a natural elevation difference of more than 2,000 meters, the Wujiang River was deep and fast flowing, and the cliffs on both sides were steep. The enemy tried to use natural barriers to stop the Red Army from crossing the river northward. They destroyed all the ships and boats, without leaving even a single piece of wood, and built a fortification on the north bank of the river. The Red Army could only use materials available on the spot to make rafts for crossing the river.

1月2日上午,红一军团第2师第4团1营3连连长毛振华率领7名战士拉绳泅渡,计划将缆绳拉过江去,以便主攻部队渡江,然而缆绳被敌人炮火炸断,未能成功。晚上,部队又组织18名战士乘竹筏偷渡,只有毛振华等5人偷渡成功,在对岸隐伏了下来。1月3日上午9时,强渡开始。

On the morning of January 2, Mao Zhenhua, the commander of the Third Company, First Battalion, Fourth Regiment, Second Division of the First Red Army Legion, led seven soldiers to swim across the river with a rope and planned to set up the rope across the river to facilitate the later crossing by the main force. However, the rope was severed by gunfire and the attempt failed. In the evening, another 18 soldiers were organized again to sneak across the river on bamboo rafts. Only five people including Mao Zhenhua succeeded and then hid on the north side of the river. At 9 a.m. on January 3, the forcible crossing began.

由第1营第1、第2、第3连官兵组成的突击队在密集火力掩护下乘竹筏从新渡口冲向对岸。当竹筏接近北岸时,头天晚上偷渡成功的毛振华等5人突然奋起接应,在岸上向敌军发起猛烈进攻。敌军乱作一团,江中竹筏借机加速靠岸。同时,红军趁势在渡口迅速架设浮桥,后续部队陆续冲过浮桥过江,并对敌军猛攻猛打,撕开了江防的口子。与此同时,另外2个渡口也成功强渡。

The strike force, consisting of officers and soldiers from the first, second, and third companies of the First Battalion, rushed to the opposite riverbank from the New Ferry on bamboo rafts under the cover of intensive gunfire. When the bamboo rafts approached the north riverbank, the five soldiers including Mao Zhenhua who had succeeded in sneaking across the river the previous night, suddenly rose up to collaborate with the strike force and launched a strong attack on the enemy army on the bank. As the enemy troops were shocked into chaos, the Red Army strike force took the chance to cross the river rapidly, and a pontoon bridge was quickly erected at the ferry. The follow-up troops rushed across the river through the pontoon bridge one after another and attacked the enemy furiously, eventually tearing open the enemy defense at the river. At the same time, the forcible crossings at the other two ferries also succeeded.

登岸勇士顽强进攻，冲入守军阵地，与敌展开了近距离战斗。其中，第1营第1连官兵在攻入敌人主阵地后，立即展开追击，长途奔袭40多里，攻占了黔军"前敌指挥部"，为乌江战斗的胜利奠定了基础。至1月6日，中央红军和军委纵队全部渡过乌江，随即占领遵义城。

The Red Army warriors who successfully reached the opposite riverbank fought tenaciously, storming the enemy's defenses for close combat. The officers and soldiers of the First Company of the First Battalion launched an immediate pursuit of the enemy after entering the enemy's primary position. They pursued for more than 12 miles and captured the "front command headquarters" of the KMT Guizhou Army, laying the foundation for the Red Army's victory in the Wujiang Battle. By January 6, all the columns of the Central Red Army and the Military Commission had crossed the Wujiang River and subsequently occupied Zunyi City.

为表彰红一军团红2师第4团第1营第1连在此次战斗中的突出战绩，红一军团授予该连"强渡乌江模范连"的称号。在之后的革命岁月中，该连始终高举战旗、冲锋在前。在庆祝中华人民共和国成立70周年阅兵式上，这面战旗与中国人民解放军100面英雄的战旗在天安门前走过,彰显了人民军队的英雄气概。

In recognition of the outstanding achievements of the First Company of the First Battalion of the Fourth Regiment of the Second Division of the First Red Army Legion, the First Red Army Region awarded the company the title of "Model Company for Crossing the Wujiang River". In the following revolutionary years, the company always held the battle flag high and charged ahead. At the military parade celebrating the 70th anniversary of the founding of the People's Republic of China, this flag was one of the 100 heroic battle flags of the Chinese PLA that paraded through Tiananmen Square. It is a true demonstration of the heroic spirit of the people's army.

青杠坡战斗——四渡赤水之序幕
The Battle of Qinggangpo — The Prelude to Crossing the Chishui River

遵义会议之后,蒋介石调集40万兵力合围遵义城,中革军委决定在敌军合围之前撤离遵义,从赤水北渡长江,进入川西北与红四方面军会合。红军兵分三路,陆续抵达土城。此时川军刘湘一面调重兵封锁长江,一面向赤水、合江、叙永一线推进。川军郭勋祺部紧追而来,盘踞在土城北部青杠坡周围的山上,企图在此围歼中央红军。面临着前有阻敌,后有追兵的不利形势,中革军委决定集中优势兵力,歼灭郭军的4个团后再全力北进。

After the Zunyi Meeting, Chiang Kai-shek mobilized 400,000 troops to encircle Zunyi City. The Central Revolutionary Military Commission decided to evacuate from Zunyi before the enemy troops tightened the encirclement, and to cross the Yangtze River northward from the Chishui River so that the Red Army could enter northwest Sichuan to join forces with the Fourth Red Army. The Red Army troops arrived in Tucheng Town in three routes in succession. At that time, Liu Xiang, the commander-in-chief of the KMT Sichuan Army, deployed a large number of troops to block the Yangtze River, while also directing the army to advance towards the region of Chishui, Hejiang, and Xuyong. Meanwhile, the Red Army was pursued by the Sichuan troops led by Guo Xunqi, which were entrenched on the mountains around the Qinggangpo Village of North Tucheng attempting to encircle and annihilate the Central Red Army. Faced with the treacherous situation of being blocked by the enemy in the front and chased by enemy troops in the back, the Central Revolutionary Military Commission decided to concentrate its superior Red Army forces to wipe out the four regiments of troops led by Guo Xunqi before marching north with all their strength.

1935年1月28日凌晨,青杠坡战斗打响了。红三军团、红五军团首先向郭勋祺部发起了进攻,而此时郭部占据青杠坡制高点,凭借有利的地形和援军的配合,猛烈反击。红军部分阵地被突破,敌军直逼红军指挥部前沿。紧急关头,总司令朱德、总参谋长刘伯承亲自上前线指挥战斗,并命令已到达赤水、元厚的红一军团2师火速回援。同时,干部团团长陈赓、政委宋任穷也率领干部团投入战斗中。

On the early morning of January 28, 1935, the Qinggangpo battle started. The Third and the Fifth Red Army Legions first launched an attack on the Sichuan Army troops commanded by Guo Xunqi. At that time, Guo's troops occupied the commanding heights of Qinggangpo. With the favorable terrain and the cooperation of reinforcements, Guo's army fought back violently. Some of the Red Army's positions were broken through, and the enemy was approaching the front of the Red Army headquarters. At this critical juncture, Commander-in-Chief Zhu De and Chief of General Staff Liu Bocheng went to the front line to personally direct the battle, while they also ordered the Second Division of the First Red Army Legion, which had reached Yuanhou in Chishui, to quickly return to give aid. At the same time, commander Chen Geng and political commissar Song Renqiong of the Cadre Regiment also led their troops to engage in the battle.

最终,红军在付出极大牺牲后,夺取了敌军主阵地营棚顶,战斗进入到胶着状态。而此时敌人的增援部队源源不断赶来,火力越来越猛,寡不敌众的红军即将陷入敌军重围。面临险境,中革军委、中央政治局紧急召开了"土城会议",毛泽东当机立断,决定暂缓执行北渡长江的计划,撤出战斗,改为西渡赤水河。1935年1月29日凌晨,红军分三路渡过赤水河,拉开了"四渡赤水、出奇制胜"的序幕。

In the end, after making great sacrifices, the Red Army captured Yingpengding, the primary position of the enemy, and the battle entered a stalemate. However, the enemy's reinforcements arrived in a steady stream, and their increasingly fierce firepower was threatening to plunge the outnumbered Red Army into a siege. Faced with this peril, the Central Revolutionary Military Commission and the Political Bureau of the Central Committee urgently held the "Tucheng Meeting". In that meeting, Mao Zedong made a decisive decision for the Red Army to suspend the implementation of the plan to cross the Yangtze River northward and withdraw from the battle. Instead, they would cross the Chishui River westward. On the early morning of January 29, 1935, the Red Army crossed the Chishui River in three different routes, opening the prelude to the surprising triumph of the four crossings of Chishui.

四渡赤水出奇兵
Crossing the Chishui River Four Times with Ingenious Military Move

遵义会议后,中央红军仍然面临十分严峻的形势。此时,蒋介石为阻止中央红军北进四川与红四方面军会合,或东出湖南与红二、红六军团会合,部署其嫡系部队和川、黔、湘、滇、桂五省地方部队的数十万兵力,从四面八方向遵义地区进逼包围,企图在遵义一带围歼红军。而红军只有3万多人,双方在兵力、装备上对比悬殊。1935年1月19日,中央红军由遵义地区北进,计划夺取川黔边的土城和赤水县城,从四川的泸州和宜宾之间北渡长江,与红四方面军会合。蒋介石急调重兵布防于川黔边境,封锁长江。

After the Zunyi Meeting, the Central Red Army still faced a very severe situation. At that time, in order to prevent the Central Red Army from advancing northward to Sichuan to join forces with the Fourth Front Red Army, or going east to Hunan to join up with the Second and the Sixth Red Army Legions, Chiang Kai-shek mobilized the troops under his direct control in addition to the hundreds of thousands of local troops in Sichuan, Guizhou, Hunan, Yunnan and Guangxi provinces to attack and besiege the Zunyi region from all directions. In this way, he attempted to encircle and wipe out the Red Army there. In contrast, the Red Army had only 30,000 troops. There was a great disparity both in strength and equipment. On January 19, 1935, the Central Red Army marched northward from Zunyi, planning to seize the Tucheng and Chishui regions at the junction of Sichuan and Guizhou, and to cross the Yangtze River northward between Luzhou and Yibin in Sichuan to join forces with the Fourth Front Red Army. Chiang Kai-shek hurriedly deployed many troops on the border between Sichuan and Guizhou to block the Yangtze River.

1月28日,红军在土城与尾追的国民党军川军发生激战。由于战前敌情侦查有误,红军战斗陷入极其不利的境地。毛泽东当机立断,果断放弃原定北渡长江进入川南的计划,决定迅速撤出战斗,西渡赤水,向川南古蔺、叙永地区转移。1月29日凌晨,红军除以少数部队阻击国民党军外,主力部队在土城、元厚两地一渡赤水,跳出蒋介石在黔北布下的包围圈,向川滇黔三省边境国民党军设防空虚的云南扎西挥师西进。这一行动,显示了毛泽东善于从不利战局寻找有利因素,化被动为主动的指挥艺术。

On January 28, the Red Army fought fiercely with the chasing KMT Sichuan Army in Tucheng. Due to inaccurate intelligence about the enemy, the Red Army was ensnared in a perilous battle. Mao Zedong acted decisively and resolutely abandoned the original plan to cross the Yangtze River to the south of Sichuan, and directed the Red Army to quickly withdraw from the battle that night and cross the Chishui River westward to make for the Gulin and Xuyong areas in Southern Sichuan. On the early morning of January 29, except for a small number of troops left to block the KMT army, the main force of the Red Army, with light packs, all crossed the Chishui River for the first time from the Yuanhou and Tucheng areas. In this way they broke out of the encirclement deployed by Chiang Kai-shek in northern Guizhou and marched westward to Zhaxi at the junction of Sichuan and Yunnan. This strategic shift demonstrated Mao Zedong's brilliant military maneuver of seeking advantages from disadvantages and turning passivity into initiative.

2月9日,红军摆脱川军的追击,在扎西地区集结并进行整编。中央红军除干部团以外,改编为16个团,一个团兵力达2000多人,基层的战斗力明显提高。通过整编和加强政治工作,红军得以精简,部队士气高涨。此时,国民党各路军纷纷向川滇边境地区急进,企图夹击红军。鉴于敌军主力已被红军吸引到川滇黔边境,黔北兵力空虚,毛泽东决定暂缓执行北渡长江的计划,原路返回,于 2 月 18 日至 21 日二渡赤水,重入贵州,奇袭娄山关,再战遵义城。

On February 9, the Red Army rid itself of the pursuit of the KMT Sichuan Army and assembled and reorganized in the Zhaxi area. Apart from the Cadre Regiment, the Central Red Army was all re-organized into 16 regiments with over 2,000 troops for each regiment, and the combat effectiveness of the grassroots system was significantly improved. Through the reorganization and strengthening of political work, the Red Army was streamlined, and the morale of the troops rose. At that time, the KMT troops were rushing to the border areas between Sichuan and Yunnan, attempting to flank the Red Army. Knowing that most of the enemy's main force had been attracted by the Red Army to the borders between Sichuan, Yunnan and Guizhou, and that northern Guizhou was empty of enemy troops, Mao Zedong decided to suspend the plan for the Red Army to cross the Yangtze River northward, and instead directed the army to backtrack. From February 18 to 21, the Red Army crossed the Chishui River for the second time and reentered Guizhou. Following a surprise attack on Loushan Pass, the Red Army re-engaged in a battle with the KMT force in Zunyi.

在遵义战役中,红军歼灭国民党军两个师又八个团,俘敌 3000 余人,缴获大批军用物资,取得中央红军长征以来最大的一次胜利,沉重地打击了敌军的气焰,鼓舞了红军的斗志。娄山关大捷后,毛泽东奋笔写下了著名的诗篇《忆秦娥·娄山关》。

忆秦娥·娄山关

西风烈,长空雁叫霜晨月。
霜晨月,马蹄声碎,喇叭声咽。
雄关漫道真如铁,而今迈步从头越。
从头越,苍山如海,残阳如血。

In the Battle of Zunyi, the Red Army annihilated two divisions and eight regiments of the KMT army, captured more than 3,000 enemies, and seized large amounts of the enemy's military supplies. The battle marked the biggest victory for the Red Army since the start of the Long March, which heavily demoralized the enemy and greatly lifted the spirits of the Red Army. After the Loushan Pass victory, Mao Zedong wrote the famous poem "The Pass of Mount Lou".

Tune: Dream of a Maid of Honor
The Pass of Mount Lou

(Translated by Xu Yuanchong)

The wild west wind blows strong;

The morning moon shivers at the wild geese's song.

On frosty morn,

Steeds trot with hooves out worn,

And bugles blow forlorn.

Fear not the strong pass iron-clad on all sides!

The summit's now surmounted with big strides.

Surmounted with big strides,

Green mountains like the tide;

The sunken sun blood-dyed.

三渡赤水:声东击西
The Third Crossing of Chishui: Feinting to the East and Attacking in the West

遵义战败,让蒋介石感到奇耻大辱,于是调整部署,指挥多路国民党军向遵义、鸭溪一带合围。毛泽东将计就计,指挥红军在遵义地区徘徊,引诱更多国民党军前来围攻。当各路国民党军云集而来时,红军迅速跳出敌军的合围圈,再次转兵西进,于3月16日至17日,在茅台镇及其附近地区三渡赤水,重入川南。为在运动中调动敌人,红军故意在白天渡河,大张旗鼓地行军。

The defeat of the KMT army in Zunyi struck Chiang Kai-shek as a burning shame, and he consequently adjusted his deployment and commanded multiple enemy troops to encircle the areas of Zunyi and Yaxi. Mao Zedong counterplotted and directed the Red Army to hover around the Zunyi area, intending to lure more KMT troops to come to the siege. As the KMT troops were converging on Zunyi, the Red Army quickly withdrew from the enemy's encirclement and moved westward again. From March 16 to 17, the Red Army crossed the Chishui River for the third time through Maotai Town and its surrounding areas, and re-entered southern Sichuan. In order to "mobilize" the enemy during the move, the Red Army deliberately crossed the river during the day and marched with great fanfare.

四渡赤水：乘隙而进
The Fourth Crossing of Chishui: Exploiting the Enemy's Gaps

蒋介石以为红军又要北渡长江，急忙调动重兵围堵，企图一举歼灭红军。此时，毛泽东派一支部队伪装成主力继续诱敌西进，给敌人造成红军要北渡长江的假象，吸引敌人所有部队。而真正的红军主力却在敌军新的合围将成未成之际，再次杀了一个回马枪，挥师东进，折返贵州，于3月21日晚至22日四渡赤水，将敌人甩在了身后。

Believing that the Red Army was again planning to cross the Yangtze River northward, Chiang Kai-shek hurriedly deployed many troops to intercept and attempt to annihilate the Red Army in one fell swoop. In response, Mao Zedong dispatched a force disguised as the main force to continue to lure the enemy to the west, giving the enemy the illusion that the Red Army was going to cross the Yangtze River northward, which attracted all the enemy troops. However, the real main force of the Red Army made yet another swing back before the enemy's new encirclement was about to complete. They marched east and reentered Guizhou again. From the evening of March 21 to March 22, the Red Army crossed the Chishui River for the fourth time, leaving the enemy far behind.

威逼昆明，巧渡金沙江
Feinting towards Kunming and Swiftly Crossing the Jinsha River

随后，红军南渡乌江，佯攻贵阳，诱出滇军来援。当滇军赶往贵阳时，毛主席又指挥红军向敌人兵力空虚的云南疾进,直逼昆明,国民党军被迫从滇北和金沙江急调兵力回防,削弱了金沙江防务。趁金沙江南岸敌人防御薄弱之际,红军突然调头向北,于5月9日渡过金沙江,跳出敌人包围圈。至此,中央红军摆脱了数十万敌军的追堵拦截,取得了战略转移中具有决定意义的胜利。

Afterwards, the Red Army crossed the Wujiang River southward and staged a feint attack on Guiyang, which lured out the KMT Yunnan army to come to aid. When the Yunnan army were rushing to Guiyang, Mao Zedong commanded the Red Army to advance towards Yunnan, where the enemy troops were thin, and the Red Army troops were soon approaching Kunming. The KMT was forced to urgently recall the troops from northern Yunnan and the Jinsha River back for defense, which weakened the defense on the Jinsha River. Taking advantage of the opportunity window of weak defense on the south bank of the Jinsha River, the Red Army suddenly turned north and crossed the Jinsha River on May 9, finally breaking away from the enemy's encirclement. So far, the Central Red Army got rid of its pursuers and avoided interception by several hundreds of thousands of enemy troops, and achieved a decisive victory in the strategic shift of the Red Army.

四渡赤水扭转了红军自长征以来的被动局面
Crossing the Chishui River Four Times Overturned the Passive Situation for the Red Army

四渡赤水战役,从1935年1月19日红军离开遵义开始,到5月9日巧渡金沙江为止,历时3个多月,行程5000多公里,是遵义会议后,中央红军在长征途中,处于国民党几十万重兵围追堵截的艰险条件下,进行的一次决定性运动战战役,也是红军自第五次反"围剿"失败后取得的第一个重大胜利。红军从此扭转了长征以来的被动局面,为实现北上的战略目标创造了有利条件。

From January 19, 1935, when the Red Army left Zunyi, to May 9 that year, when the army crossed the Jinsha River, the Red Army crossed the Chishui River four times, which lasted more than three months and covered more than 5,000 kilometers. It was a crucial mobile warfare campaign undertaken by the Central Red Army during the Long March after the Zunyi Meeting. Despite facing daunting challenges, including encirclement, pursuit, obstruction and interception by hundreds of thousands of KMT troops, the Red Army emerged victorious. This triumph marked the first major success of the Red Army following the failure of its Fifth Campaign against KMT Encirclement and Suppression, effectively overturning the previous passive situation. The battle created favorable conditions for the Red Army's strategic objective of advancing northward.

在毛泽东、周恩来、朱德等人的指挥下,中央红军采取高度机动的运动战战术,纵横驰骋于川黔滇边境广大地区,积极创造和寻找战机,有效地调动和歼灭敌人,从而牢牢地掌握战场的主动权,彻底粉碎了蒋介石围歼红军于川黔滇边境的企图,取得了战略转移中具有决定意义的胜利。

四渡赤水是中央红军长征中最惊心动魄而又最精彩的一次军事行动,是红军长征史上以少胜多,变被动为主动的光辉战例,是"毛主席用兵真如神"的真实写照,也因此被毛泽东本人认为是他军事生涯中的"得意之笔"。

Under the command of Mao Zedong, Zhou Enlai, Zhu De and other Party leaders, the Red Army flexibly shifted between courses of action and promptly created battle opportunities, which made it possible for the Red Army to gallop across the vast areas along the borders between Sichuan, Guizhou and Yunnan and to outflank and manipulate hundreds of thousands of enemy troops. The Red Army firmly grasped the initiative on the battlefield by effectively "mobilizing" and annihilating enemy forces during the movement, which helped the Red Army break the enemy's siege, confound their pursuit and interception, and shatter the enemy's arrogant plan to encircle and wipe out the Red Army in the border areas between Sichuan, Guizhou, and Yunnan. The victory of this battle marked a decisive triumph in the strategic shift of the Red Army.

The battle of the four crossings of the Chishui River stands as a breathtaking and glorious military campaign in the history of the Red Army's Long March in which the army defeated enemy troops with a force much inferior in number and turned passivity into initiative. It fully demonstrates the superb military maneuver of the leaders of the CPC, and it is the most glorious and miraculous chapter in the history of the Long March. Mao Zedong once said that the Four Crossings of the Chishui River were the "most brilliant stroke" in his life.

长征路上的独腿将军：钟赤兵
The One-Legged General in the Long March: Zhong Chibing

娄山关是大娄山脉主峰上的险要关隘，海拔1576米，位于遵义与桐梓的交界处，北拒巴蜀，南扼黔桂，是川黔交通要塞，历来为兵家必争之地。1935年1月遵义会议后，中共中央和中革军委决定北渡长江到四川与红四方面军会合，由于在习水土城发生的青杠坡战斗中失利，红军果断一渡赤水改向扎西集结，之后又决定趁黔北敌军兵力空虚，回师贵州，二渡赤水，重占娄山关、再占遵义城，摆脱敌军的围堵。由此打响了娄山关战斗，揭开了遵义战役的序幕。

Loushan Pass, with an elevation of 1,576 meters, is a precipitous mountain pass located on the main peak of the Daloushan Mountains. It is situated at the border between Zunyi and Tongzi, serving as a critical junction that controls access between the regions of Sichuan to the north and Guizhou and Guangxi to the south. It has been a crucial battleground for military strategists since ancient times. After the Zunyi Meeting in January 1935, the Central Committee of the Party and the Central Revolutionary Military Commission decided that the Red Army would cross the Yangtze River northward to march to Sichuan and join forces with the Fourth Front Red Army. Due to the loss of the battle of Qinggangpo in Tucheng, Xishui, the Red Army decisively crossed the Chishui River for the first time and shifted to a new plan to assemble in Zhaxi. Afterwards, perceiving the opportunity to take advantage of the thin enemy forces in northern Guizhou, the Red Army backtracked to Guizhou, crossed the Chishui River for the second time, re-seized Loushan Pass, and then captured Zunyi City, which all helped the Red Army to break away from the enemy's siege and interception. The battle of Loushan Pass was a prelude to the crucial battle of Zunyi.

第四章 遵义:历史转折 出奇制胜

1935年2月25日,彭德怀、杨尚昆率领的红三军团主力对先行抢占娄山关的黔军发动强攻,彭雪枫、李干辉率领的红十三团三营夺取娄山关东侧的点金山。黔军疯狂反扑,经过反复争夺,十三团最终攻下点金山及大小尖山,控制了娄山关。面对严峻的形势,彭德怀决定采取正面进攻和两翼包抄的迂回战术,并由红十二团接替红十三团担任正面主攻。26日拂晓,敌军为夺回失去的娄山关阵地进行疯狂反扑。

红十二团团长谢嵩和政委钟赤兵带领部队向娄山关的制高点点金山发起猛攻。在激烈的争夺中,钟赤兵的右腿被敌人的子弹击中,鲜血直流。不顾团长谢嵩让其赶紧撤离的命令,还未等警务员为其包扎好伤口,钟赤兵又强忍疼痛拖着伤腿继续指挥战斗,直到失血过多晕了过去。最后红军牢牢占领了关口,取得娄山关战斗的胜利。敌军溃散南逃,红军乘胜追击,歼灭残敌,占领遵义。

On February 25, 1935, the main force of the Third Red Army Legion led by Peng Dehuai and Yang Shangkun launched a strong attack on the KMT Guizhou army that had occupied Loushan Pass. Peng Xuefeng and Li Ganhui led the Third Battalion of the 13th Regiment to first seize the Dianjin Mountain to the east of Loushan Pass. The Guizhou army counterattacked frantically. After repeated struggles, the 13th Regiment finally captured the mountains of Dianjin, Dajian and Xiaojian, taking control of Loushan Pass. During the perilous battle, Peng Dehuai decided to adopt detour tactics, combining frontal assault with flanking on both sides, and the 12th Regiment was deployed to substitute for the 13th Regiment for major attacks on the front line. On the dawn of February 26, the enemy made a frantic counterattack to reclaim the lost positions of Loushan Pass.

Commander Xie Song and political commissar Zhong Chibing of the 12th Regiment led the troops to launch a fierce attack on the Dianjin Mountain, the commanding height of Loushan Pass. In the fierce battle, Zhong Chibing suffered a bullet shot in the right leg, from which blood trickled out. Regardless of the order of regimental commander Xie Song for him to evacuate, and even before a medic could bandage his wound, Zhong Chibing dragged his injured leg and endured pain to continue commanding the battle, until he lost too much blood and fainted. In the end, the Red Army firmly occupied the pass and won the battle of

Loushan Pass. The enemy was routed and dispersed to the south. The Red Army followed up the victory by pursuing and annihilating the fleeing enemy troops, and ultimately occupied Zunyi.

占领遵义后,医生立即为钟赤兵进行治疗。由于伤势严重,受伤后又未及时包扎,必须从小腿以下进行截肢。当时,红军医院的条件极其简陋,没有医疗器械,也没有麻药,只得用锯木头的锯子进行手术,强忍剧痛的钟赤兵手术中几度昏死。手术后,由于伤口反复感染,短短半个月内,钟赤兵便做了三次截肢手术,直至截掉整只右腿。部队领导建议钟赤兵留在当地疗伤,可他坚持要继续长征。凭着顽强的毅力,钟赤兵跟随红军爬雪山、过草地,最终到达了长征的终点陕北。

After the Red Army occupied Zunyi, Zhong Chibing was immediately treated by a doctor. Unfortunately, due to the serious injury, and since his wound had not been bandaged in time, his lower right leg had to be amputated. The conditions of the Red Army Hospital were extremely poor at that time. There was no medical equipment or anesthesia, so the amputation had to be performed with a wood saw. Zhong Chibing fainted several times during the operation while enduring the severe pain. After the operation, the wound became repeatedly infected. Within just half a month, Zhong Chibing underwent three amputations until the entire right leg was cut off. The army leaders advised Zhong Chibing to stay in the local area to heal his wound, but he insisted on continuing with the Long March. With tenacious perseverance, Zhong Chibing followed the Red Army in climbing snow-capped mountains and crossing grasslands, and eventually reached the destination of the Long March in northern Shaanxi.

第三节 红色景点
Section Ⅲ Red Tourism Attractions

黎平会议会址
The Liping Meeting Site

黎平,位于湘黔交界,是中央红军长征进入贵州的第一城。1934年10月中旬,中央红军从中央苏区开始进行战略转移,同年11月底至12月初,红军主力血战湘江,以惨重的代价突破了敌军的封锁线,到达湘黔边界时,中央红军人数已由长征出发时的8.6万余人锐减到3万余人。蒋介石集结兵力,妄图趁红军由通道北出湘西与红二、红六军团会合之机一举围歼红军。

图4-1 黎平会议会址
Figure 4-1 The Liping Meeting Site

在此危急关头,12月12日,中革军委在通道召开了紧急会议。在会上,毛泽东提出避实就虚,转向贵州前进的主张。在得到大多数人的赞同后,红军改变行军计划,分两路急转贵州,于12月14日一举攻克黎平县城,中共中央在黎平召开了长征途中的第一次中央政治局会议——黎平会议。

Liping, located at the junction of Hunan and Guizhou, was the first city to witness the Central Red Army's Long March into Guizhou. In mid-October of 1934, the Central Red Army began a strategic shift from the Central Soviet Zone. From the end of November to the beginning of December of that year, the main force of the Red Army fought the bloody Battle of Xiangjiang River and broke through the enemy's blockade at a massive cost. The 86,000 troops of the Red Army at the departure of the Long March were reduced to little more than 30,000. Chiang Kai-shek assembled his forces and attempted to encircle and destroy the Red Army in one fell swoop while the Red Army was planning to exit western Hunan through Tongdao and advance to join forces with the Second and the Sixth Red Army Legions.

At that critical juncture, the Central Military Commission held an urgent meeting in Tongdao on December 12. Mao Zedong proposed in the meeting that the Red Army should strike where the enemy was the weakest and avoid its strongholds and that the army should make a shift to march into Guizhou instead. After Mao's proposal obtained the approval of the majority of the Military Commission, the Red Army changed its marching plan, and branched out in two forces to quickly advance to Guizhou through two routes. On December 14, the Red Army captured Liping County in one stroke. The Party Central Committee then held the first meeting of the Political Bureau in the Long March—the Liping Meeting.

会上,博古等人坚持进入湘西、同红二和红六军团会合的原定计划,而毛泽东则主张在川黔边地区创建新的根据地。经过激烈争论,政治局采纳了毛泽东的正确主张,通过了《中央政治局关于战略方针之决定》,按照此决议,中央红军分左、右两路纵队,向以遵义为中心的黔北地区进军,开启了长征以来具有决定意义的战略方向转变。

At the meeting, Bo Gu and some other Red Army leaders insisted on the original plan to enter western Hunan and join up with the Second and the Sixth Red Army Legions, while Mao Zedong advocated the establishment of a new base in the Sichuan-Guizhou border area. After heated debate, the Political Bureau adopted Mao Zedong's correct proposition and passed the "Decision of the Political Bureau of the Central Committee on the Strategic Policies". According to this resolution, the Central Red Army was split into two columns, left and right, to march towards the northern Guizhou area with Zunyi as the center. This meeting marked a decisive shift in the strategic direction of the Red Army since the start of the Long March.

黎平会议是中共中央红军长征以来,中共中央召开的第一次政治局会议,它完全接受了毛泽东的正确意见,否定了博古、李德的错误主张,从根本上实现战略转移,扭转了红军长征以来的被动挨打局面,为遵义会议的召开奠定了基础,是长征伟大转折的序曲。

The Liping Meeting was the first Political Bureau meeting convened by the Central Committee of the CPC since the Red Army initiated the Long March. It completely accepted Mao Zedong's correct suggestions and rejected Bo Gu and Li De's wrong propositions, which fundamentally realized the strategic shift of the troops and reversed the situation in which the Red Army had been in a passive position of having to receive blows after the beginning of the Long March. The Liping Meeting laid the foundation for the Zunyi Meeting, and was the prelude to the great turning point in the Long March.

黎平会议会址所在的翘街,位于贵州省黔东南苗族侗族自治州黎平县的县城德凤镇。德凤镇始建于明朝洪武年间,距今已有600多年的历史,现在古镇风貌依旧、保存完好。古镇中央的翘街,全长一公里,因两头高、中间低,形如翘起的扁担而得名,自古就是黎平的繁华之地。站在街头放眼望去,整条街尽收眼底。翘街不仅有两湖会馆等历史悠久的古城文化,更有厚重的红色文化。

黎平会议会址坐落在翘街的中间,是一座始建于清代中叶的古建筑,占地面积近1000平方米。原为胡氏住宅和商号,即"胡荣顺"店铺,现今墙面上仍留有"苏洋广货绸缎布疋"等字迹。会址大门门楣上方悬挂着陈云同志题写的"黎平会议会址"黑底金字横匾,会址内有周恩来、朱德住室等7个小展室和一个藏品堂,陈列文物共370件。

Qiaojie Street, where the Liping Meeting site is located, is situated in the Defeng Town of Liping County, Qiandongnan Miao and Dong Autonomous Prefecture, Guizhou Province. The Defeng Town, with a history of over 600 years, was intially built during the Hongwu era of the Ming Dynasty. The historical charm of this ancient town remains well-preserved. At the heart of the town lies a one-kilometer-long street, named Qiaojie street. "Qiao" means "curling", and the street earned its name because it is higher at both ends and lower in the middle, resembling the shape of a weight-bearing shoulder pole. This street has always been the bustling center of Liping since ancient times. Standing at the end of the street and looking ahead, one will be able to take a panoramic view of the whole street. Qiaojie Street not only features the ancient city culture with a long history as marked by the Lianghu Guild Hall, but also features profound red culture.

The Liping Meeting site is located at the middle of Qiaojie Street. It is an ancient building first erected in the middle of the Qing Dynasty and covers an area of nearly 1,000 square meters. The building was originally a Hu family's residence and shop, namely the "Hu Rongshun" shop, on the walls of which there are still such legible signs as "Goods from Suzhou, Guangzhou and Abroad; Silks, Satins and Cloths". Above the lintel of the gate of the meeting site hangs a horizontal plaque with gold characters on a black background inscribed by Comrade Chen Yun, "Li Ping Hui Yi Hui Zhi"［黎平会议会址］(Liping Meeting Site). There are seven small exhibition rooms including the living chambers of Zhou Enlai and Zhu De and a collection hall, with a total of 370 cultural relics on display.

黎平会议纪念馆位于会址正对面,于2009年正式落成,展厅由"战略转移北上抗日""黎平会议伟大转折的起点""走向胜利""红色记忆""今日黎平"五个部分组成,生动形象地展现了黎平会议在中国革命史上的地位及作用,记忆红军长征艰苦卓绝的光辉历程。此外,翘街各处还散布着红军广场、红军干部休养连住址、毛泽东同志住址等革命遗址,成为黎平古城文化与红色文化的聚集地,2020年,黎平翘街被贵州省人民政府列为贵州省历史文化街区。

The Liping Meeting Memorial Hall, officially completed in 2009, is located directly opposite the meeting site. The exhibition hall is composed of five parts, respectively named "Strategic Shift, Proceed North to Fight Against Japanese Aggression", "Liping Meeting, the Starting Point of the Great Turn", "Towards Victory", "Red Memories" and "Today's Liping". They vividly encapsulate the status and role of the Liping Meeting in the history of China's revolution, serving as a memory of the glorious course of the Red Army's extremely arduous and heroic Long March. Qiaojie Street is also dotted with revolutionary sites such as Red Army Square, the residence of the Recuperation Company of the Central Red Army Cadres, and Mao Zedong's Dwelling. The Liping Meeting Memorial Hall has become the hub of Liping's ancient city culture and red culture, and was listed as a Historical and Cultural Street of Guizhou Province by the People's Government of Guizhou Province in 2020.

猴场会议会址
The Houchang Meeting Site

黎平会议后,中央红军按照黎平会议决议精神,挥戈西进,连克数镇,直抵乌江南岸,但处境仍很不利,前有乌江天险的阻拦,后有国民党追兵的步步紧逼。1934年12月31日,中央红军抵达贵州瓮安猴场。面对严峻的形势,为消除分歧、统一思想,进一步明确红军进入黔北建立根据地的战略方针和行动方向,中共中央于进抵猴场的当天召开长征途中的第二次中央政治局会议——猴场会议。

图 4-2 猴场会议纪念馆
Figure 4-2 The Houchang Meeting Memorial Hall

After the Liping Meeting, the Central Red Army, in accordance with the spirit of the Liping Meeting resolution, led the troops westward, and conquered several towns. They reached the south bank of the Wujiang River, but the situation for the Red Army was still very unfavorable. The perilous terrain of the Wujiang River formed a natural blockade ahead while the KMT troops chased from behind. On December 31, 1934, the Central Red Army arrived at

Houchang, Weng'an, Guizhou. In the face of the severe situation, in order to resolve differences, unify thoughts, and further clarify the strategic policy and course of action concerning the Red Army's plan to enter northern Guizhou to establish a base area there, the Party Central Committee held the second meeting of the Political Bureau in the Long March the day they arrived at Houchang—the Houchang Meeting.

会议再次讨论了红军的进军方向等问题,毛泽东反驳了博古、李德提出的不过乌江,留在乌江南岸打游击,回头再东进与红二、红六军团会合的主张,具体分析各方形势,坚持北渡乌江,在黔北建立川黔边新苏区根据地。

会议从1934年12月31日下午一直持续到次日凌晨,是中国共产党历史上唯一一次跨年的中央政治局会议。最终,会议重申了黎平会议的决定,再次肯定了毛泽东同志渡江北上的正确主张,并且通过了《中央政治局关于渡江后新的行动方针的决定》,命令红军立即强渡乌江,北上遵义。

The Red Army's strategic course of action and other issues were discussed at the meeting. Mao Zedong refuted Bo Gu and Li De's proposition that the Central Red Army should not cross the Wujiang River but stay south of the Wujiang River to engage in guerrilla activities and then make for the east to join up with the Second and the Sixth Red Army Legions. Based on specific analyses of the situations of the relevant parties, Mao Zedong insisted on crossing the Wujiang River northward and establishing the new Soviet base area in northern Guizhou near the Sichuan-Guizhou border.

The meeting began on the afternoon of December 31, 1934, and extended into the early morning of January 1, 1935, making it the only meeting of the Political Bureau of the Central Committee in the history of the CPC held at the turn of the year. In the end, the meeting reiterated the resolution of the Liping Meeting and reaffirmed Comrade Mao Zedong's correct proposition of crossing the river and heading north. The "Decision of the Political Bureau of the Central Committee on the New Policies of Action after Crossing the River" was also passed, ordering the Red Army to immediately cross the Wujiang River by force and advance northward to Zunyi.

第四章 遵义:历史转折 出奇制胜

会议特别强调了军事指挥权问题,明确了军事决策必须置于中央政治局的集体领导之下,实际上限制了李德的军事指挥权,开始把最高"三人团"①的军事领导权收回由政治局集中统一领导,使党对军队的指挥正常化。这项决定,为渡江后的遵义会议明确取消博古、李德的军事领导权和指挥权,事实上确立毛泽东在党中央和红军的领导地位夯实了基础。

The issue of military command was particularly emphasized at the meeting, and it was also made clear that military decision-making must be placed under the collective leadership of the Political Bureau of the Central Committee, which, in effect, limited Li De's power of military command and began to reclaim military leadership from the supreme "three-person group" back to the centralized and unified leadership of the Political Bureau.②This decision normalized the party's command over the army. It laid a solid foundation for the resolution made at the Zunyi Meeting after crossing the river, which explicitly revoked the military leadership and command of Bo Gu and Li De and established Mao Zedong's leadership within the Party Central Committee and the Red Army.

猴场会议后,中央红军按照会议部署,以势不可挡之势,强渡乌江,占领遵义。猴场会议重申了黎平会议应以遵义为中心建立根据地的战略决定,为遵义会议的召开奠定了坚实的基础,被周恩来誉为"伟大转折的前夜"。

After the Houchang Meeting, the Central Red Army, in accordance with the deployment of the meeting, crossed the Wujiang River with an unstoppable force and occupied Zunyi. The Houchang Meeting reiterated the strategic decision of Liping Meeting to establish a base with Zunyi as its center, and laid a solid foundation for the holding of the Zunyi Meeting. It was acclaimed by Zhou Enlai as the "eve of the great turn".

---

① 长征初期,为筹划战略转移事宜,成立了由博古、李德、周恩来组成的"三人团",政治上由博古做主、军事上由李德做主,周恩来负责督促军事准备计划的实施。

② In the early days of the Long March, in order to plan for the strategic shift, a "three-person group" was established consisting of Bo Gu, Li De, and Zhou Enlai. Bo Gu took charge of political affairs, Li De was responsible for military affairs, and Zhou Enlai oversaw the implementation of military preparation plans.

猴场会议会址位于瓮安县猴场镇宋家湾,距县城20公里。原为宋泽生住宅。建于1912年,为木结构四合院,俗称"一颗印"房子,总占地面积6667平方米。会址西侧有猴场会议纪念馆,于2014年建成并对外开放。纪念馆以红军四过瓮安为主题,以时间为主线,分"运筹帷幄战黔中、承前启后迎曙光、鱼水情深感瓮安"三个部分,将红军四过瓮安期间发生的所有历史事件串联起来,重点突出中央红军从黎平会议到猴场会议、再到遵义会议的过程,以及猴场会议历史转折的伟大意义。纪念馆内展存了大量红军长征期间留下的文物。

The Houchang Meeting site is in Songjiawan Village, Houchang Town, Weng'an County, 20 Kilometers from the county town. The site, built in 1912, was originally the private residence of Song Zesheng. The standard wooden-structured quadrangle courtyard house, covering a total area of 6,667 square meters, is commonly known as a "one stamp" house. The Houchang Meeting Memorial Hall, located on the west side of the meeting site, was completed and opened to the public in 2014. The memorial hall, which primarily records the Red Army's four passages through Weng'an, is chronologically divided into three parts, namely "mapping out strategies to fight in the middle of Guizhou, inheriting the past and ushering in the dawn of the future, and the army and the Weng'an people being close as fish and water". The exhibitions knit together all the historical events that occurred during the Red Army's four passages through Weng'an, focusing on the process and context in which the Central Red Army proceeded from the Liping Meeting to the Houchang Meeting and then to the Zunyi Meeting, and the great significance of the Houchang Meeting as a historic turning point. A large number of cultural relics left by the Red Army during the Long March are displayed in the memorial hall.

猴场会议会址区域除了猴场会议会址、猴场会议纪念馆外,还有毛泽东行居、红军干部团休养连旧址等革命遗址。2009年,猴场会址被中宣部列入全国爱国主义教育示范基地。2019年10月,被中华人民共和国国务院公布为第八批全国重点文物保护单位。

In addition to the Houchang Meeting site and the Houchang Meeting Memorial Hall, the Houchang Meeting site area also includes other revolutionary sites. Among them are the residence where Mao Zedong lived and the site of the dwellings of the Recuperation Company of Red Army Cadres. It is a National Demonstration Base for Patriotism Education approved by the Publicity Department of the CPC Central Committee in 2009 and a National Key Cultural Relics Protection Unit approved by the State Council in 2019.

遵义会议会址
The Zunyi Meeting Site

1935年1月，红军突破乌江后，1月7日凌晨占领遵义，暂时摆脱了敌人的围追堵截，获取了进行短暂休整的机会。这为中央召开会议，总结经验教训提供了必要条件。1935年1月15日至17日，中共中央政治局扩大会议（即遵义会议）在遵义召开。会议改组了中央领导机构，选举毛泽东为中央政治局常委。

图 4-3　遵义会议会址
Figure 4-3　The Zunyi Meeting Site

In January 1935, the Red Army forcibly crossed the Wujiang River, and captured Zunyi in the early hours of January 7, temporarily defending itself from encirclement, pursuit, obstruction and interception by the enemy, which provided the necessary conditions for the Party Central Committee to hold a meeting, review experience, and draw lessons. From January 15 to 17, 1935, the enlarged meeting of the Political Bureau of the Party Central Committee (the Zunyi Meeting) was held in Zunyi. It was decided in the meeting to reorganize the central leadership and elect Mao Zedong as a member of the Standing Committee of the Political Bureau of the Central Committee.

遵义会议在红军第五次反"围剿"失败和长征初期严重受挫的历史关头召开,结束了"左"倾教条主义在党中央的统治,事实上确立了毛泽东在党中央和红军的领导地位,开始形成以毛泽东为核心的第一代中央领导集体,开启了党独立自主解决中国革命实际问题的新阶段,标志着中国共产党在政治上逐步走向成熟。从此,中国共产党在以毛泽东为代表的马克思主义正确路线领导下,克服重重困难,一步步地引导中国革命走向胜利。

The Zunyi Meeting was held at a historical juncture after the Red Army had failed in its Fifth Campaign against KMT Encirclement and Suppression, and in the wake of the serious setbacks of the early period of the Long March. It ended the rule of the "Left" leaning dogmatism within the CPC Central Committee, and effectively established Mao Zedong as leader of the CPC Central Committee and the Red Army. The meeting led to the formation of the first generation of central collective leadership with Mao Zedong at its core, set the stage for the Party to independently solve the practical problems of the Chinese revolution, and marked the gradual political maturity of the Party. Since then, under the leadership of the correct Marxist line chiefly represented by Mao Zedong, the Party has overcome numerous difficulties and guided the Chinese revolution step by step to victory.

遵义会议会址,位于贵州省遵义市红花岗区子尹路96号,原为国民党第25军第二师师长柏辉章的私邸,故名"柏公馆",建于20世纪30年代初,是一座坐北朝南、砖木结构的两层楼房。整个建筑分主楼、跨院两部分,是长征期间红军总部的所在地。遵义会议召开的会议室,位于会址主楼的2楼,面积约为27平方米。

会议室墙上有一个挂钟和两个壁柜,壁柜上有一面穿衣镜。房间中心摆放着一张长200厘米、宽100厘米、高80厘米的板栗色长方形木桌,四周藤椅环绕,桌下有一只古老的炭火盆。此木桌漆色略退,见证了遵义会议的成功召开,见证了中国共产党和红军的一个生死攸关的历史转折点。1994年,经国家文物局专家组鉴定,被确定为国家一级革命文物,成为遵义会议纪念馆的"镇馆之宝"。

The Zunyi Meeting site is located at No. 96 Ziyin Road, Honghuagang District, Zunyi City, Guizhou Province. It was originally the private residence of Bai Huizhang, the commander of the Second Division of the 25th Army of the KMT, hence the name "Bai Mansion". The two-story brick and wood building facing south was built in the early 1930s. The entire building of the meeting site, divided into two parts (the main building and the side buildings), was the location of the Red Army's headquarters during the Long March in Zunyi. The meeting room where the Zunyi Meeting was held was on the second floor of the main building. It is about 27 square meters.

On the wall of the meeting room, there is a wall clock as well as two wall cabinets with a full-length mirror on one of them. In the center of the room is a chestnut-colored rectangular wooden table with a length of 200 cm, a width of 100 cm and a height of 80 cm. The table is surrounded by rattan chairs, and there is an antique charcoal brazier under it. This slightly paint-faded wooden table has witnessed the successful holding of the Zunyi Meeting and a life-and-death historic turning point for the CPC and the Red Army. In 1994, it was determined as a national first-class revolutionary cultural relic by the expert group of the National Cultural Heritage Administration, and became the "most treasured piece of the collection" of the Zunyi Meeting Memorial Hall.

遵义会议纪念馆是为纪念中国共产党历史上具有伟大历史意义的遵义会议而建立的,是中华人民共和国成立后最早建立的21个革命纪念馆之一。1951年7月开始筹备,1955年1月开放,1961年,被国务院公布为全国第一批重点文物保护单位。纪念馆总占地面积6万多平方米,总建筑面积近4万平方米,展室面积6083平方米。纪念馆包括遵义会议会址、遵义会议陈列馆、红军总政治部旧址、中华苏维埃共和国国家银行旧址、遵义红军街以及遵义会议期间毛泽东、张闻天、王稼祥故居等十余个红色景点。

The Zunyi Meeting Memorial Hall was completed and opened in 1955 to commemorate the significant historic Zunyi Meeting in the history of the CPC. It was one of the 21 earliest revolutionary memorial halls established after the founding of New China. Covering a total area of more than 60,000 square meters, the memorial hall has a total construction area of nearly 40,000 square meters and an exhibition room area of 6,083 square meters. The Memorial Hall encompasses more than ten red spots, including the Zunyi Meeting site, the Zunyi Meeting Exhibition Hall, the site of the General Political Department of the Red Army, the site of the State Bank of the Chinese Soviet Republic, the Zunyi Red Army Street, and the dwellings of Mao Zedong, Zhang Wentian, and Wang Jiaxiang during the Zunyi Meeting.

馆内收藏了遵义会议会议室挂钟、遵义会议会议桌、中国工农红军第一军团总指挥部特务连印章等珍贵藏品。目前,馆藏文物共1551件,其中包括726件原物、667件复制品、158件仿制品。遵义会议会址是遵义会议纪念馆的最核心部分。1964年1月,毛泽东为遵义会议纪念馆题写"遵义会议会址"的馆名。这是毛泽东唯一一次为革命历史纪念馆题写馆名。

The memorial hall houses precious collections such as the wall clock and the table of the Zunyi Meeting room and the stamp of the Secret Service Company of the General Headquarters of the First Army Legion of the Chinese Workers' and Peasants' Red Army. There are a total of 1,551 cultural relics, including 726 originals, 667 replicas and 158 imitations. The Zunyi Meeting site is the core part of the Zunyi Meeting Memorial Hall. In January 1964, Mao Zedong inscribed the name of "Zun Yi Hui Yi Hui Zhi"(遵义会议会址) for the Zunyi Meeting Memorial Hall. That was the only time Mao Zedong inscribed the name for a revolutionary history museum.

苟坝会议会址
The Gouba Meeting Site

1935年2月,中央红军二渡赤水、强攻娄山关、再战遵义,取得了长征以来最大的一次胜利。之后于3月9日行军来到苟坝。3月10日1时,红一军团军团长林彪、政委聂荣臻发来一封万急电报,建议攻打打鼓新场(今金沙县城),歼灭驻扎在那里的黔军。接到电报后,张闻天随即召集毛泽东、周恩来、朱德等20余人召开会议,讨论是否要进攻打鼓新场。

图 4-4 苟坝会议会址
Figure 4-4 The Gouba Meeting Site

In February 1935, the Central Red Army crossed the Chishui River for the second time, forcibly took the Loushan Pass, and battled again with the KMT army in Zunyi, winning the biggest victory since the start of the Long March. On March 9, the Red Army marched to Gouba. At one o'clock on March 10, the commander Lin Biao and the political commissar Nie Rongzhen of the First Red Army Legion sent an urgent telegram, suggesting to launch a strike on Daguxinchang (now Jinsha County). After receiving the telegram, Zhang Wentian immediately convened a meeting of more than 20 people including Mao Zedong, Zhou Enlai, and Zhu De to discuss whether or not to attack Daguxinchang.

会议在苟坝一处民宅内召开,除毛泽东外,所有与会者都一致主张进攻打鼓新场。但正如毛泽东所预见和担忧的那样,蒋介石已令重兵驰援打鼓新场。危险正一步一步向红军袭来。会后,毛泽东回到自己住所,依然十分担忧党和红军的前途及命运。尽管已是深夜,毛泽东仍手提马灯,沿着崎岖不平的田埂小道,来到2公里外周恩来的住处,再次向周恩来分析了攻打打鼓新场面临的巨大危险,希望周恩来能够暂缓下发作战命令。周恩来接受了毛泽东的建议,积极支持毛泽东的正确判断,并决定于3月11日清早继续召开会议,重新讨论进攻打鼓新场的问题。

The meeting was held in a residential house in Gouba. All the participants, except Mao Zedong, unanimously advocated the strike on Daguxinchang. However, just as Mao Zedong anticipated and worried, Chiang Kai-shek had already deployed substantial troops to rush to Daguxinchang. A great danger was approaching the Red Army. After the meeting, Mao Zedong was still concerned about the safety of the Party and the Red Army and the future of the revolution. In the middle of the night, he carried a lantern and walked along the rugged ridge trail to Zhou Enlai's dwelling two kilometers away, reiterating the great danger of striking Daguxinchang and advising Zhou Enlai against hastily issuing the battling order. Zhou Enlai was persuaded by Mao Zedong. He then proactively supported Mao Zedong's correct judgment, and decided to convene a further meeting in the early morning of March 11 to rediscuss the issue of striking Daguxinchang.

在此期间,中革军委二局截获了敌军电报,确认国民党各方军队正从四面八方迅速向打鼓新场集结,意图围歼红军,新的敌情验证了毛泽东的正确预判。最终,中央撤销了进攻打鼓新场的计划。毛泽东的正确主张又一次在关键时候挽救了红军、挽救了党、挽救了中国革命。

During that period, the Second Bureau of the Central Revolutionary Military Commission intercepted a telegram from the enemy, confirming that the KMT troops were rapidly converging on Daguxinchang and intending to surround and destroy the Red Army. The new intelligence about the enemy verified Mao Zedong's correct prediction. In the end, the Central Committee canceled the plan to attack Daguxinchang. Mao Zedong's correct proposition once again saved the Red Army, the Party, and the Chinese revolution at a critical time.

3月12日,在继续召开的中央政治局会议上,决定成立由毛泽东、周恩来、王稼祥组成的三人小组,代表中央政治局全权指挥军事。由此,毛泽东真正掌握了红军的指挥权,在党中央和红军中的领导地位进一步得到巩固。从此以后,中国革命节节走向胜利。

On March 12, at the continued meeting of the Political Bureau of the Central

Committee, it was decided to set up a new three-member group composed of Mao Zedong, Zhou Enlai and Wang Jiaxiang to represent the Political Bureau of the Central Committee with full authority to command the entire military. As a result, Mao Zedong truly took the command of the Red Army, and his leadership within the Party Central Committee and the Red Army was further consolidated. After that, the Chinese revolution steadily advanced from victory to victory.

苟坝会议会址位于贵州省遵义市播州区枫香镇苟坝村马鬃岭山脚,距遵义60公里。苟坝是一块三面高山环绕的坝子,苟坝会议会址是一座老式黔北农家三合院。三合院正中处有一个2米高的朝门,朝门瓦檐下面挂着一块刻有"苟坝会议会址"的黑底金字木匾。走进朝门,一栋长三间的木质结构房屋,左右两边配有厢房,房屋坐北朝南,显得质朴简略。房屋的正中央是一间堂屋,房屋的堂屋内摆放着2张方形木桌,木桌四周围着数根木凳,桌上放着2个茶壶及10来个瓷碗,桌下有两个炭火盆。四周墙上的红色标语依稀可辨。当年,红军就是在这个堂屋内,围坐在木桌旁召开了"苟坝会议"。

The Gouba Meeting Site is located at the foot of the Mazongling Mountain, Gouba Village, Fengxiang Town, Bozhou District, Zunyi City, Guizhou Province, 60 kilometers away from downtown Zunyi. Gouba is a flat land surrounded by high mountains on three sides. The Gouba Meeting Site is an old-fashioned three-sided courtyard farmhouse in northern Guizhou. There is a two-meter-high entrance gate in the middle of the courtyard, featuring a wooden plaque with the gold characters "Gou Ba Hui Yi Hui Zhi"[苟坝会议会址] (Gouba Meeting Site), on a black background hanging below the tiled eave. Walking through the entrance, one will see a three-room wooden house at the front. There are two square wooden tables placed in the main room, namely the middle room of the house, and those tables are surrounded by several wooden stools. Two porcelain teapots and about a dozen porcelain bowls are scattered on the table, and two charcoal braziers rest under the table. On the surrounding walls, some red slogans are vaguely recognizable. Back then, the Red Army officials held the "Gouba Meeting" in this very room sitting around these wooden tables.

2014年10月,距离苟坝会议会址3公里的苟坝会议陈列馆全面建设完工。陈列馆占地面积2143平方米,室外广场17000平方米。馆中展陈了大量的历史文物、文献、图片资料,通过雕塑、绘画、场景以及声光影像多媒体等现代技术手段,全面再现了中国工农红军在苟坝的活动情况。2017年1月,苟坝会议会址入选中国红色旅游经典景区名录,被中宣部命名为全国爱国主义教育示范基地,2019年10月,被中华人民共和国国务院公布为第八批全国重点文物保护单位。

In October 2014, the construction of the Gouba Meeting Exhibition Hall, three kilometers away from the Gouba Meeting site, was completed. The exhibition hall covers an area of 2,143 square meters, and the affiliated square outside the hall covers 17,000 square meters. A large number of historic relics, documents, and pictures are displayed in the hall, and the activities of the Red Army in Gouba are comprehensively reproduced through modern technical means such as sculpture, painting, scene display, and multimedia combining sound, light, and video. The Gouba Meeting site is a National Demonstration Base for Patriotism Education approved by the Publicity Department of the CPC Central Committee in January, 2017 and a National Key Cultural Relics Protection Unit approved by the State Council in October, 2019.

四渡赤水纪念馆
The Memorial Hall of Crossing the Chishui River Four Times

四渡赤水纪念馆位于贵州省遵义市习水县土城镇长征街,于2007年7月建成并开放,由中央军委原副主席张震题写馆名。四渡赤水纪念馆为黔北民居建筑风格,占地面积7700多平方米,共九个展厅。纪念馆序厅正面墙为50多个红军人物形象与红军渡赤水河情景的浮雕,浮雕高7米,宽18.8米,场面宽阔,气势恢宏。浮雕上刻有"四渡赤水是毛泽东军事生涯中的得意之笔"几个大字,为纪念馆整个陈列的主题词。浮雕前为四渡赤水战役的主要领导人毛泽东、周恩来、朱德、张闻天、王稼祥的雕像。

The Memorial Hall of Crossing the Chishui River Four Times is located in

图 4-5 四渡赤水纪念馆
Figure 4-5　The Memorial Hall of Crossing the Chishui River Four Times

Changzheng Street, Tucheng Town, Xishui County, Zunyi City, Guizhou Province. It was completed and opened in July 2007. The name of the memorial hall was inscribed by Zhang Zhen, the former vice chairman of the Central Military Commission. The memorial hall, built in the style of northern Guizhou residential buildings, covers an area of more than 7,700 square meters and consists of a total of nine exhibition halls. On the front wall of the preface hall of the Memorial Hall, there is a relief sculpture of more than 50 Red Army figures depicting the scene of the Chishui River crossing. The relief sculpture is 7 meters high and 18.8 meters wide, presenting a spacious and imposing spectacle. On the relief sculpture, there are several big characters reading "Crossing the Chishui River Four Times were the most brilliant stroke in Mao Zedong's military career", which is the theme of the entire display of the hall. In front of the relief sculpture are statues of Mao Zedong, Zhou Enlai, Zhu De, Zhang Wentian and Wang Jiaxiang, the main commanders of the battle of Crossing the Chishui River Four Times.

纪念馆分战史陈列和辅助陈列两部分。战史陈列通过"土城战役四度序曲""一渡赤水扎西整编""二渡赤水再战遵义""三渡赤水调虎离山""四渡赤水出奇制胜"五个篇章,翔实地再现了红军四渡赤水河,巧渡金沙江,摆脱40万敌军围追堵截,取得战略转移伟大胜利的光辉历史。辅助陈列包括"四渡赤水精神,光耀革命老区"专题书画展,彭德怀、杨尚昆的住室复原等。

馆内收藏红军文物 300 余件。

The memorial hall is divided into two parts: the battle history exhibition and the supplementary exhibition. The battle history exhibition was materialized through the five chapters of "Tucheng Battle—the Prelude to the Four Crossings", "The First Crossing of Chishui River—Reorganization of the Army in Zhaxi", "The Second Crossing of Chishui River—Battling Again in Zunyi", "The Third Crossing of Chishui River— Luring the Enemy away from its Base", and "The Fourth Crossing of Chishu Riveri—Winning the Victory with Ingenious Military Move". These chapters of the exhibition reproduced the glorious history of the Red Army's four crossings of the Chishui River and the surprising crossing of the Jinsha River, which helped the Red Army break away from the siege and pursuit of 400,000 enemy troops and achieve a great victory in its strategic shift. The supplementary exhibition includes the special displays of calligraphy and paintings themed "The Spirit of Crossing the Chishui River Four Times Shines in the Old Revolutionary Area", and the restoration of the dwellings of Comrade Peng Dehuai and Yang Shangkun. There is a collection of more than 300 cultural relics of the Red Army in the memorial hall.

四渡赤水纪念馆包括四渡赤水纪念馆主馆、中国女红军纪念馆、红军医院纪念馆、红九军团陈列馆、土城古镇博物馆等馆群,以及毛泽东、周恩来、朱德等领导人住居,红军总司令部驻地、红三军团司令部驻地、青杠坡战斗遗址等十多处全国重点文物保护单位,是全国爱国主义教育示范基地、国家国防教育示范基地、全国青少年教育基地、全国十大红色旅游景区,2020 年 12 月,被评定为国家一级博物馆。

The Memorial Hall of Crossing the Chishui River Four Times is a group of halls including the Main Hall, the Chinese Women Red Army Soldiers' Memorial Hall, the Red Army Hospital Memorial Hall, the Ninth Red Army Legion Exhibition Hall, and the Tucheng Ancient Town Museum. It also includes the dwellings of Mao Zedong, Zhou Enlai, Zhu De and other Red Army leaders, the site of the Red Army General Headquarters, the site of the command headquarters of the Third Red Army Legion, the site of the Qinggangpo Battle, and a few other major historical and cultural sites protected at the national level. The Memorial Hall of Crossing the Chishui River Four Times is a National Demonstration Base for Patriotism Education, a National Demonstration Base for National Defense Education, a National Education Base for Adolescents, and one of the Top Ten National Red Tourist Spots. In December 2020, it was rated as a national first-class museum.

专栏 4：遵义会议精神
Special Column IV: The Spirit of the Zunyi Meeting

2021年春节来临之际,习近平总书记第六次亲临贵州考察时强调,遵义会议的鲜明特点是坚持真理、修正错误,确立党中央的正确领导,创造性地制定和实施符合中国革命特点的战略策略。2022年4月25日,中国共产党贵州省第十三次代表大会隆重开幕,会议强调,要大力弘扬伟大建党精神,大力弘扬长征精神和"坚定信念、坚持真理、独立自主、团结统一"的遵义会议精神。历史证明,遵义会议精神是中国共产党的宝贵精神财富,是中国革命、建设和改革的"内生动力",为实现中华民族伟大复兴提供了强大精神动力,在今天仍然具有十分重要的意义。

As the Spring Festival of 2021 was approaching, General Secretary Xi Jinping paid his sixth visit to Guizhou in person and emphasized during the visit that the distinctive features of the Zunyi Meeting were to uphold the truth and fix mistakes, establish the correct leadership of the CPC Central Committee, and creatively formulate and implement strategies and tactics that conform to the characteristics of the Chinese revolution. On April 25, 2022, the 13th CPC Guizhou Provincial Congress grandly opened. The conference emphasized the importance of vigorously carrying forward the great founding spirit of the Party, the spirit of the Long March, and the spirit of the Zunyi Meeting of "strengthening beliefs, upholding truth, staying independent, and promoting solidarity and unity". History has proved that the Spirit of the Zunyi Meeting is the precious spiritual wealth of the CPC and the "endogenous driving force" for China's revolution, construction, and reform. It has provided strong spiritual momentum for the realization of the great rejuvenation of the Chinese nation, and it is still of great significance today.

第五章 延安:革命圣地 抗战中心

Chapter V　Yan'an: The Chinese Revolutionary Holy Land and the Command Center of the CPC

延安,古称肤施,是中华民族重要的发祥地,也是民族圣地、中国革命圣地。从1935年至1948年,中共中央和毛泽东等老一辈无产阶级革命家在此生活和战斗了13个春秋,宝塔山、清凉山、凤凰山、枣园、杨家岭、南泥湾……一段段红色记忆、一个个革命故事,透过厚重的黄土和斑驳的岁月印记,向我们走来。

Yan'an, formerly known as Fushi, is an important birthplace of the Chinese nation and a sacred land for the Chinese people. It is also a holy site of revolution in China. From 1935 to 1948, the CPC Central Committee and the older generation of proletarian revolutionaries, such as Mao Zedong, lived and fought here for 13 years. Baota Mountain, Qingliang Mountain, Phoenix Mountain, Zaoyuan, Yangjialing, Nanniwan... Each carries a red memory, and holds a revolutionary story, all emerging through the thick yellow soil and the mottled traces of time.

第一节　历史回眸
Section I　A Glimpse of History

一二·九运动和抗日救亡运动的新高潮
The December 9th Movement and the New Culmination of the Resistance Against Japan to Save the Nation from Extinction Movement

九一八事变后,日本侵略者侵占了东北,同时加紧了对华北的争夺。

1935年5月,日本寻找借口向国民政府提出对华北统治权的无理要求,并调动日本关东军入关,以武力相威胁。国民政府妥协退让,使华北主权大部分丧失,华北危在旦夕。正如北平学生所说:"华北之大,已经安放不得一张平静的书桌了!"

After the September 18th Incident, Japanese forces invaded Northeast China while at the same time intensifying their aggression towards North China. In May 1935, Japan made unreasonable demands on the Nationalist Government for dominion of North China as an excuse to mobilize the Japanese Kwantung Army into the area with the threat of force. The Nationalist Government compromised and retreated, causing it to lose much of its sovereignty over North China, and putting the entire region at stake. As the Beiping students eloquently stated, "In such a vast expanse as North China, is there really no quiet spot left to place a desk?"

1935年12月9日,在中国共产党的领导下,北平学生数千人举行了声势浩大的抗日游行示威,遭到国民党军警的镇压。学生一边同军警搏斗,一边向群众进行抗日救国宣传。翌日,北平全市学生举行总罢课,抗议国民党反动政府的暴行。12月16日,北平1万多名学生和市民群众举行了更大规模的抗日游行。北平学生的爱国行动得到全国各地学生、工人和知识分子的广泛响应和支持,全国抗日救亡运动空前高涨。一二·九运动粉碎了日本吞并华北进而独占中国的阴谋,打击了国民党的妥协退让政策,极大促进了中华民族的觉醒,标志着中国人民抗日救亡运动新高潮的到来。

On December 9, 1935, under the leadership of the CPC, thousands of students in Beiping staged a spectacular anti-Japanese demonstration, which was suppressed by the Nationalist military and police. The students fought against them while calling on the people to save the nation by resisting Japanese aggression. Students in Beiping held a general strike to protest against the atrocities committed by the reactionary KMT Government on the following day. On December 16, more than 10,000 students and citizens of Beiping staged an even larger protest march. The patriotic actions of these students were widely acknowledged and supported by other students, workers and intellectuals from all over the country, and support for the national anti-Japanese aggression movement rose to an unprecedented level. The December 9th Movement shattered Japan's plot to annex North China and thus monopolize China, and dealt a blow to the Nationalist Party's policy of compromise and concession, greatly contributing to the awakening of the Chinese nation and marking the arrival of a huge climax to the Chinese people's anti-Japanese aggression movement.

抗日民族统一战线策略的制定
The Formulation of the Chinese United Front Against Japanese Aggression Strategy

在中华民族遭遇空前危机的紧要关头,中国共产党率先举起了武装抗日旗帜,广泛开展抗日救亡运动。1935年8月1日,中共驻共产国际代表团发表了《中国苏维埃政府、中国共产党中央为抗日救国告全体同胞书》(八一宣言),主张停止内战,组织国防政府和抗日联军,对日作战。12月,毛泽东在党的活动分子会议上,作了《论反对日本帝国主义的策略》的报告,号召建立广泛的抗日民族统一战线。但是,蒋介石却顽固地坚持"攘外必先安内"的方针,坚持先消灭共产党,再抵抗日本侵略者的政策。

At the critical moment when the Chinese nation was plunged into an unprecedented crisis, the CPC was the first to propose that China should fight against Japanese aggression with armed resistance and launched extensive resistance movements. On August 1, 1935, the Party's delegation to the Comintern issued the "Message of the Chinese Soviet Government and the Central Committee of the CPC to All Compatriots on Resistance Against Japanese and National Salvation" (the August lst Declaration), which advocated the cessation of the civil war and the organization of the Nationalist Government for an amalgamated army to fight against Japan. In December, Mao Zedong delivered a report entitled "On Tactics Against Japanese Imperialism" at a meeting of Party activists, calling for the establishment of a broad Chinese United Front Against Japanese Aggression. However, Chiang Kai-shek stubbornly adhered to the policy of "Internal Pacification before External Resistance", insisting on eliminating the Communists before resisting Japanese invaders.

西安事变的和平解决
The Peaceful Settlement of the Xi'an Incident

1936年12月4日,蒋介石亲赴西安,逼迫张学良、杨虎城率部"剿共"。已经丢失了自己的故乡东北三省的张学良请求蒋介石不要再打内战,救国要紧,却遭到蒋介石的训斥。张学良、杨虎城看劝说无效,只好另想办法,逼蒋抗日。12月12日凌晨,张学良、杨虎城发动兵变,在临潼华清池扣留了蒋介石。这便是震惊中外的西安事变。

On December 4, 1936, Chiang Kai-shek flew to Xi'an to force Zhang Xueliang and Yang Hucheng to lead their troops to "suppress the Communists". Zhang Xueliang, who had already lost three provinces in his hometown in the Northeast of China, requested Chiang stop the civil war and help save the nation, but he was rebuked. As such, they had to find another way to force Chiang to resist the Japanese invasion. In the early hours of December 12, Zhang Xueliang and Yang Hucheng launched a mutiny and detained Chiang Kai-shek in Huaqingchi, Lintong, which was the Xi'an Incident that shocked the world.

事变发生后,应张学良、杨虎城的邀请,共产党派周恩来去西安商讨解决问题的办法。经过各方面的努力,终于迫使蒋介石答应"停止剿共,联红抗日",西安事变和平解决。西安事变的和平解决,对促成以国共两党合作为基础的抗日民族统一战线的建立起到了重要作用。此后,十年内战的局面基本结束,抗日民族统一战线初步形成。

After the Incident, at the invitation of Zhang Xueliang and Yang Hucheng, the Party sent Zhou Enlai to Xi'an to discuss a solution to the problem. With the efforts of all parties, Chiang Kai-shek was finally forced to agree to "end the policy of suppressing the Communists and enter into an alliance with the Red Army to resist Japan", and the Xi'an Incident was peacefully resolved. The peaceful settlement of the Xi'an Incident played an important role in the establishment of the Chinese United Front Against Japanese Aggression based on the collaboration between the two parties. After that, the ten-year civil war was basically over and the anti-Japanese national united front was formally established.

卢沟桥事变
The Lugou Bridge Incident

1937年7月7日夜,驻扎在北平郊区卢沟桥一带的日本军队举行军事演习。演习结束后,日军借口有一个士兵失踪,又说好像听到卢沟桥附近的宛平城内有枪声,要强行进入宛平县城搜查,遭到中国守军的拒绝。日军随即炮轰卢沟桥,向宛平城发起进攻。中国军队奋起还击,驻守卢沟桥的100多名士兵战斗到只剩4人,其余全部牺牲,终于打退了日军的进攻。这便是卢沟桥事变。因发生于7月7日,又叫"七七事变"。

On the evening of July 7, 1937, a small Japanese force on maneuvers near Lugou Bridge demanded entry to Wanping Fortress to search for one of their soldiers who was said to be missing. Additionally, the Japanese claimed that they had heard gunshots within the Fortress, near the vicinity of Lugou Bridge. However, the Chinese garrison refused the Japanese entry. The Japanese then shelled Lugou Bridge and launched an attack on Wanping Fortress. The Chinese army, about 100 soldiers, stationed at Lugou Bridge fought back until only four were left alive, yet still repelled the Japanese attack. This was the Lugou Bridge Incident. It is also known as the July 7th Incident, named after the day upon which it took place.

第二次国共合作的形成
The Establishment of the Second Cooperation Between the KMT and the CPC

卢沟桥事变发生的第二天,中共中央向全国发出通电:"平津危急!华北危急!中华民族危急!只有全民族实行抗战,才是我们的出路!"呼吁"立刻给进攻的日军以坚决的反攻!立刻放弃任何与日寇和平苟安的希望和估计!"。全国各界群众、爱国党派和团体、海外华侨也纷纷举行集会,强烈要求政府抗战。

The day after the Lugou Bridge Incident, the CPC Central Committee issued a telegram to the whole country: "Pingjin (now Beijing and Tianjin) is in danger! North China is in danger! The Chinese nation is in dire straits! Only a nation-wide war of resistance is our way out!" It called for "an immediate and resolute counter-attack on the attacking of Japanese army! Immediately abandon any hope or expectation of peace with the Japanese invaders!" As the call went up, people from all walks of life, patriotic parties and groups, including overseas Chinese, also held rallies to strongly urge the government to resist Japan.

在严峻的形势和全国人民高昂的抗日热情面前,1937年7月17日,蒋介石发表第二次庐山谈话,表示了准备抗战的决心。国共两党经过谈判,决定将共产党领导的主力红军改编为国民革命军第八路军(简称"八路军"),开赴华北抗日前线。南方八省的红军游击队则被改编为国民革命军陆军新编第四军(简称"新四军")。9月,国共合作宣言发表,国共两党重新合作,抗日民族统一战线正式形成。

Facing a dire situation and a high level of enthusiasm against Japan from the Chinese people, on July 17, 1937, Chiang Kai-shek issued the Second Lushan Statement, announcing his determination to prepare for the war. After negotiations between the Communist Party and the KMT, it was decided that the main bulk of the Red Army, led by the Communist Party, would be reorganized into the Eighth Route Army of the National Revolutionary Army (the Eighth Route Army for short) and move to the anti-Japanese front in North China. Meanwhile, the Red Army guerrillas in eight southern provinces were transformed into the New Fourth Army of the National Revolutionary Army (the New Fourth Army for short). In September, a declaration of cooperation was issued, signifying the resumption of cooperation between the two parties and the establishment of a national united front against Japanese aggression.

南京大屠杀
The Nanjing Massacre

1937年12月13日上午,以松井石根为司令官的日军侵入当时中国的首都南京城内,南京沦陷。日军采用极其野蛮的手段,对中国平民和解除武装的军人进行了长达6周的血腥屠杀,制造了震惊中外的"南京大屠杀"。

On the morning of December 13, 1937, the Japanese army, under the command of Iwane Matsui (SongJing Shigen), invaded the city of Nanking (later known as Nanjing), then the capital of China, which promptly fell. With extremely barbaric methods, the Japanese invaders massacred Chinese civilians and disarmed soldiers for six weeks, committing the "Nanjing Massacre" that shocked people across the globe.

日军在南京下关江边、草鞋峡、煤炭港、上新河、燕子矶、汉中门外等地制造了多起集体屠杀事件,还实行了分散屠杀。日军的屠杀手段残忍至极,人类史上罕见。主要有砍头、刺杀、枪击、活埋、火烧等,还有惨无人道的杀人比赛。屠杀后,日军又采取了抛尸入江、火化焚烧、集中掩埋等手段,毁尸灭迹。据调查统计,被日军屠杀的人数达30万以上。在日军的屠刀下,南京这座昔日繁华的古都成了阴森可怕的人间地狱。侵华日军在南京的反人类罪行,为人类历史上十分黑暗的一页。

The Japanese army committed a number of mass killings in several sites in Nanjing, including the riverside of Nanjing's Xiaguan District, Caoxie Gorge, Coal Port, Shangxin River, Yanziji and the outside of Hanzhong Gate, as well as many scattered massacres. The Japanese massacres were brutal to a level rarely seen in human history, including beheading, stabbing, shooting, burying alive, burning, and inhumane killing contests. After the massacre, the Japanese army took measures to destroy the bodies by throwing them into the Yangtze River, cremating them, and burying them together. Investigation shows that, more than 300,000 people were massacred. The massacre in Nanjing turned this metropolis, which had been prosperous and peaceful, into a ghastly hell on earth. The crimes against humanity committed by the Japanese army in Nanjing are a very dark chapter in human history.

1945年8月15日,日本无条件投降。其后,中国军事法庭及东京军事法庭都对南京大屠杀进行了严肃认真的调查、审理并作出审判。集体屠杀列为28案,零散屠杀列为858案。东京军事法庭对东条英机等28名日本甲级战犯进行了审判。至此,国际社会对侵华日军南京大屠杀事件定下了铁案。2014年2月27日,第十二届全国人民代表大会常务委员会第七次会议表决通过,决定将12月13日设立为南京大屠杀死难者国家公祭日。中国以立法形式设立南京大屠杀死难者国家公祭日,表明中国人民反对侵略战争、捍卫人类尊严、维护世界和平的坚定立场。

On August 15, 1945, Japan surrendered unconditionally. Subsequently, both the Chinese Military Court and the Tokyo Military Tribunal conducted serious investigations and trials, and handed down judgments on the Nanjing Massacre. The courts came to the conclusion that there had been 28 cases of collective massacre and 858 cases of scattered massacre. The Tokyo Military Tribunal tried Class A war criminals, including Toujou Hideki (Dongtiao Yingji) and 27 others. With this trial, the international community rendered a definitive judgment on the Nanjing Massacre perpetrated by the invading Japanese forces. On February 27, 2014, the seventh meeting of the Standing Committee of the 12th National People's Congress voted to set the 13th of December as the National Memorial Day for Nanjing Massacre Victims. By legislation, China has demonstrated the Chinese people's firm stance on opposing wars of aggression, defending human dignity and safeguarding world peace.

80余年过去了,一些日本军国主义者仍想否认侵略中国犯下的罪行,甚至为那些双手沾满鲜血的刽子手唱赞歌。但是,南京大屠杀铁证如山,侵略者的名字将永远被钉在历史的耻辱柱上。

More than 80 years later, some Japanese militarists still want to deny the crimes committed in the invasion of China, and even sing the praises of those executioners whose hands are stained with blood. But the evidence of the Nanjing Massacre is indisputable, and the names of the invaders will forever be nailed to the pillar of shame in history.

持久战之战略
The Strategy of a Protracted War

在抗日战争初期,"亡国论"和"速胜论"等观点都有相当大的市场。为批驳这些错误观点,向全国人民指出抗日战争的正确道路,必须明确提出抗战的军事战略,系统阐明党的抗日持久战方针。

At the beginning of the War of Resistance Against Japanese Aggression, many people held views such as "the theory of national subjugation" and "the theory of quick victory", which the Party considered erroneous. In order to refute these views and to show the people of China the correct path for the war, it was necessary to set out a clear military strategy and systematically clarify the Party's approach to protracted fighting.

1938年5月26日至6月3日,毛泽东在延安抗日战争研究会上发表了题为《论持久战》的长篇演讲。毛泽东在演讲中驳斥了"亡国论"和"速胜论":"抗战十个月以来,一切经验都证明下述两种观点的不对:一种是中国必亡论,一种是中国速胜论。前者产生妥协倾向,后者产生轻敌倾向。他们看问题的方法都是主观的和片面的,一句话,非科学的。"在此基础上,毛泽东指出:"于是问题是:中国会亡吗?答复:不会亡,最后胜利是中国的。中国能够速胜吗?答复:不能速胜,抗日战争是持久战。"

From May 26 to June 3, 1938, Mao Zedong delivered a long speech entitled "On Protracted War" at the Yan'an Anti-Japanese War Research Conference. In his speech, Mao refuted these two main beliefs: "All the experience of the ten months of the war proves the error in both of 'the theory of China's inevitable subjugation' and 'the theory of China's quick victory'. The former gives rise to the tendency to compromise and the latter to the tendency to underestimate the enemy. Both approaches to the problem are subjective and one-sided, or, in a word, unscientific." On this basis, Mao Zedong pointed out, "The question is now: Will China be subjugated? The answer is: No, she will not be subjugated, but will win the final victory. Can China win quickly? The answer is: No, she cannot win quickly and the War of Resistance will be a protracted war."

毛泽东在《论持久战》中深刻地分析了中日双方的形势,科学地预见了抗日战争将具体地表现为三个阶段:第一个阶段,是敌之战略进攻、我之战略防御的时期;第二个阶段,是敌之战略保守、我之准备反攻的时期;第三个阶段,是我之战略反攻、敌之战略退却的时期。简言之,论持久战将经过战略防御、战略相持、战略反攻三个阶段。《论持久战》论述了只有实行人民战争,才能赢得胜利的思想;强调为了胜利,必须坚持抗战、坚持统一战线、坚持持久战。《论持久战》对中国取得抗日战争的最终胜利起到了重要的理论指导作用。此外,毛泽东还撰写了《抗日游击战争的战略问题》(1938年)一文,强调了游击战在抗日战争全过程中的重要战略地位。

In "On Protracted War", Mao Zedong deeply analyzed the situation between China and Japan and scientifically foresaw that the War of Resistance would manifest itself in three specific stages: "The first stage covers the period of the enemy's strategic offensive and our strategic defensive. The second stage will be the period of the enemy's strategic consolidation and our preparation for a counter-offensive. The third stage will be the period of our strategic counter-offensive and the enemy's strategic retreat. In short, the war will go through three stages: strategic defensive, strategic stalemate and strategic counter-offensive." "On Protracted War" discusses the idea that victory can only be won through the implementation of the people's war. It stresses that in order to win, it is necessary to persist, present a united front and be prepared for a protracted war. "On Protracted War" played an important theoretical guiding role in China's final victory in the War of Resistance Against Japanese Aggression. In addition, Mao Zedong also wrote an article entitled "Problems of Strategy in Guerrilla War Against Japan" (1938), emphasizing the important strategic positions of guerrilla warfare during the War of Resistance Against Japanese Aggression.

抗日根据地军民的反扫荡斗争
The Anti-Mopping-up Campaign of the Army and the People in Anti-Japanese Base Areas

抗日战争进入战略相持阶段后,日本侵略军对中国共产党领导下的敌后抗日根据地进行了疯狂"扫荡",推行烧光、杀光、抢光的"三光"政策。在日军的疯狂攻击下,抗日根据地的面积缩小,八路军、新四军由50万人减少到约40万人,总人口由1亿人减少到5000万人以下。在此背景下,敌后军民创造了很多有效的歼敌方法,如麻雀战、地道战、地雷战、破袭战、水上游击战等,开展了形式多样的抗日斗争。

After the war entered a phase of strategic stalemate, Japanese invaders launched a frenzied "mopping-up" in CPC-led anti-Japanese base areas behind enemy lines, implementing a barbarous "Three Alls" policy — burning all, killing all and looting all. Under these wild attacks, the anti-Japanese base areas shrank in size, the Eighth Route Army and the New Fourth Army were reduced from 500,000 members to about 400,000, and the total population of these areas was reduced from 100 million to less than 50 million. Against this backdrop, the military and civilians behind the enemy lines devised many effective strategies to combat the enemy, such as sparrow warfare①, tunnel warfare, and mine warfare, sabotage warfare and guerrilla warfare on the lakes, all of which took various forms during the resistance against Japanese aggression.

华侨与抗日战争
Overseas Chinese and the War of Resistance Against Japanese Aggression

海外华侨有着爱国的光荣传统,是中华民族抗日战争中的重要力量。从1931年的九一八事变到1945年抗日战争胜利,他们同祖国人民一起,为世界反法西斯战争作出了不可磨灭的贡献。

Overseas Chinese have a glorious tradition of patriotism and played an important role in the Chinese people's War of Resistance Against Japanese Aggression. From the September 18th Incident in 1931 to the victory in the War of Resistance Against Japanese Aggression in 1945, they made indelible contributions to the world Anti-Fascist War together with the people of their homeland.

华侨利用自己侨居海外的便利条件,在欧洲、美洲、大洋洲以及东南亚组织抗日团体,开展各种各样的爱国抗日活动,为抗日战争争取广泛的国际

---

① Sparrow warfare is a popular method of fighting created by the Communist-led anti-Japanese guerrilla units and militia behind the enemy lines. It was called sparrow warfare because, first, it was used diffusely, like the flight of sparrows in the sky; and second, it was used flexibly by guerrillas or militiamen, operating in threes or fives, appearing and disappearing unexpectedly and wounding, killing, depleting and wearing out the enemy forces.

同情和援助。他们积极捐款捐物,支持祖国抗战;他们还积极宣传抗日,支持团结抗战,反对分裂投降。

Taking advantage of their residence abroad, overseas Chinese organized anti-Japanese groups in Europe, America, Oceania and Southeast Asia and had launched a variety of patriotic anti-Japanese activities to gain widespread international sympathy and assistance. They donated money and materials to support their motherland, and also actively promoted resistance against Japanese aggression, supported the united resistance and opposed secession and surrender.

全面抗战开始后,很多华侨回国参战。1938年10月以后,中国东南的海陆交通被日军切断,新开辟的滇缅公路工程完成后,亟需大批汽车司机和修理工。爱国华侨陈嘉庚先生在新加坡成立的"南洋华侨筹赈祖国难民总会"(简称"南侨总会")受国民政府的委托,招募3200名华侨机工回国效力。1940年5月31日,陈嘉庚先生冲破国民政府重重阻挠到访延安。在延安实地考察期间,陈嘉庚先生亲眼见到共产党人艰苦奋斗、清正廉洁的优良作风,意味深长地说:"中国的希望在延安!"

After the start of the full-scale war, many overseas Chinese returned to China to join the fighting. After October 1938, land and sea transportation in southeast China was cut off by the Japanese army, so when work on the newly opened Yunnan-Burma Highway was completed, a large number of car drivers and mechanics were urgently needed. The Federation of China Relief Funds of Southeast Asia(FCRFSA), founded in Singapore by the Chinese patriot Chen Jiageng (also known as Tan Kah Kee) was commissioned by the Nationalist Government to recruit 3,200 overseas Chinese mechanics back to serve China. On May 31, 1940, Chen Jiageng overcame obstructions of the KMT Government to visit Yan'an. During his visit there, Chen Jiageng personally observed the hard work, integrity and honesty of the Communists. He profoundly stated, "The hope of China lies in Yan'an!"

中国人民经过14年艰苦卓绝的斗争,终于取得了抗日战争的伟大胜利,爱国华侨为祖国抗战作出了巨大贡献。毛泽东曾高度赞扬陈嘉庚先生的爱国主义精神,称他为"华侨旗帜,民族光辉"。

After 14 years of hard struggle, the Chinese people finally won the War of Resistance Against Japanese Aggression, for which the patriotic Chinese people abroad made great contributions. Mao Zedong once highly praised the patriotism of Mr. Chen Jiageng, calling him "the banner of the overseas Chinese and the glory of the nation".

大生产运动与南泥湾
The Production Campaign and Nanniwan

1941年,由于日本侵略军的疯狂"扫荡"及国民党顽固派的军事包围和经济封锁,中国共产党领导下的敌后抗日根据地面临前所未有的经济困难。为克服经济上的严重困难,中共中央制定了"发展经济、保障供给"的总方针,在抗日根据地掀起军民大生产运动。

In 1941, the CPC-led anti-Japanese base areas behind enemy lines faced unprecedented economic difficulties due to the frenzied "mopping-up" by the Japanese, and also a military encirclement and economic blockade by a stubborn clique of the KMT. In order to overcome these difficulties, the Central Committee of the CPC formulated the general policy of "developing the economy and ensuring supplies" and launched a large-scale production campaign involving both the army and the people in these areas.

1941年春,王震率领的八路军第一二〇师第三五九旅开进南泥湾垦荒屯田。他们发扬自力更生、奋发图强的精神,使昔日荒无人烟的南泥湾变成了"陕北的好江南",而三五九旅也被誉为大生产运动的模范。抗日根据地开展大生产运动后,根据地实现了粮食等物资的自给自足,度过了严重的经济困难,为争取抗日战争的胜利奠定了物质基础。

In the spring of 1941, the 359th Brigade of the 120th Division of the Eighth Route Army, led by Wang Zhen, moved into an area of wilderness called Nanniwan to cultivate the fields. They embraced the spirit of self-reliance and perseverance, transforming the once-deserted Nanniwan into the "Fertile

Jiangnan of Northern Shaanxi", and thus, the 359th Brigade was hailed as a model for the Production Campaign. After the Production Campaign was launched in anti-Japanese base areas, food and other materials became sufficient, thus overcoming economic difficulties and laying the material foundation for victory in the War of Resistance Against Japanese Aggression.

"革命圣地"延安
Yan'an: the Holy Land of the Chinese Communist Revolution

1937年1月13日,毛泽东率领中共中央机关进驻延安,直至1948年3月23日东渡黄河前往华北,党中央在延安度过了十三年。延安既是红军"北上抗日"长征的"落脚点",也是建立抗日民族统一战线、取得抗日战争胜利的"出发点"。全民族抗战开始后,党中央所在地延安成为革命者向往的"圣地"。大批爱国志士和知识青年背着行李,燃烧着希望,冲破敌占区的重重封锁,冒着生命危险,从全国各地来到延安寻求救国真理和道路。为培养革命干部,开展文化教育,党中央先后创办了抗日军政大学、陕北公学、鲁迅艺术学院、中共中央党校、中国女子大学、民族学院、卫生学校等一批学校,取得了显著成绩。

On January 13, 1937, Mao Zedong led the Central Committee of the CPC to Yan'an, where the Party spent 13 years until March 23, 1948, after which they crossed the Yellow River eastward to North China. Yan'an was both the "landing point" of the Red Army's long march north and the "starting point" for the establishment of the Anti-Japanese National United Front and the eventual victory. When the war began, Yan'an, the location of the Party's Central Committee, became the "holy land" where revolutionaries aspired to visit. A large number of patriotic and intellectual youths from all over the country, carrying their luggage and burning with hope, broke through the blockade of enemy-occupied areas and risked their lives to come to Yan'an, seeking truth and a way to save the nation. In order to train revolutionary cadres and provide cultural education, the Party Central Committee founded a variety of schools, including the Anti-Japanese Military and Political College, the Shaanbei Public School, Luxun Academy of Fine Arts, the Party School of the Central Committee

第五章 延安：革命圣地 抗战中心

of CPC, the Chinese Women's College, the Nationalities Institute, and the Health School. These schools all achieved remarkable results.

抗日战争的伟大胜利
The Great Victory of the Resistance Against Japanese Aggression

1945年上半年,世界反法西斯战争进入最后胜利阶段。4月25日,联合国制宪会议在美国旧金山举行,包括中国解放区代表董必武在内的中国代表团出席会议。中国成为联合国的创始会员国之一和安理会五个常任理事国之一。

In the first half of 1945, the Global War Against Fascism entered the stage of final victory. The United Nations Conference on International Organization (UNCIO) was held in San Francisco on April 25. A Chinese delegation, including Dong Biwu, a representative of the liberated areas of China, was in attendance. China became a founding member of the United Nations and one of the five permanent members of the Security Council.

1945年5月8日,纳粹德国无条件投降,欧洲战场的反法西斯战争胜利结束。8月15日,日本天皇裕仁以广播《终战诏书》的形式,宣布接受《波茨坦公告》,无条件投降。9月2日,日本代表在投降书上签字。9月3日成为中国人民抗日战争胜利纪念日。

On May 8, 1945, Nazi Germany surrendered unconditionally and the war against fascism in Europe ended victoriously. On August 15, the Japanese Emperor Hirohito announced his acceptance of the Potsdam Declaration and unconditional surrender by broadcasting the Imperial Rescript on the Termination of the War, and on September 2, the Japanese representative signed the surrender. The 3rd of September became the anniversary of the victory of the Chinese People's War of Resistance Against Japanese Aggression.

2020年9月3日,习近平总书记在纪念中国人民抗日战争暨世界反法西斯战争胜利75周年座谈会上的讲话中指出:"中国人民经过14年不屈不挠的浴血奋战,打败了穷凶极恶的日本军国主义侵略者,取得了中国人民抗日战争的伟大胜利！这是近代以来中国人民反抗外敌入侵持续时间最长、规模最大、牺牲最多的民族解放斗争，也是第一次取得完全胜利的民族解放斗争。这个伟大胜利，是中华民族从近代以来陷入深重危机走向伟大复兴的历史转折点也是世界反法西斯战争胜利的重要组成部分，是中国人民的胜利也是世界人民的胜利。中国人民抗日战争的伟大胜利，将永远铭刻在中华民族史册上！永远铭刻在人类正义事业史册上！"

On September 3, 2020, a symposium was held in Beijing to commemorate the 75th Anniversary of the Victory of the Chinese People's War of Resistance Against Japanese Aggression and the World Anti-Fascist War. General Secretary Xi Jinping delivered a speech at the symposium, noting that: "After 14 years of indomitable and bloody struggle, the Chinese people defeated the vicious Japanese militarist invaders and achieved great victory! This was the longest, largest and most sacrificial national liberation struggle against foreign invasion in modern times, and the first national liberation struggle to achieve complete victory. This great victory was a turning point in the history of the Chinese nation, from a deep crisis in modern times to a great renaissance, and it played an important role in the victory over fascism in the World Anti-Fascist War, a victory for both the Chinese people and people all over the world. The great victory of the Chinese people in the war against Japan will forever be engraved in the history of the Chinese nation! It will forever be engraved in the history of the just cause of mankind!"

第二节　红色故事
Section Ⅱ　Red Stories

瓦窑堡革命故事

Story of the Wayaobao Revolution

1935年7月25日，共产国际召开第七次代表大会，制定了建立世界反法西斯统一战线的方针。此时中国红军尚在长征途中，与共产国际的联系在长征前便已中断。为恢复联系，共产国际在做出多次努力之后，最终决定派遣中国共产党党员林育英带回最新的电讯密码。化名"张浩"的林育英还肩负另一项更为重要的责任：向中共中央传达共产国际第七次代表大会的会议精神。

On July 25, 1935, the Seventh Congress of the Comintern was held, at which the policy of establishing a globally united anti-fascist front was set down. At this time, the Chinese Red Army was still on its Long March, and communication with the Comintern had already been severed prior to the start of the march. After many unsuccessful attempts to contact the CPC, Comintern finally decided to send Lin Yuying (alias Zhang Hao), a representative of the CPC Central Committee to Comintern, back to China with the latest telecommunication codes. The other more important task for Lin was to convey the spirit of the Seventh Congress of the Comintern to the Central Committee of the CPC.

林育英牢记会议内容和电讯密码跋山涉水、南下归国的时候,红军三大主力尚在艰难险阻的长征途中。1935年10月,中共中央终于带领中央红军到达陕北,完成了长征。11月,进驻陕西省安定县(今子长县)瓦窑堡。林育英也终于到达了安定县,与党中央取得了联系。林育英的到来,让中共中央与共产国际重新取得了联系,加速了抗日民族统一战线的确立。

While Lin Yuying embarked on a grueling journey back to China with both the contents of the meeting and the telecommunication codes, the three main forces of the Red Army were still on the arduous and perilous Long March. In October 1935, the Central Committee of the CPC finally led the Central Red Army to northern Shaanxi, completing the Long March. In November, they stationed themselves in Wayaobao, Anding County (now Zichang County), Shaanxi Province. Lin Yuying also arrived there and established contact with the CPC Central Committee. The arrival of Lin Yuying brought the Central Committee back into contact with the Comintern and accelerated the establishment of the anti-Japanese national united front.

1935年,日本在华北制造了一系列事端,加紧了对华北的侵略。面对日益加深的民族危机,中国很多大中城市爆发了大规模的抗日学生运动。各地工人在全国总工会的号召下,纷纷举行罢工,支援学生斗争。爱国人士、爱国团体也纷纷成立各界救国会,要求停止内战,一致抗日。抗日救亡斗争迅速发展成为全国规模的群众运动。在此背景下,中共中央于12月17日至25日,在瓦窑堡举行了政治局扩大会议,毛泽东、张闻天、周恩来等出席了会议。会议讨论了军事战略问题、全国的政治形势和党的策略路线问题,通过了《中央关于军事战略问题的决议》和张闻天起草的《中央关于目前政治形势与党的任务决议》。

In 1935, the Japanese fabricated a series of incidents in North China, escalating its invasion of the region. In the face of the deepening national crisis, large-scale anti-Japanese protests erupted in many major and medium-sized cities across China. Workers throughout the country, under the call of the All-China Federation of Trade Unions, initiated strikes in solidarity with the students' movements. Patriotic individuals and groups alike began forming a myriad of associations for national salvation, advocating for an end to the civil war and a united resistance against Japan. The struggle for anti-Japanese resistance and national salvation quickly blossomed into a nationwide mass movement. Against this backdrop, from December 17 to 25, the CPC Central Committee convened an enlarged Politburo meeting in Wayaobao. Attendees of the meeting included Mao Zedong, Zhang Wentian, Zhou Enlai, and others. The meeting deliberated on issues concerning military strategy, the nationwide political situation, and the Party's strategic direction. The "Resolution on Military Strategy of the Party" was approved, as was the "Resolution on the Present Political Situation and the Tasks of the Party", which was drafted by Zhang Wentian.

会后,毛泽东在12月27日召开的党的活动分子会议上作了《论反对日本帝国主义的策略》的报告,阐明了抗日民族统一战线的策略方针。为准备东渡黄河进入山西抗击日寇,中共中央组织了东征部队,由毛泽东亲自率领。1936年2月,东征部队途经清涧县袁家沟时,毛泽东提笔写下了被柳亚子先生推为千古绝唱的《沁园春·雪》。

After the meeting, Mao Zedong delivered a report entitled "On Tactics

Against Japanese Imperialism" at another meeting of Party activists held on December 27, outlining the strategic policy for the anti-Japanese national united front. In preparation for crossing the Yellow River eastwards into Shanxi to combat Japanese forces, the Central Committee of the CPC organized an eastern expeditionary force, personally led by Mao Zedong. In February 1936, as the expeditionary force was passing through Yuanjiagou in Qingjian County, Mao Zedong penned "Snow", a work later proclaimed as an unparalleled masterpiece by Liu Yazi.

沁园春·雪

北国风光,千里冰封,万里雪飘。
望长城内外,惟余莽莽;
大河上下,顿失滔滔。
山舞银蛇,原驰蜡象,
欲与天公试比高。
须晴日,
看红装素裹,分外妖娆。

江山如此多娇,
引无数英雄竞折腰。
惜秦皇汉武,略输文采;
唐宗宋祖,稍逊风骚。
一代天骄,成吉思汗,
只识弯弓射大雕。
俱往矣,
数风流人物,还看今朝。

Tune: Spring in a Pleasure Garden
Snow

(Translated by Xu Yuanchong)

See what the northern countries show:
Hundreds of leagues ice-bound go;

Thousands of leagues flies snow.
Behold! Within and without the Great Wall
The boundless land is clad in white,
And up and down the Yellow River, all
The endless waves are lost to sight.
Mountains like silver serpents dancing,
Highlands like waxy elephants advancing,①
All try to match the sky in height.
Wait till the day is fine
And see the fair bask in sparkling sunshine,
What an enchanting sight!
Our motherland so rich in beauty
Has made countless heroes vie to pay her their duty.
But alas! Qin Huang② and Han Wu③
In culture not well bred,
And Tang Zong④ and Song Zu⑤
In letters not wide read.
And Genghis Khan,⑥ proud son of Heaven for a day,
Knew only shooting eagles by bending his bows.
They have all passed away;
Brilliant heroes are those
Whom we will see today!

---

① Author's notes: Highlands of Shaanxi and Shanxi.

② Qin Huang or Qin Shihuang (259 – 210 BC) was the first emperor of the Qin Dynasty, who had founded a unified empire in 221 BC.

③ Han Wu or Han Wudi (156 – 87 BC) was the fifth emperor of Han Dynasty, who had resisted foreign aggression.

④ Tang Zong or Tang Taizong (599 – 649) was the second emperor of the Tang Dynasty, who had made China one of the strongest countries in the world.

⑤ Song Zu or Song Taizu (927 – 976) was the first emperor of the Song Dynasty.

⑥ Genghis Khan (1162 – 1227) was the first emperor of the Yuan Dynasty, who has made a western expedition as far as Europe.

《黄河大合唱》的诞生
The Birth of the "Yellow River Cantata"

《黄河大合唱》是冼星海、光未然创作的一部极具影响力的大型合唱声乐套曲。1938年10月,武汉沦陷后,诗人光未然带领抗敌演剧队第三队,从陕西宜川县的壶口附近东渡黄河,转入吕梁山抗日根据地。他在途中目睹了黄河船夫们与狂风恶浪搏斗的情景,聆听了高亢、悠扬的船工号子。

1939年1月,光未然抵达延安后,创作了朗诵诗《黄河吟》,并在这年的除夕联欢会上朗诵此作。冼星海听后非常兴奋,表示要为演剧队创作《黄河大合唱》。同年3月,在延安一座简陋的土窑里,冼星海抱病连续写作6天,于3月31日完成了《黄河大合唱》八个乐章的作曲。全曲由《黄河船夫曲》《黄河颂》《黄河之水天上来》《黄水谣》《河边对口曲》《黄河怨》《保卫黄河》和《怒吼吧!黄河》八个乐章组成。

The "Yellow River Cantata" is an influential, large-scale choral vocal suite composed by Xian Xinghai and Guang Weiran. In October 1938, after the city of Wuhan fell to Japanese invaders, the poet Guang Weiran led the third group of the Anti-Japanese drama team across the Yellow River near Hukou Town, Yichuan County, Shaanxi Province, and eastwards into the anti-Japanese base in the Luliang Mountains. During his journey, Guang witnessed local boatmen battle against heavy gales and torrential waves, and heard their spirit-lifting songs.

Upon his arrival in Yan'an in January 1939, Guang composed a poem entitled "Chanting of the Yellow River". He recited it at the Chinese New Year's Eve celebration that year. After hearing the recitation, Xian Xinghai was so inspired that he expressed his intention to compose the "Yellow River Cantata" for the drama team. In March of the same year, in a humble earthen cave dwelling in Yan'an, Xian Xinghai composed for six consecutive days despite his ill health. He completed the composition of the "Yellow River Cantata" on March 31. The whole piece consisted of eight movements: "Song of the Yellow River Boatmen", "Ode to the Yellow River", "Yellow River's Water from Heaven Descends," "Yellow River Ballad", "Musical Dialogue on the Bank of the

Yellow River", "Yellow River Lament", "Defend the Yellow River" and "Roar! Yellow River!"

《黄河大合唱》表现了抗日战争年代里中国人民的苦难与顽强斗争精神,讴歌了中华儿女不屈不挠,保卫祖国的必胜信念。它以我们民族的发源地——黄河为背景,展示了黄河岸边曾经发生过的事情,以启迪人民来保卫黄河、保卫华北、保卫全中国。《黄河大合唱》以其独特的个性,恢宏的气势,催人奋进的强烈号召力和凝重深刻的哲学气息征服了世界。就如埃德加·斯诺所言:"《黄河大合唱》永永远远,都属于明日的中国。"

The "Yellow River Cantata" depicts the hardships and resilient struggle of the Chinese people during the period of the War of Resistance Against Japanese Aggression. It pays tribute to the relentless fortitude and unwavering conviction of the Chinese in defending their motherland and their certainty of ultimate victory. Set against the backdrop of the Yellow River, the birthplace of our nation, it shows what happened on those banks to inspire people to defend the Yellow River, North China, and then all of China. The "Yellow River Cantata" has captivated the world with its unique character, magnificence, strong call to action, along with a solemn and profound philosophical undertone. As the American journalist Edgar Snow once said, "The 'Yellow River Cantata' will always belong to tomorrow's China."

斯诺与《红星照耀中国》
Edgar Snow and the *Red Star Over China*

北大未名湖南岸,有一座长方形汉白玉墓碑,碑上镌刻着"中国人民的美国朋友埃德加·斯诺之墓"。埃德加·斯诺是一名美国记者,1905年出生于密苏里州堪萨斯,大学毕业后从事新闻工作。1928年23岁时抵达上海,其后遍访南京、天津、东北、内蒙古等地,足迹几乎踏遍中国大地。1930年,作为美国统一新闻协会记者远行至缅甸、印度,随后又返回中国。1934年在燕京大学担任新闻系讲师。也就是在燕京大学任职期间,他去了陕北,真实地记录了当时红军的状况,写下了著名的《红星照耀中国》。

On the south bank of the Weiming Lake in Peking University, there is a rectangular white jade tombstone, upon which is engraved "The Tomb of Edgar Snow, the American Friend of the Chinese People". Edgar Snow was an American journalist born in Kansas, Missouri in 1905. After graduating from university, he worked in journalism. In 1928, at the age of 23, he arrived in Shanghai, and then visited Nanjing, Tianjin, Northeast China, Inner Mongolia and other places, traversing most of China. In 1930, as a reporter for the Consolidated Press Association of the United States, he traveled to Myanmar and India, then returned to China. In 1934, he became a lecturer in the Department of Journalism at Yenching University (now Peking University). During his tenure at Yenching University, he went to Northern Shaanxi, where he accurately documented the conditions of the Red Army at that time. This experience led him to write the renowned *Red Star over China*.

自从1927年第一个苏维埃政权诞生以来，国民党就对红军进行了新闻封锁，并在报纸上肆意抹黑共产党。这导致了外界对于苏区、对共产党一无所知。斯诺就是在这种重重封锁下，得到了前往延安的机会。为打破国民党的新闻封锁，向全世界报道中国红军和苏区的真相，1936年6月，斯诺带着他的采访工具，冒险前往延安。

Since the establishment of the first Soviet regime in 1927, the KMT imposed a press blockade on the Red Army and wantonly smeared the Communist Party in the newspapers. This led to the outside world not knowing anything about the Soviet Area and the Communist Party. It was under this blockade that Snow found himself with the opportunity to go to Yan'an. In order to break the KMT's news blockade and report the truth about the Chinese Red Army and the Soviet Area to the world, in June 1936, Snow, equipped with his reporting tools, bravely journeyed alone to Yan'an.

在宋庆龄的引荐下，斯诺突破重重关卡，最终于1936年7月13日抵达当时中共中央驻地保安（现志丹县）。斯诺在苏区的采访被给予了高度自由。周恩来亲自为斯诺确定好了在苏区采访的日程安排。原计划共有92天，实际上斯诺在苏区待满了四个月。他在保安采访了毛泽东、彭德怀等中共领导人,成为第一位到达陕甘宁边区进行采访的外国记者。

Thanks to the endorsement of Song Qingling, Edgar Snow was able to navigate through numerous challenges and finally arrived at the headquarters of the CPC in Bao'an (now known as Zhidan County) on July 13, 1936. Snow was granted extensive freedom during his stay in the Soviet Areas. Zhou Enlai personally organized Snow's schedule for his time in the Soviet Areas. Originally planned to last 92 days, Snow's visit extended to a full four months. During his stay in Bao'an, he interviewed key Communist leaders such as Mao Zedong and Peng Dehuai, thereby becoming the first foreign journalist to conduct interviews in the Shaanxi-Gansu-Ningxia Border Region.

斯诺对根据地和工农红军进行了深入的采访,采访了红军将士和当地百姓,对根据地的军民生活、地方政治改革以及风俗习惯等作了广泛深入的调查。斯诺还多次受到毛主席的会见,从而使他获得了许多关于毛泽东个人和中国共产党以及工农红军的第一手珍贵资料。在斯诺的再三请求之下,毛泽东还讲述了自己从童年到长征的革命经历。这也是毛泽东唯一一次比较完整地详谈自己的经历。

Snow conducted in-depth interviews with members of the Red Army and local inhabitants within the revolutionary bases. He carried out extensive and comprehensive investigations into the lives of the military personnel and civilians, the local political reforms, as well as the customs, and traditions of the area. Snow had multiple meetings with Chairman Mao, which granted him access to invaluable first-hand information about Mao Zedong himself, the CPC, and the Red Army. At Snow's persistent requests, Mao Zedong recounted his revolutionary experiences from his childhood to the Long March, providing the most comprehensive account of his personal history ever recorded.

斯诺把他的采访详细记录在了他的笔记本上,四个月的采访,他密密麻麻写满了 14 个笔记本。此外,他当时还带了 2 架相机,24 卷胶卷,在苏区拍了大量的照片。他的照片大致有以下几类:① 领导人照片;② 苏区生活照片;③ 红军的照片;④ 苏区文化生活和少先队的照片。这些照片真实地记载了当时的历史,给后人留下了珍贵的图像资料。

Snow meticulously documented his interviews in his notebooks filling up 14 of them during the four-month period. He also brought two cameras with 24 rolls of film and took a large number of photos in the Soviet Area. His photographs can be divided roughly into the following categories: ① photos of leaders; ② photos of life in the Soviet Area; ③ photos of the Red Army; ④ photos of the cultural scene and the Young Pioneers in the Soviet Area. These photos provide a truthful account of the history of the time and leave precious visual documents for future generations.

当年10月底,斯诺带着他的采访资料、胶卷和照片,从陕北回到北平。他将他在苏区的所见所闻写了多篇报道,随后汇集成一部纪实性很强的报道性作品——《红星照耀中国》,于1937年10月在伦敦出版。为了能在国民党统治区出版发行,中文译名改为《西行漫记》。这本书让世界初窥中国革命根据地、中国共产党、中国红军的真实面貌,粉碎了外界对于中国共产党和中国红军的不实谣言。《红星照耀中国》发表后,国际社会掀起了支援中国人民抗日战争的热潮。加拿大医生白求恩、印度医生柯棣华、美国记者艾格尼丝·史沫特莱、安娜·路易斯·斯特朗等纷纷来到中国,帮助中国人民进行抗战。

At the end of October of that year, Snow returned to Beiping from Northern Shaanxi with his interview materials, film rolls and photos. He wrote a number of reports on what he saw and heard in the Soviet Area, which were later compiled into a highly informative work, *Red Star Over China*. It was published in London in October 1937. In order to publish and distribute it in the areas ruled by the KMT, the name of the book was translated into Chinese as *Journey to the West*. This book provided the world with the first glimpse of the true face of the Chinese revolutionary base areas, the CPC, and the Chinese Red Army, and shattered false rumors about them. After the publication of *Red Star Over China*, the international community rallied in support of the Chinese people's resistance against Japanese aggression. Notable individuals such as Canadian doctor Norman Bethune, Indian doctor Ke Dihua (known as Dwarkanath Kotnis), American journalist Agnes Smedley, along with Anna Louise Strong and many others, came to China to assist the Chinese people in their fight.

新中国成立后,斯诺先后三次来访中国。1972年逝世后,他的夫人遵照他的遗嘱,将他的部分骨灰带到了中国,埋葬在了北大未名湖湖畔,埋葬在了他曾留下浓墨重彩的印记的红色土地。

After the founding of New China, Snow visited China three more times. After his death in 1972, some of his ashes were brought to China by his wife in accordance with his will. They were interred on the shores of the Weiming Lake in Peking University, returning him to the land where he had left such an indelible mark.

第三节　红色景点
Section Ⅲ　Red Tourism Attractions

延安革命纪念馆
Yan'an Revolutionary Memorial Hall

在陕西省延安市宝塔区西北延河东岸,距离市区1公里之处,坐落着新中国成立后最早建立的革命纪念馆之一的延安革命纪念馆。延安革命纪念馆始建于1950年,1951年正式对外展出。纪念馆建成后几经更名,在1955年正式定名为"延安革命纪念馆",馆名为1971年郭沫若前来参观时题写。纪念馆前方是占地面积2.7万平方米的广场。广场正中耸立着巍峨的毛主席青铜像,铜像高5米,加上3.15米的底座,总高8.15米。

On the east bank of the Yan River in northwest Baota District, Yan'an City, Shaanxi Province, one kilometer away from the city, sits the Yan'an Revolutionary Memorial Hall, one of the earliest revolutionary memorial halls established after the founding of New China. The Yan'an Revolutionary Memorial Hall was established in 1950 and officially opened to the public in 1951. After completion, it was renamed several times, and was officially named as "Yan'an Revolutionary Memorial Hall" in 1955. The name was penned by Guo Moruo

图 5-1 延安革命纪念馆
Figure 5-1 Yan'an Revolutionary Memorial Hall

during his visit in 1971. In front of the memorial hall is a plaza covering an area of 27,000 square meters. In the middle of the square stands a towering bronze statue of Chairman Mao, rising to a total height of 8.15 meters when including the 5-meter-high statue and the 3.15-meter base.

延安革命纪念馆总建筑面积约为29853平方米。主体建筑呈"门"字形，东西长222米，南北共119米，宛如张开的手臂欢迎游客的光临。2021年6月，在第10次陈列提升改造工作之后，纪念馆重新免费开放，陈列面积10677平方米。正对广场的主楼的序厅由主题雕塑和环绕浮雕组成。主题雕塑有毛泽东、朱德、刘少奇、周恩来、任弼时塑像以及工农阶级、国际友人等群像。其背后的浮雕为冉冉升起的红日及沐浴在阳光下的延安宝塔，左上侧写着"1935—1948 延安"字样。右侧浮雕是黄帝陵及长城，左侧浮雕为大禹治水的黄河壶口瀑布。

The total construction area of Yan'an Revolutionary Memorial Hall is about 29,853 square meters. The main building, with an east-to-west length of 222 meters and 119 meters from north to south, is in the shape of the Chinese character "门" (meaning "gate"), resembling an open arm gesturing to welcome visitors. In June 2021, following its 10th renovation and upgrade, the memorial hall with an exhibition area of 10,677 square meters reopened and offered free admission. The entrance hall of the main building faces the square, and consists of themed sculptures and reliefs on three walls. The themed sculptures include statues of Mao Zedong, Zhu De, Liu Shaoqi, Zhou Enlai, and Ren Bishi, as well as group statues of the workers' and peasants' class and international friends. The relief in the background is of a rising red sun and the Yan'an Pagoda in sunlight, with the words "1935 - 1948 Yan'an" written on the upper left side. The relief on the right is the Mausoleum of the Yellow Emperor and the Great Wall, and the relief on the left is the Hukou Waterfall on the Yellow River, where King Yu tamed the flood.

这里共有两层展区,展出内容分为5个单元:第一单元红军长征的落脚点;第二单元抗日战争的政治指导中心;第三单元新民主主义的模范实验区;第四单元延安精神的发祥地;第五单元毛泽东思想的形成与发展。共展出文物2000余件,照片900余张。同时还有红军长征胜利到陕北、大生产、干部学习等26项艺术品场景。还用3D裸眼技术展现了直罗镇战役,还有瓦窑堡会议、延安文艺座谈会等科技多媒体互动展40项。

There are two exhibition areas here, and the exhibition content is divided into 5 units, which are Unit 1, the Foothold of the Long March of the Red Army; Unit 2, the Political Guidance Center of the War of Resistance Against Japanese Aggression; Unit 3, the Model Experimental Area of New Democracy; Unit 4, the Birthplace of the Yan'an Spirit; and Unit 5, the Formation and Development of Mao Zedong Thought. A total of more than 2,000 cultural relics and more than 900 photos are exhibited. Additionally, there are 26 artistic scenes, such as the victory of the Red Army's Long March to northern Shaanxi, the Production Campaign, and Cadre Learning. It also shows the Battle of Zhiluo Town using naked-eye 3D technology, as well as other 40 interactive exhibitions including the Wayaobao Meeting, the Yan'an Conference on Literature and Art, and others.

广场左右两侧的纪念馆还有4个大型专题展。右侧为《伟大长征辉煌史诗》《强基:延安时期党的组织建设》,左侧是《铸魂:延安时期的从严治党》《学习用典:中国优秀经典故事全国连环画作品展》两个专题展。延安革命纪念馆2008年3月,被国家文物局评定为国家一级博物馆,2016年12月,被列入全国红色旅游经典景区名录。2017年入选教育部首批全国中小学生研学实践教育基地营地名单。

There are also four large-scale thematic exhibitions at the memorial halls on the left and right sides of the square. On the right are "The Great Long March, A Brilliant Epic" and "Strengthening the Foundation, the Party's Organizational Construction During the Yan'an Period". On the left are two special exhibitions, "Casting the Soul, Strict Governance over the Party in the Yan'an Period" and "Learning from Classics: National Exhibition of Outstanding Chinese Comic Strip Stories". The Yan'an Revolutionary Memorial Hall was designated as a national first-class museum by the National Cultural Heritage Administration in March 2008. In December 2016, it was included in the national list of red tourism attractions and scenic areas. In 2017, it was selected by the Ministry of Education as one of the first national educational bases and campgrounds for experiential learning by primary and secondary school students.

见证历史的宝塔山
Baota Mountain: A Witness to History

宝塔山,古称丰林山,宋时改名为嘉岭山,现在人们又称宝塔山。宝塔山位于延安城东南方,海拔1135.5米,为周围群山之冠。宝塔山上视野开阔,林木茂盛,山林空气清新,凉爽宜人,夏季平均气温较市内低3~4摄氏度,是人们消夏避暑的好地方。

Precious Pagoda Hill, known as Fenglin Mountain in ancient times, was renamed Jialing Mountain in the Song Dynasty (960 – 1279), and is now also known as Baota Mountain. It is located in the southeast of Yan'an City, with an altitude of 1,135.5 meters, making it the tallest of the surrounding mountains. It is a good place to escape the summer heat, as the average temperature in summer is three to four degrees lower than that of urban areas. You can enjoy the cool fresh air and take in the lush views on the mountain.

宝塔始建于唐代宗大历年间(766—779),距今已有1200多年的历史。

图 5-2　延安宝塔山
Figure 5-2　Baota Mountain in Yan'an

塔用砖砌筑,平面呈八角形,九层,通高 44 米。登上塔顶,全城风貌可尽收眼底。宝塔是历史名城延安的标志,是引领中国革命走向胜利的熊熊火炬和航标灯。在塔旁边有一口明代铸造的铁钟,1938 年,日本飞机轰炸延安时,这口钟曾被多次敲响,为保卫延安人民的生命安全作出过特殊贡献。

The pagoda was first constructed during the reign of Emperor Daizong of the Tang Dynasty (766 - 779), making it over 1,200 years old. It is an octagonal brick tower with nine floors, reaching a height of 44 meters. When you climb to the top of the pagoda, you can enjoy a panoramic view of the whole city. It is the symbol of the historic city of Yan'an, a torch and beacon light that led the Chinese Revolution to victory. Next to the tower is an iron bell cast in the Ming Dynasty (1368 - 1644). This bell was repeatedly rung in 1938 when Japanese planes bombed Yan'an, playing a unique role in safeguarding the lives of the people there.

此外,山上还有长达 260 米的摩崖石刻群和碑林,占地面积 2864 平方米,高 6~7 米。石刻大部分是北宋时期的石刻,有"嘉岭山""云生幽处""嘉岭胜境称第一""先忧后乐""一韩一范、泰山北斗""胸中自有数万甲兵"等九组。摩崖石刻中最具有历史意义的是毛泽东手书"实事求是"和"发扬革命传统、争取更大光荣"等,体现了中国共产党的初心使命。

In addition, there are also stone carvings spanning 260 meters and stele forests on the mountain cliff, covering an area of 2,864 square meters, and being six to seven meters high. Most of these stone carvings date back to the Northern Song Dynasty (960 – 1127) and they include nine sets of inscriptions such as "嘉岭山(meaning 'Jialing Mountain')", "云生幽处(meaning 'where clouds gather in tranquility')", "嘉岭胜境称第一(meaning 'Jialing's splendid scenery ranks first')", "先忧后乐(meaning 'Being the foremost in bearing burdens, the ultimate in savoring bliss')", "一韩一范、泰山北斗(meaning 'Han Qi and Fan Zhongyan: Towering Mount Tai and Guiding Big Dipper')", and "胸中自有数万甲兵('tens of thousands of armored soldiers reside in my heart')". Among the cliff carvings, the most historically significant are those in Mao Zedong's handwriting, "实事求是" (meaning "seek truth from facts") and "发扬革命传统争取更大光荣" (meaning "carry forward the revolutionary tradition for greater glory"), which embody the original aspiration and the mission of the CPC.

杨家岭革命旧址
The Yangjialing Revolutionary Site

杨家岭革命旧址位于陕西省延安市西北约3公里的杨家岭村。1938年至1940年、1942年至1943年,中共中央曾在此领导中国革命。毛泽东1938年11月至1943年5月在此居住,1940年秋,因修建中央大礼堂等工程,环境嘈杂,毛泽东等领导人和中央一些机关搬到枣园居住,1942年又搬回杨家岭。

The Yangjialing Revolutionary Site is located in Yangjialing village, about three kilometers northwest of Yan'an city in Shaanxi province. From 1938 to 1940 and again from 1942 to 1943, this site was the headquarters from which the Central Committee of the CPC led the Chinese revolution. Mao Zedong resided here from November 1938 to May 1943. In the autumn of 1940, due to the noise caused by the construction of the Great Auditorium and other projects, Mao Zedong and the other leaders, as well as some departments of the Central Committee, relocated to Zaoyuan, and then returned to Yangjialing in 1942.

图 5-3 杨家岭革命旧址
Figure 5-3 Yangjialing Revolutionary Site

1943年,毛泽东等领导人又从这里陆续搬往枣园。毛泽东在此写下了《五四运动》《青年运动的方向》《被敌人反对是好事而不是坏事》《〈共产党人〉发刊词》《纪念白求恩》《中国革命和中国共产党》《新民主主义论》《抗日根据地的政权问题》《目前抗日统一战线中的策略问题》《〈农村调查〉的序言和跋》《改造我们的学习》《整顿党的作风》《反对党八股》《经济问题与财政问题》等光辉著作。

In 1943, Mao Zedong and other leaders moved again to Zaoyuan. During this period, Mao Zedong wrote a variety of impressive works, including "The May Fourth Movement", "The Orientation of the Youth Movement", "To be Attacked by the Enemy Is Not a Bad Thing but a Good Thing", "Introducing *The Communist*", "In Memory of Norman Bethune", *The Chinese Revolution and the Chinese Communist Party*, *On New Democracy*, "On the Question of Political Power in the Anti-Japanese Base Areas", "Current Problems of Tactics in the Anti-Japanese United Front", "Preface and Postscript to *Rural Surveys*", "Reform Our Study", "Rectify the Party's Style of Work", "Oppose Stereotyped Party Writing", and "Economic and Financial Problems".

枣园革命旧址
The Zaoyuan Revolutionary Site

枣园革命旧址位于延安城西北 8 公里处,占地面积 80 亩,环境清幽,景色秀丽。园林中央坐落着中央书记处礼堂,依山分布着 5 座独立的院落,分别是毛泽东、朱德、周恩来、刘少奇、任弼时、张闻天、彭德怀等中央领导的旧居。

图 5-4　枣园革命旧址
Figure 5-4　The Zaoyuan Revolutionary Site

The Zaoyuan Revolutionary Site is located eight kilometers northwest of Yan'an City, covering an area of 13.18 acres, with a quiet environment and beautiful scenery. In the center is the auditorium of the Secretariat of the Central Committee. Five independent courtyards are distributed along the mountain, in which the former residences of Mao Zedong, Zhu De, Zhou Enlai, Liu Shaoqi, Ren Bishi, Zhang Wentian, Peng Dehuai and other central leaders are located.

1943 年 10 月至 1947 年 3 月,枣园是中共中央书记处所在地。其间,中共中央书记处继续领导了全党的整风运动和解放区军民大生产运动,筹备了中国共产党第七次全国代表大会。抗日战争胜利后,为争取和平建国,毛泽东、周恩来等从这里启程前往重庆,同国民党政府进行了针锋相对的斗争,领导解放区军民,为粉碎国民党发动的全面内战作了充分准备。

From October 1943 to March 1947, Zaoyuan was the seat of the Secretariat of the Central Committee of the CPC. During this period, the Secretariat continued to lead the party's Rectification Movement and the Production Campaign of the army and the people in the Liberated Areas, and prepared for the Seventh National Congress of the CPC. After the victory in the War of Resistance Against Japanese Aggression, Mao Zedong, Zhou Enlai and others set off from here to Chongqing. Their aim was to strive for peaceful nation-building and to engage in fierce negotiations with the KMT government. This endeavor, led by the leadership of the Liberated Areas, was in preparation for successfully countering the impending civil war instigated by the KMT.

枣园内有一座苏式小礼堂,是中共中央书记处的会议室,也是俱乐部。中央书记处和中央政治局的许多重要会议都在这里召开。1945年毛泽东接受蒋介石的邀请去重庆谈判的决策就是在这里召开的政治局扩大会议上做出的。

There is a small Soviet-style auditorium in Zaoyuan, which served as the conference room of the Secretariat of the Central Committee and also functioned as a club. Many important meetings of the Secretariat and the Political Bureau of the Central Committee were held here. The decision of Mao Zedong to accept Chiang Kai-shek's invitation to Chongqing for negotiations was made here in 1945, during an enlarged meeting of the Political Bureau of the CPC Central Committee.

在枣园后沟西山脚下,有一方简陋的土平台。1944年9月8日,在这里举行了张思德追悼会,毛泽东在会上发表著名的题为《为人民服务》的演讲。张思德出生在四川仪陇一个穷苦农民家庭,1933年参加红军,1937年加入中国共产党。他曾爬雪山、过草地,作战机智勇敢,奋不顾身,屡立战功,后到中央警备团当战士,在延安枣园毛泽东等中央领导工作的地方执行警卫任务。

At the foot of the west mountain of Zaoyuan, there is a simple earthen platform. On September 8, 1944, the memorial service to Zhang Side was held here, at which Mao Zedong delivered his famous speech entitled "Serve the

People". Born into a poor peasant family in Yilong County, Sichuan province, Zhang Side joined the Red Army in 1933 and the CPC in 1937. He climbed snow-capped mountains and traversed meadows in the Long March, fought with wit and bravery, and accomplished many military achievements. He later became a soldier in the Central Guard Regiment, performing guard duties in Zaoyuan where Mao Zedong and the other central leadership worked.

1944年夏,张思德去安塞执行烧炭任务,在工作中不怕苦累,充分发挥了共产党员的先锋模范作用。1944年9月5日,即将挖成的炭窑突然坍塌,张思德奋力把战友推出洞外,自己却被埋在洞里,牺牲时年仅29岁。

In the summer of 1944, Zhang Side was dispatched to Ansai County to undertake the task of making charcoal. Fully commitment to his responsibility, he was not afraid of hardship or fatigue, and became an exemplary role model to the Communist Party members. On September 5, 1944, a near-completed charcoal kiln suddenly collapsed. Zhang Side managed to push his fellow comrades out of the danger zone, but tragically, he was buried in the process, losing his life at the young age of 29.

得知张思德牺牲的消息后,毛泽东心情十分悲痛,提出要为张思德开追悼会,他要参加并讲话。据1944年9月21日《解放日报》的报道记载,9月8日下午"到会者千余人"。毛泽东以沉痛、激动的语气向大家说:"我们的共产党和共产党所领导的八路军、新四军,是革命的队伍。我们这个队伍完全是为着解放人民的,是彻底地为人民的利益工作的。张思德同志就是我们这个队伍中的一个同志。"毛泽东的演讲,由中央速记室主任认真记录,后由胡乔木整理成文,经毛泽东审阅,被收入《毛泽东选集》第三卷。

After learning the news of Zhang Side's death, Mao Zedong was deeply saddened and suggested to hold a memorial service in honor of Zhang, at which he intended to give a speech. According to a report in the *Liberation Daily* on September 21st, 1944, on the afternoon of September 8, "more than a thousand people attended the meeting". Mao Zedong said to the gathering in a deep and impassioned tone, "Our CPC, together with the Eighth Route Army and New

Fourth Army under its leadership, are revolutionary forces. Our entire mission is dedicated to liberating the people and working for the complete benefit of the people. Comrade Zhang Side is amongst us." Mao Zedong's speech was carefully transcribed by the director of the Central Stenographic Office. It was then compiled by Hu Qiaomu and, after being reviewed by Mao Zedong himself, was included in the third volume of the *Selected Works of Mao Tse-Tung*.

1953年,枣园革命旧址开始修复,1959年正式对外开放。1961年3月4日,国务院公布为第一批全国重点文物保护单位。1996年被中宣部命名为全国爱国主义教育示范基地之一。

In 1953, the restoration work on the Zaoyuan Revolutionary Site began, and it was officially opened to the public in 1959. On March 4, 1961, the State Council announced that it was listed in the first batch of National Key Cultural Relics Protection Units. In 1996, the Zaoyuan Revolutionary Site was named by the Publicity Department of CPC as one of the National Patriotism Education Demonstration Bases.

中国抗日军政大学纪念馆
The Memorial Hall of the Anti-Japanese Military and Political College of China

中国人民抗日军政大学旧址位于延安城内二道街,是抗日战争时期,由中国共产党创办的培养军事和政治干部的学校。古色古香的校门上方书写着"中国抗日军政大学"的字样,校门两边墙上写着"团结、紧张、严肃、活泼"的校训。抗大的前身是1933年11月在江西瑞金成立的中国工农红军大学,1936年6月恢复开学后,更名为中国抗日红军大学,校址设在瓦窑堡,后迁至保安,更名为中国人民抗日军政大学。抗大开办第五期时,总校于1936年7月迁出延安,到达晋东南敌后根据地,1943年返回陕北绥德,抗战胜利后迁往东北,改为东北军政大学。1949年后迁到北京,改为中国人民解放军军政大学。

The former site of the Chinese People's Anti-Japanese Military and Political College, also commonly known as Kangda, is located on Erdao Street in Yan'an

图 5-5　抗日军政大学纪念馆
Figure 5-5　The Anti-Japanese Military and Political College of China

City. Established by the CPC during the period of the War of Resistance Against Japanese Aggression, this institution served as a training ground for military and political cadres. Above its antique gate are the inscription "中国抗日军政大学" (meaning "Anti-Japanese Military and Political College of China"), and the school motto of "团结、紧张、严肃、活泼" (meaning "togetherness, alertness, seriousness, and liveliness") was inscribed on the walls to both sides of the gate. The predecessor of Kangda was the Chinese Workers' and Peasants' Red Army College, established in Ruijin, Jiangxi Province in November 1933. After the reopening of the school in June 1936, it was renamed the Chinese People's Anti-Japanese Red Army University. Its campus was located in Wayaobao, and later moved to Bao'an, where it was renamed the Anti-Japanese Military and Political College of China. When Kangda recruited the fifth batch of students, the main campus moved out of Yan'an in July 1936, and settled at the base area behind enemy lines in southeastern Shanxi. Later in 1943, it moved back to Suide County in northern Shaanxi. After the victory of the War of Resistance, it moved once again to northeast China, and was renamed the Northeast Military and Political College. After 1949, it was relocated to Beijing and became the PLA Military and Political College.

在延安抗大纪念馆里,有一幅复原的会场画面:会场上方悬挂着"造就成千成万的铁的干部"的横幅,毛泽东、朱德等党中央领导同志的塑像站在画面的中央。这是1939年6月1日抗大隆重举行纪念成立三周年庆祝活动时的一个感人场面。而"造就成千成万的铁的干部"正是党中央的伟大战略决策。

In the Yan'an Kangda Memorial Hall, there is a restored scene vividly depicting the activities on June 1, 1939 when Kangda held a grand celebration to commemorate the third anniversary of its founding. A banner that reads "Zao Jiu Cheng Qian Cheng Wan De Tie De Gan Bu"［造就成千成万的铁的干部］(meaning train large numbers of cadres to be as strong as iron in their belief and faith) hangs high in the scene, and in the center stand statues of Mao Zedong, Zhu De, and other leading comrades of the Party Central Committee. "Train large numbers of cadres to be as strong as iron in their belief and faith" is precisely the great strategic decision of the Party Central Committee at that time.

1937年7月7日夜,日本侵略军制造了震惊中外的卢沟桥事变,日本帝国主义的全面侵华战争开始。延安成为全国人民抗战的中心,抗大也成为全国人民心目中的抗战堡垒,成为进步青年向往的革命熔炉。一批又一批的爱国青年从全国各地纷纷奔赴延安,报考延安各抗日院校。抗大每天都要接待几十名甚至上百名的新学员。从抗战爆发到1938年底,就有15000多名爱国青年涌入抗大学习。在投奔抗大的人流中,除了青年学生外,还有东北军张学良部和西北军杨虎城部的进步军官和抗日志士。

On the night of July 7, 1937, the Japanese invading army instigated the Lugou Bridge Incident that shocked the world, which marked the beginning of the full-scale invasion of China by Imperial Japan. Yan'an became the center of the people's War of Resistance, and Kangda became the fortress of the war in the minds of people across the whole country, and the crucible of the revolution to which progressive young people aspired. Progressive patriots rushed successively from all over the country to Yan'an to apply for the counter-Japanese academies and colleges. Every day, Kangda received dozens or even hundreds of new students. From the outbreak of the war to the end of 1938, more than 15,000 patriotic young people poured into Kangda to study. Amongst the flow of people who went to Kangda, there were not only young students but also progressive officers and anti-Japanese patriots from Zhang Xueliang's Northeast Army and Yang Hucheng's Northwest Army.

1955年,在被共和国授予的10名元帅、10名大将、57名上将、177名中将和1359名少将中,就有7名元帅、8名大将、26名上将、47名中将和129名少将是曾在抗大工作、学习的干部和学员。抗大之所以能成功地为中国革命培养出大批德才兼备的人才,关键是理论与实践相结合、教学与战局相结合、党和军队建设相结合。灵活多样的办学方式,也为新中国办学积累了经验。今天,中国共产党和人民军队形成的优良作风,就是在大批抗大干部的影响下形成的;中国共产党治党、治军的经验也是从抗大学来的。

In 1955, some PLA officers were awarded different ranks by the People's Republic of China. There were altogether 10 marshals, 10 senior generals, 57 generals, 177 lieutenant generals and 1359 major generals. Among them, 7 marshals, 8 senior generals, 26 generals, 47 lieutenant generals and 129 major generals had worked and studied in Kangda. The key to the success of Kangda in cultivating a wealth of talents with both moral integrity and professional ability for the Chinese revolution lies in blending theory with practice, integrating teaching with wartime situations, and merging the development of the party and the army. Kangda's flexible and diverse education methods also accumulated valuable experience for educational practices in New China. Today, the commendable work style of the CPC and the PLA is a result of the influence exerted by numerous Kangda-trained cadres. Furthermore, the significant experience garnered by the CPC in party governance and military administration was largely derived from the teachings of Kangda.

专栏 5：延安精神与伟大抗战精神

Special Column Ⅴ：The Yan'an Spirit and the Great Spirit of Resisting Aggression

延安精神

The Yan'an Spirit

党中央在延安十三年,形成了伟大的延安精神。延安精神的主要内容是"坚定正确的政治方向、解放思想实事求是的思想路线、全心全意为人民服务的根本宗旨、自力更生、艰苦奋斗的创业精神"。

During the thirteen years in Yan'an, the Central Committee of the CPC cultivated the profound Yan'an Spirit. The main contents of the Yan'an Spirit are "commitment to the right political direction, the ideological line of emancipating the mind and seeking truth from facts, the basic principle of serving the Chinese people heart and soul, and the pioneering spirit of self-reliance and hard work".

2020 年 4 月,习近平总书记在陕西考察时指出"延安精神培育了一代代中国共产党人,是我们党的宝贵精神财富。要坚持不懈用延安精神教育广大党员、干部,用以滋养初心、淬炼灵魂,从中汲取信仰的力量、查找党性的差距、校准前进的方向"。

In April 2020, during his inspection in Shaanxi, General Secretary Xi Jinping pointed out that "The Yan'an Spirit has cultivated generations of Chinese Communists and is a precious spiritual wealth of our party. It is necessary to unremittingly use the Yan'an Spirit to educate the vast number of party members and cadres, so as to nourish the original intention, temper the soul, draw the strength of faith from it, find out the gap in the party spirit, and calibrate the direction of progress."

伟大抗战精神
The Great Spirit of Resisting Aggression

中国人民在抗日战争的壮阔进程中孕育出伟大抗战精神,其主要内容是"天下兴亡、匹夫有责的爱国情怀,视死如归、宁死不屈的民族气节,不畏强暴、血战到底的英雄气概,百折不挠、坚忍不拔的必胜信念"。

In the course of the War of Resistance Against Japanese Aggression, the Chinese people bred a great spirit of resisting aggression, the main contents of which are: patriotism that inspires the individual to work for the well-being of the country; the dauntless national character that is prepared to sacrifice oneself for the greater good; heroic valor that nurtures a national will to confront brute force and fight to the last with great perseverance, and an unfailing belief in victory.

2020年9月3日,习近平总书记在纪念中国人民抗日战争暨世界反法西斯战争胜利75周年座谈会上的讲话中指出:"伟大抗战精神,是中国人民弥足珍贵的精神财富,将永远激励中国人民克服一切艰难险阻、为实现中华民族伟大复兴而奋斗。"

On September 3, 2020, in his speech at the symposium commemorating the 75th anniversary of the victory of the Chinese People's War of Resistance Against Japanese Aggression and the World Anti-Fascist War, General Secretary Xi Jinping pointed out that "The Great Spirit of Resisting Aggression is the precious spiritual wealth of the Chinese people, and will always inspire the Chinese people to overcome every difficulty and obstacle, and strive for the great rejuvenation of the Chinese nation."

第六章　重庆：艰苦斗争　红岩精神

Chapter Ⅵ　Chongqing：The Red Rock Spirit Through Hardship and Struggle

巴蜀之地，人杰地灵，其独特的人文地理令人神往。沿着四川、陕西边界的苏维埃区域走进有着光荣革命传统的历史文化名城重庆，一路都可以感受到璀璨的历史文化和红色文化。1937年11月，国民党政府迁都重庆，使得这座位于大后方的城市一跃成为中国战时首都和世界反法西斯战争东方战场的指挥中心。1947年前后，由于敌人破坏和叛徒出卖，重庆地下党组织遭到严重挫折，大批地下党员被捕，关押在重庆市西北郊歌乐山的白公馆和渣滓洞集中营。这些共产党人在身陷囹圄的情况下依然坚持原则，在狱中与敌人英勇斗争，为重庆留下了一段可歌可泣的英雄故事。从这里诞生的红岩精神，成为中国共产党人和中华民族宝贵的精神财富。

Ba-Shu, known as a land rich in natural resources and a cradle for creative minds, has long been fascinating to many. Traveling along Sichuan-Shaanxi Soviet Areas into Chongqing, a famous historical and cultural city with a glorious revolutionary tradition, you will be well exposed to China's historical culture as well as "red culture". In November 1937, the KMT government moved to Chongqing, transforming this city from an inland port to the war-time capital of China, and Command Center of the Anti-Fascist War in the Far East during the World War Ⅱ. Around 1947, the sabotage and betrayal of traitors dealt a heavy blow to the CPC underground in Chongqing, with the result that many underground communists were arrested and detained in Bai Mansion and Zhazi Cave at the foot of Gele Mountain in the northwest suburb of Chongqing. However, these imprisoned communists adhered to their principles and fought against their enemies. Their heroic deeds gave rise to the "Red Rock Spirit" that will always be an invaluable asset to the party and the country.

第一节　历史回眸
Section Ⅰ　A Glimpse of History

1937 年 11 月 20 日,在日军进攻首都南京之前,国民政府发表迁都重庆宣言,直至抗战胜利后的 1946 年 5 月,重庆成为国民政府的陪都,是当时中国的政治、经济、军事、文化中心。重庆郊外的红岩,作为抗日战争时期和解放战争初期中共中央南方局领导机关所在地和重庆谈判期间中共代表团驻地,与中国革命的历史紧密联系在了一起。

When the Japanese Army was about to attack Nanjing on November 20, 1937, the Nationalist Government announced that its capital would be evacuated to Chongqing. Until May 1946, Chongqing had been its provisional capital and the political, economic, military and cultural center of the nation. Hongyan Village in the suburb of Chongqing served as the site of the leadership of the Southern Bureau of the CPC Central Committee during the War of Resistance Against Japanese Aggression and the early Civil War periods. It was also the residence of the CPC delegation during the Chongqing Negotiation. As such, it is closely linked with the history of the Chinese revolution.

中共中央南方局在红岩的斗争
The Southern Bureau of the CPC Central Committee in Hongyan

1938 年,抗日战争进入相持阶段。这年秋天召开了中共中央六届六中全会,决定成立以周恩来为书记的中共中央南方局,加强党对国民党统治区工作的领导。1939 年 1 月 16 日,中共中央南方局在重庆正式成立,最初在机房街 70 号和八路军重庆办事处一起办公,同年 5 月因驻地被日军炸毁搬迁到红岩嘴。

In 1938, the War of Resistance Against Japanese Aggression reached a virtual stalemate and the Sixth Plenary Session of the Sixth CPC Central

Committee was held in the fall. The plenary session decided to establish the Southern Bureau of the CPC Central Committee with Comrade Zhou Enlai serving as its Secretary, aiming to strengthen the leadership in the KMT-controlled areas. On January 16, 1939, the Southern Bureau of the CPC Central Committee was officially established at No.70, Jifang Street, Chongqing, which also housed the Chongqing Office of the Eighth Route Army. In May, the office was destroyed by a Japanese air attack and relocated to Hongyan Village.

在党中央的坚强领导下,中共中央南方局通过长期艰苦卓绝的工作,为将南方国统区共产党组织建设成为坚强战斗堡垒、巩固抗日民族统一战线、发展人民民主统一战线、争取民族独立和人民解放,为最终赢得抗日战争的全面胜利和世界反法西斯战争胜利都作出了重大历史性贡献。

Through prolonged tenacious struggle under the strong leadership of the CPC, the Southern Bureau of the CPC Central Committee made significant contributions to the overall victory in the War of Resistance Against Japanese Aggression and the Anti-Fascism War, particularly in terms of building the Party organization in southern KMT controlled areas, consolidating a united front against Japanese aggression, developing the People's Democratic United Front, and striving for the independence of the nation and the liberation of the people.

重庆谈判和"双十协定"
Chongqing Negotiations and the October 10th Agreement

抗战胜利后,蒋介石一方面准备发动内战,一方面又受到国内外要求和平、反对内战的舆论压力,于是采取了"假和平,真内战"的策略。1945年8月14日、20日、23日,蒋介石三次邀请毛泽东去重庆"商讨"国内和平问题。他的真实意图是:如果毛泽东不去,就宣传共产党没有和平诚意,把发动内战的责任加在共产党身上;如果去了,就可以借谈判逼共产党交出人民军队和解放区政权。

After the victory over Japan, Chiang Kai-shek prepared for civil war while adopting the strategy of "fake peace talks and real civil war" under internal and external pressures of calling for peace and opposing civil war. On August 14, 20, and 23, 1945, Chiang sent Mao Zedong three telegrams, inviting him to "discuss state affairs" in Chongqing. In Chiang's estimation, if Mao Zedong did not accept the invitation, he would be free to get on with prosecuting a civil war while putting all the blame on the CPC. If the negotiation was held, he would make a bid for commanding the CPC's armed forces and Liberated Areas administration.

1945年8月28日,为谋求和平,毛泽东、周恩来、王若飞等中共领导人毅然从延安前往重庆,与国民党谈判。国民党派王世杰、张治中、邵力子为谈判代表。这次谈判共进行了43天。中共代表团提出了和平建国的基本方针,即坚决避免内战,在和平、民主、团结的基础上实现全国统一,建立独立、自由、富强的新中国。蒋介石不得不表面同意结束专制统治,召开各党派政治协商会议,保障民主自由,保障各党派平等合法地位等主张,并于10月10日公布了《政府与中共代表会谈纪要》,即"双十协定"。

On August 28, 1945, Mao Zedong, joined by Zhou Enlai and Wang Ruofei, flew from Yan'an to Chongqing with a sincere desire for peace to enter negotiations with the KMT delegation represented by Wang Shijie, Zhang Zhizhong, and Shao Lizi. During the 43-day negotiations, the CPC delegation, with the aim of avoiding another civil war, put forward the basic policy of peace and national reconstruction to build China into an independent, free and prosperous country on the principle of peace, democracy and unity. Chiang agreed ostensibly to end his autocratic political regime and convene a political consultative conference to ensure democracy and equal and legal status of other political parties. The two sides signed The Summary of Conversations Between the Representatives of the KMT and the CPC on October 10, which is also known as the October 10th Agreement.

这次谈判,国共双方在解放区的政权问题和军队问题上争论激烈。中共代表团要求承认人民军队和解放区民主政权的合法地位,蒋介石则要求中共交出军队和解放区。为了争取和平,中共代表团作出让步,将人民解放军减少为24个师,并退出广东、湖南等8个解放区。重庆谈判期间,毛泽东在红岩村亲自指挥上党战役,揭穿了国民党假和平、真内战的阴谋,使得中国共产党在政治上取得主动,国民党在政治上陷入孤立。

Throughout the negotiations, the two parties held heated discussions about the political power of the Liberated Areas and the army. The CPC delegation asked the KMT government to recognize the legitimacy of the people's army and political power of the Liberated Areas while Chiang Kai-shek, on the other hand, demanded that the CPC surrender their armed forces and control over the Liberated Areas. With a sincere desire for peace, the CPC made concessions to reduce the CPC military to 24 divisions and withdraw troops from eight Liberated Areas including Guangdong, Hunan, and others. During the talks, Mao Zedong commanded the Shangdang Campaign in Hongyan Village, which uncovered the KMT's plot of "fake peace talks and real civil war", thus winning the political initiative for the CPC and making the KMT fall into a political isolation.

《红岩》中的革命先烈
The Revolutionary Martyrs in *Red Rock*

《红岩》是罗广斌、杨益言创作的一部长篇革命小说,以1949年人民解放军进军大西南,全国胜利在即,山城重庆处于"黎明前的白色恐怖"为背景,讲述了在白公馆、渣滓洞集中营里,身陷囹圄的共产党员许云峰、江姐、成岗等,与国民党反动派英勇斗争的故事。

Red Rock was a full-length revolutionary novel written by Luo Guangbin and Yang Yiyan. It was set in Chongqing in 1949 when the PLA marched into the southwest and the War of Liberation drew to a victorious close. Chongqing was still under "white terror before dawn" at that time. The novel tells the stories of underground communists represented by Xu Yunfeng, Sister Jiang and Cheng Gang fighting heroic battles against the KMT reactionaries in Bai Mansion and Zhazi Cave.

罗广斌、杨益言曾于1948年被国民党反动派逮捕,囚禁在重庆渣滓洞、白公馆集中营。他们和小说中的英雄人物共同经历了监狱中的斗争生活。新中国成立后,为了"把这里的斗争告诉后代",罗广斌、杨益言把狱中亲历写成小说,于1961年12月出版。截至目前,该书再版51次,发行量逾1000万册,堪称新中国建国以来最畅销的图书。《红岩》中最动人的情节、最令人崇拜的英雄,都有现实依据和人物原型,如江姐的主要原型是中共重庆市委江竹筠,许云峰的主要原型是中共重庆市委工运委员许建业。

Luo Guangbin and Yang Yiyan were arrested by KMT reactionaries in 1948 and detained in Zhazi Cave and Bai Mansion in Chongqing. Similar to the heroes in the novel, they experienced soul-stirring struggles in prison. After the founding of New China, with the aim of "telling future generations about the struggle here", Luo and Yang wrote the novel *Red Rock* based on their experiences in prison. The novel was first published in December 1961, and to date, it has been republished fifty-one times with a total distribution of more than 10 million, making it a contemporary best-seller. The most touching plot and admired characters in the novel were reality-based, such as Sister Jiang, who was based on Jiang Zhuyun, secretary of the CPC Chongqing Municipal Committee; and Xu Yunfeng, based on Xu Jianye, an officer of the Workers Committee of the CPC Chongqing Municipal Committee.

《红岩》后来被改编成歌剧《江姐》、电影《烈火中永生》,还被拍成电视剧等。1963 年,日本共产党中央将《红岩》翻译成日文,发行量达 100 万部。此外,《红岩》还先后被译成英、德、法、朝、越等多种语言。

The novel was later adapted to such operas and movies as *Sister Jiang* and *Eternity in Flames*, and was later made into a television series. In 1963, the novel was translated into Japanese by the Japanese Communist Party, with a distribution of up to one million. Moreover, the novel was translated into many other languages, such as English, German, French, Korean, and Vietnamese.

第二节　红色故事
Section II　Red Stories

江竹筠:红梅傲雪红岩上
Jiang Zhuyun: the Plum Blossom on Red Rock

江竹筠,1920 年 8 月 20 日出生于四川省自贡市大山铺江家湾的一个农民家庭。人们习惯称她江姐,以表敬爱之情。她于1939年秘密加入共产党,1946年到重庆参加和领导学生运动。1947年春,中共重庆市委创办《挺进报》,江竹筠具体负责校对、整理、传送电讯稿和发行工作。《挺进报》在几个月的时间,就发行到1600多份,引起了敌人的极大恐慌。

Jiang Zhuyun was born into a peasant's family in Dashanpu, Zigong, Sichuan Province on August 20, 1920. She was also affectionately called "Sister Jiang". In 1939, Jiang secretly joined the CPC and devoted herself to patriotic student movements in Chongqing in 1946. In spring 1947, *Tingjin Newspaper* ("Tingjin" means "march forward") was founded by the CPC Chongqing Municipal Committee and Jiang was responsible for proofreading, collating and arranging for the articles to be published. Within several months, the newspaper, with a print circulation of up to 1,600, threw their enemies into a great panic.

1948年6月14日,由于叛徒的出卖,江姐不幸被捕,被关押在重庆渣滓洞监狱。国民党军统特务用尽各种酷刑折磨江姐。然而,江姐始终坚贞不屈,并领导狱中的难友同敌人展开坚决的斗争。1949年11月14日,在重庆解放的前夕,江姐被国民党军统特务杀害于渣滓洞监狱,为共产主义理想献出了年仅29岁的生命。江姐就像傲立雪中的红梅花一样,在中国的革命史上永放光彩。

On June 14, 1948, betrayal by traitors led to Jiang's arrest and subsequent trial in Zhazi Cave where Jiang underwent an array of brutal tortures. However, Jiang remained steadfast in her determination to fight the battle against the enemy with her inmates. On November 14, 1949 when Chongqing was about to be liberated, she was brutally killed by the KMT agents in the prison. Even as her life dedicated to fighting for the Communist cause ended at 29, Jiang remained an inspiration in the history of the Chinese revolution, perpetually signifying tremendous courage and strong will, like the plum blossom braving snow and frost.

"小萝卜头":共和国年龄最小的烈士
"Little Radish Head": the Youngest Communist Martyr of China

"小萝卜头"名叫宋振中,是共和国年龄最小的烈士,牺牲时年仅8岁。

1941年，宋振中出生于江苏邳州，是中国共产党党员、革命烈士宋绮云、徐林侠夫妇的幼子。宋振中8个月的时候，就随父母被带进监狱，由于终年住在阴暗、潮湿的牢房里，加之长期营养不良，8岁的孩子却只有4、5岁孩子那么高，成了一个大头细身、面黄肌瘦的孩子，难友们都疼爱地叫他"小萝卜头"。

"Little Radish Head", whose real name was Song Zhenzhong, is the youngest communist martyr in the history of the People's Republic of China, who sacrificed his life at the tender age of eight. Song Zhenzhong, the youngest child of the revolutionaries Song Qiyun and Xu Linxia, was born in Pizhou, Jiangsu Province in 1941. Along with his parents, he was put into prison at eight months old. Sealed into a dark and damp prison cell all year around, Song experienced stunted growth due to malnutrition. By the age of eight, he was just as tall as kids aged four or five, with a large head and a tiny body, thus the inmates kindly referred to this child as "Little Radish Head".

虽然年纪很小，但宋振中在父母及狱中爱国志士的教导下学会了明辨是非，他对国民党反动派深恶痛绝，小小年纪就帮着地下党传递消息。敌人觉得"小萝卜头"年纪小不懂事，恰恰利用这一点，宋振中帮助地下党做了很多成年人做不了的事情，为打倒反动派，建立新中国立下了不可磨灭的功劳。因此，重庆解放后，"小萝卜头"宋振中被追认为革命烈士，成为共和国最小的烈士。

Under the guidance of his parents and patriotic inmates, Song, though at a tender age, could distinguish right from wrong and showed hatred for KMT reactionaries. He even passed on information for the underground communists. The enemy thought Song was too young to pose a threat, so he took advantage of the opportunities and accomplished various tasks impossible for many adults. Song made indelible contributions to the overthrow of reactionaries and the establishment of New China. After the liberation of Chongqing, he was posthumously recognized as a revolutionary martyr, the youngest in China.

《狱中八条》:血与泪的嘱托
"Eight Articles in Prison": Lessons Learned at the Cost of Blood and Tears

1949年11月27日,在重庆解放前夕,国民党特务对关押在白公馆、渣滓洞监狱内的共产党员和其他进步人士进行了残酷的大屠杀。当天夜里,共产党人罗广斌带领十多位革命者成功脱险后,将大家在狱中总结出的意见进行了梳理,完成了这部饱含英烈血泪的《关于重庆组织破坏经过和狱中情况的报告》,报告的第七部分就是广为人知的《狱中八条》:

第一条:防止领导成员的腐化;

第二条:加强党内教育和实际斗争锻炼;

第三条:不要理想主义,对上级也不要迷信;

第四条:注意路线问题,不要从"右"跳到"左";

第五条:切勿轻视敌人;

第六条:注意党员,特别是领导干部的经济、恋爱和生活作风问题;

第七条:严格整党整风;

第八条:严惩叛徒特务。

On the eve of the liberation of Chongqing, many communists imprisoned in Bai Mansion and Zhazi Cave were brutally killed by KMT agents on November 27, 1949. That night, Luo Guangbin led a few dozen prisoners to make a narrow escape, and then sort out the discussions and summaries of the comrades in prison in a narrative entitled "A Report on the Sabotage of Chongqing's CPC Underground Organizations and the Situation in the Prison" including lessons learned by revolutionary martyrs at the cost of blood and tears. The seventh part is the well-known "Eight Articles in Prison".

Article 1: Prevent the corruption of leading members.

Article 2: Strengthen inner-party education and training in practical struggle.

Article 3: Do not be idealistic, and do not be superstitious about your superiors.

Article 4: Pay attention to the route problem, and do not jump from "right" to "left".

Article 5: Do not despise the enemy.

Article 6: Attach importance to the economic life, romantic life and lifestyle of party members, especially the leaders.

Article 7: Strictly carry out the rectification of the party.

Article 8: Punish traitors and spies.

《狱中八条》内容的背后,是共产党人面对信仰的抉择,是革命先烈用生命换来的经验与教训,是一份沉甸甸的政治嘱托。《狱中八条》经历几十载岁月洗礼,在全力推进党的建设新的伟大工程的今天,依然闪烁着信仰与忠诚、责任与意志、忧患与担当的璀璨光芒。

The "Eight Articles in Prison" were precious lessons and experiences summed up by revolutionary martyrs in exchange for their lives, conveying their firm faiths and political exhortations. Withstanding the test of time, "Eight Articles in Prison", with emphasis on faith, loyalty, responsibility and willpower, are still of great significance in a time when Party building is being strengthened in all ways.

第三节　红色景点
Section Ⅲ　Red Tourism Attractions

红岩革命纪念馆
Hongyan Revolutionary Memorial Hall

红岩革命纪念馆位于重庆市嘉陵江畔,主要包括红岩村13号(中共中央南方局暨八路军重庆办事处旧址)、曾家岩50号(周公馆)、桂园("双十协定"签字处)、《新华日报》旧址等革命遗址。抗日战争时期,它们都是中共中央南方局的活动基地,是我党在国民党统治区巩固和发展抗日民族统一战线、领导人民群众进行革命斗争的中心。

Located on the bank of the Jialing River in Chongqing, Hongyan Revolutionary Memorial Hall consists of the following sites: No. 13 Hongyan Village (the former site of the Southern Bureau of the CPC Central Committee

图 6-1　红岩革命纪念馆
Figure 6-1　Hongyan Revolutionary Memorial Hall

and the Chongqing Office of the Eighth Route Army), No. 50 Zengjiayan (Zhou Mansion), Guiyuan Garden (where the October 10th Agreement was signed) and the Former Site of *Xinhua Daily* and others. All of them served as the activity bases of the Southern Bureau of the CPC Central Committee during the War of Resistance Against Japanese Aggression and also the command center for the CPC to consolidate and develop the national united front against Japanese aggression and lead the people in revolutionary struggle.

红岩村位于渝中区化龙桥,因为其附近为丹霞地貌,有着大片红色的岩石,红岩村因此得名。红岩村13号是一座三层简易建筑,占地面积800平方米,共有54间房,是由当时中共中央南方局和八路军驻重庆办事处机关工作人员动手改建的。一楼是八路军重庆办事处的办公室,二楼是南方局机关和领导人的办公室兼卧室,三楼则是南方局、办事处干部的工作间及宿舍,还设有秘密电台。

Located at Hualongqiao, Yuzhong District, Hongyan Village got its name from its nearby Danxia landform. No. 13 Hongyan Village is a three-story building with 54 rooms in total, covering an area of 800 square meters. It was renovated by office workers of the Southern Bureau of the CPC Central Committee and the Chongqing Office of the Eighth Route Army. Back then, at the bottom was the general office of the Eighth Route Army in Chongqing. The leaders' offices and bedrooms were on the second floor, while offices and dorms for office workers were on the third floor where a secret radio station was also located.

曾家岩50号,是八路军办事处旧址,是周恩来同志长期战斗过的地方,史称周公馆,是具有重要意义的革命纪念地。1945年8月,毛泽东同志在重庆与国民党谈判期间,曾在底楼会议室接见过中外人士,周恩来同志会见各界人士和中外记者也常在这里。

No. 50 Zengjiayan, the former site of the Chongqing Office of the Eighth Route Army where Zhou Enlai had worked for a long time, is commonly known as Zhou Mansion. It is an important revolutionary memorial with profound historical significance. During the negotiations between Mao Zedong and the KMT representatives in August 1945, Mao received guests from home and abroad in the meeting room downstairs. Also, it was the place where Zhou Enlai met journalists and figures from all walks of life.

桂园位于重庆市渝中区中山四路65号,原是国民政府军事委员会政治部部长张治中将军公馆。1945年8月重庆谈判期间,张治中将桂园让给毛泽东使用。毛泽东与周恩来白天常来这里办公和会客,著名的"双十协定"就在桂园客厅签署。1977年桂园正式对外开放,2001年被列为全国重点文物保护单位。

Located at No. 65 Zhongshansi Road, Yuzhong District, Chongqing, Guiyuan Garden was the former residence of General Zhang Zhizhong, the Minister of the Political Department of the KMT Government. During the Chongqing Negotiations in August 1945, General Zhang offered Guiyuan Garden for Mao Zedong's use. Mao Zedong and Zhou Enlai often conducted official business and received guests here during the daytime. The well-known October 10th Agreement was signed in the reception room. The garden was officially opened to the public in 1977, and it was designated as a National Key Cultural Relics Protection Unit in 2001.

歌乐山革命烈士陵园
The Gele Mountain Martyrs' Cemetery

重庆歌乐山烈士陵园原为国民党"军统"特务机关大本营(1939—1949年)和中美特种技术合作所(1943—1946年)旧址。1939年,国民党军统局用重金购来原四川军阀白驹的郊外别墅白公馆,霸占渣滓洞煤窑,将其改为监狱,同时还在这里设置了许多秘密囚室,形成了一个规模庞大的秘密集中营。这里曾经关押过爱国将领杨虎城,新四军军长叶挺,以及共产党人罗世文、车耀先、陈然、江竹筠等。1949年国民党溃逃前夕,在这里制造了系列大屠杀,300余人被杀害。新中国成立后,重庆市人民政府修建了烈士公墓。

图6-2 歌乐山革命烈士陵园
Figure 6-2 The Gele Mountain Martyrs' Cemetery

The Gele Mountain Martyrs' Cemetery in Chongqing served as the headquarters of the KMT Military Intelligence Service (1939 - 1949) and the Sino-American Special Technical Cooperative Organization (1943 - 1946). In 1939, the National Bureau of Investigation and Statistics (NBIS or BIS) paid handsomely for Bai Mansion (former villa of the Sichuan warlord Bai Ju) and then captured Zhazi Cave coalmine, and converted them into prisons with many secret cells inside. Thus, a large concentration camp was formed. Many revolutionaries detained here include General Yang Hucheng, Ye Ting (the commander of the New Fourth Army), communists Luo Shiwen, Che Yaoxian,

Chen Ran, and Jiang Zhuyun. In 1949, KMT secret agents brutally massacred more than 300 communist inmates on the eve of the rout. After the founding of New China, Chongqing Municipal People's Government built the martyrs' cemetery and monument here.

白公馆与渣滓洞
Bai Mansion and Zhazi Cave

提起重庆的白公馆、渣滓洞,在中国可谓无人不晓,很多人都是从长篇小说《红岩》中了解到并留下了深刻的印象。白公馆和渣滓洞位于重庆西北的歌乐山,这里山峰连绵,风光秀美。抗日战争和解放战争期间,国民党军统特务在这两座人间地狱里关押、迫害、屠杀了大量的革命志士。

图 6-3 歌乐山渣滓洞"小萝卜头"像
Figure 6-3 Statue of "Little Radish Head" in Zhazi Cave

Bai Mansion and Zhazi Cave are familiar to many largely due to a full-length revolutionary novel *Red Rock*. They are located at the foot of Gele Mountain on the outskirts of northwest Chongqing where the mountainous landscape is endowed with beautiful natural scenery. During the War of Resistance Against Japanese Aggression and the Civil War, the NBIS detained and prosecuted many revolutionaries at both sites which were like hell on earth.

白公馆原为四川军阀白驹的郊外别墅。白驹自诩是白居易的后代,就借用白居易的别号"香山居士",把自己的别墅取名为"香山别墅"。1939

年,戴笠在歌乐山下选址时看中了它,便用重金将它买下,改造为关押革命者的监狱。它和渣滓洞一并被人们称作"两口活棺材"。但是它们又有所区别,白公馆里关押的都是军统认为"案情严重"的政治犯。1943年"中美合作所"成立后,白公馆改为"中美合作所第三招待所",关押人员迁往渣滓洞。到1945年又作为特别看守所重新关人。

Bai Mansion used to be the suburban villa of the Sichuan warlord Bai Ju who claimed himself a descendant of Bai Juyi (a renowned Chinese poet in the Tang Dynasty), so he named his villa "Xiangshan Villa" after Bai Juyi's style name "Hermit of Xiangshan". In 1939, Dai Li, head of NBIS, picked the site at the foot of Gele Mountain, then purchased it and converted it into a prison. Bai Mansion and Zhazi Cave were known as two "living coffins", but they differed from each other in that political prisoners involved in "major cases" were detained in Bai Mansion. After the establishment of the "Sino-American Cooperative Organization" in 1943, Bai Mansion was repurposed as SACO No. 3 Guest House, and the detained revolutionaries were transferred to Zhazi Cave. However, by 1945, Bai Mansion was again used as a special detention facility.

白公馆院内的墙上写了"进思进忠、退思补过""正其宜不计其利,明其道不计其功"等标语。白公馆曾关押过抗日爱国将领黄显声、同济大学校长周均时、爱国人士廖承志、中共党员宋绮云、徐林侠夫妇及幼子"小萝卜头"等,关押的政治犯最多时达200多人。

There were a few slogans on the wall of the inner courtyard, such as "One should show loyalty when in charge of a position and make amends after taking a retrospective look at his work", "Do everything out of righteousness and justice instead of personal gain". More than 200 political prisoners were detained here, including Huang Xiansheng, Zhou Junshi (president of Tongji University), Liao Chengzhi, the couple Song Qiyun and Xu Linxia and their youngest son "Little Radish Head", as well as others.

距白公馆2.5公里的渣滓洞更是声名狼藉。这里原是重庆郊外的一个小煤窑,三面是山,一面是沟,位置较隐蔽。1939年,国民党军统特务逼死矿主,霸占煤窑,在此设立了监狱。渣滓洞分内外两院,外院为特务办公室、刑讯室等,内院一楼一底16间房间为男牢,另有两间平房为女牢。这里关押着江竹筠、许建业、何雪松等300余名革命者。

Zhazi Cave, 2.5 kilometers away from Bai Mansion, was more notorious. It was originally a small coalmine with mountains on three sides and a ditch on one side, which provided a natural shelter. In 1939, the KMT agents killed the owner and set up a detention center here which was divided into two courtyards. In the outer courtyard, there were offices and torture chambers. The inner courtyard hosted a two-story building with sixteen prison cells for male inmates and a one-story house with two prison cells for females. More than 300 revolutionaries such as Jiang Zhuyun, Xu Jianye, and He Xuesong were detained here.

1949年10月1日,当新中国成立的消息传到渣滓洞和白公馆监狱后,革命者欣喜若狂。被关押在白公馆监狱的罗广斌、陈然、丁地平等100多人难平心中的激动,他们用一床红色的被单和几个纸剪的五角星做了一面红旗。1949年11月27日,国民党特务在溃逃前夕策划了震惊中外的大屠杀,除罗广斌等15名同志脱险以外,其他同志全部光荣牺牲。革命小说《红岩》便再现了监狱内部残酷恐怖的囚禁生涯及革命党人经受住种种酷刑、矢志不渝的坚定信念。

On October 1, 1949, revolutionaries imprisoned in Zhazi Cave and Bai Mansion were ecstatic over the news of the founding of New China. Over a hundred people represented by Luo Guangbin, Chen Ran and Ding Diping made a five-star red flag out of red sheets and five-pointed stars cut from paper to express their excitement and great joy. On November 27, KMT agents planned a massacre that shocked the world before they fled to Taiwan, killing all but 15 who made a narrow escape. The revolutionary novel *Red Rock* not only recreates the cruelty and horror of prison life there, but also shows communists' steadfast beliefs and commitment.

专栏 6：红岩精神

Special Column VI: The Red Rock Spirit

红岩精神是中国共产党在国民党统治地区革命实践中形成的最具代表性的革命精神,是中国共产党人精神谱系的重要组成部分。红岩精神的主要内容是共产党人的崇高思想境界、坚定理想信念、巨大人格力量和浩然革命正气,是中华民族宝贵的精神财富。2019 年 4 月 17 日,习近平总书记在重庆考察时指出:"解放战争时期,众多被关押在渣滓洞、白公馆的中国共产党人,经受住种种酷刑折磨,不折不挠、宁死不屈,为中国人民解放事业献出了宝贵生命,凝结成'红岩精神'。"

The Red Rock Spirit forged by the CPC during their revolutionary practice in KMT-controlled areas is the most representative spirit and an important part of the spirit pedigree of Chinese Communists. With emphasis on lofty ideological realm, firm convictions, great personality power and noble revolutionary spirit, the Red Rock Spirit has become an invaluable asset to the Chinese nation. On April 17, 2019 when President Xi Jinping inspected Chongqing, he pointed out, "During the Chinese People's War of Liberation, the CPC members imprisoned in Zhazi Cave and Bai Mansion were unyielding to cruel tortures and would rather have died than surrendered. They sacrificed their lives to the Chinese people's liberation, forging the 'Red Rock Spirit'."

第七章　西柏坡：人民胜利　国旗飘扬

Chapter Ⅶ　Xibaipo: The People's Triumph, the National Flag Fluttering

"磨盘上布下了雄兵百万，土屋里奏响了胜利的凯歌。农家院捣毁一个旧世界，小山村走出了一个新中国。"1947年5月，中共中央工委来到河北省平山县，确定工委驻地以太行山深处的西柏坡为中心。1948年5月，毛泽东等来到西柏坡，与中央工委会合。从此，西柏坡成为中国革命的中心，也成为中国革命最后一个农村指挥所。在这里，党中央和毛主席指挥了震惊中外的辽沈、淮海、平津三大战役。三大战役的胜利，奠定了人民解放战争在全国胜利的基础，西柏坡也因此享有"新中国从这里走来"的美称。以毛泽东为代表的中共中央在这里铸就的"西柏坡精神"，犹如一座不熄的灯塔，激励着一代又一代人。1949年10月1日，中华人民共和国成立，庄严的五星红旗在首都北京升起。从此，在党的领导下，我们伟大的祖国意气风发地走向了新的历史时期。

"On a millstone, a mighty army of millions was arrayed. In a mud house, songs of triumph reverberated. In the farmyard, the Old World was shattered. From the small village, a New China emerged." In May 1947, the CPC Central Working Committee came to Pingshan County, Hebei Province and set the base in Xibaipo which was in the rolling Taihang Mountains. A year later, Mao Zedong along with other leaders moved to Xibaipo, which then became the command center for China's revolution and the CPC's last rural command post. It was the place where Mao Zedong and the Central Military Commission commanded the Liaoxi-Shenyang Campaign, the Huai-Hai Campaign, and the Beiping-Tianjin Campaign, which amazed China and the world. The success of these three campaigns paved the way for the nationwide victory of the Liberation War, thus Xibaipo was known as the place where New China began. The "Xibaipo Spirit" forged here by the CPC Central Committee under the leadership of Mao Zedong, serves as an enduring lighthouse, motivating successive generations. On October 1, 1949, the People's Republic of China was founded with the solemn raising of the five-star red flag in Beijing. From then on, the great nation confidently embarked on a new journey under the leadership of the CPC.

第一节 历史回眸
Section Ⅰ A Glimpse of History

全面内战爆发
The Outbreak of Full-Scale Civil War

1946年6月,蒋介石下令向中原、华东、晋冀鲁豫、晋绥等解放区全面进攻,解放区军民奋起抗击,全面内战爆发了。在战争初期,国民党军在军事和经济力量上占有明显优势,拥有430多万人的庞大军队,控制着全国所有的大城市和绝大部分交通干线,还得到美国在军事上和经济上的支持。面对严峻的形势,1946年8月,毛泽东在同美国女记者安娜·路易斯·斯特朗的谈话中提出了"一切反动派都是纸老虎"的著名论断。

In June 1946, Chiang Kai-shek ordered the mounting of large-scale offensives against the Liberated Areas including the Central Plains, East China, Shanxi-Hebei-Shandong-Henan, and Shanxi-Suiyuan. In the face of these attacks, the army and civilians in the liberated areas valiantly rose up to resist, which marked the outbreak of a full-scale civil war. At the outset of the war, the KMT had the upper hand in terms of troop strength and economy. For example, the total strength of the KMT army was about 4.3 million, and the KMT government not only controlled almost all major cities and railway lines, but also had the backing of the US government. In a grim state, Mao Zedong made the famous statement "All reactionaries are paper tigers" in a talk with the American correspondent Anna Louise Strong in August 1946.

中共中央进驻西柏坡村
The CPC Central Committee's Arrival in Xibaipo

1947年2月,解放区军民打破了国民党军的全面进攻。1947年3月起,国民党军从原来对解放区的全面进攻改为对陕甘宁和山东两个解放区的重点进攻,最终也以失败告终。至1947年7月,国共双方力量对比发生了显著变化。国民党军队总兵力从430万人下降到373万人,士气低落。国民党政府在政治上、经济上也陷入严重危机。人民解放军的总兵力则由127万人增加到195万人,武器装备也有很大改善,全军士气高涨。人民解放军开始从积极防御转入战略进攻。

In February 1947, the people's armed forces held off the KMT's large-scale attack. From March 1947 onwards, the KMT troops shifted the focus of their attacks to key sectors in Shaanxi-Gansu-Ningxia and the Shandong Liberated Areas, ending up in failures. By July 1947, the situation in the Civil War had changed dramatically. The KMT's total military strength had fallen from 4.3 million to 3.73 million accompanied by a low morale, and the KMT government got stuck in a severe political and economic crisis. In contrast, the PLA's total force had expanded from 1.27 million to 1.95 million, maintaining a high morale. Along with significant improvements in weaponry and equipment, the PLA shifted from active defensive to strategic offensive.

1948年3月23日,毛泽东率领中央机关和人民解放军总部东渡黄河,前往华北。5月27日,进驻河北建屏县西柏坡村(今属河北平山县)。党中央在这里指挥了震惊中外的辽沈、淮海、平津三大战役,召开了具有深远历史意义的七届二中全会,为新中国绘制了宏伟蓝图,成为党中央解放全中国前的最后一个农村指挥所。

On March 23, 1948, Mao Zedong led a group of CPC central officials and PLA Headquarters staff members eastward across the Yellow River into northern China. They arrived and established a base at Xibaipo Village in Jianping County (now part of Pingshan County), Hebei Province on May 27. It was from Xibaipo where the CPC Central Committee commanded the three major campaigns and convened the Second Plenary Session of the Seventh CPC Central Committee, which sketched a grand blueprint for New China. These historical events made Xibaipo the last rural command post of the CPC prior to the liberation of the country, thus lending it profound historical significance.

"进京赶考"的中国共产党人
Communists Heading for Beiping to "Take the Examination"

1949年3月23日上午,毛泽东率领中央机关离开西柏坡,向北平(现北京)进发。临行前,毛泽东对周恩来说:"今天是进京的日子,进京'赶考'去。"周恩来说:"我们应当都能考试及格,不要退回来。"毛泽东说:"退回来就失败了。我们决不能当李自成,我们都希望考个好成绩。"在不久前召开的党的七届二中全会上,毛泽东告诫全体党员:"夺取全国胜利,这只是万里长征走完了第一步……中国的革命是伟大的,但革命以后的路程更长,工作更伟大、更艰苦。这一点现在就必须向党内讲明白,务必使同志们继续地保持谦虚、谨慎、不骄、不躁的作风,务必使同志们继续地保持艰苦奋斗的作风。我们有批评和自我批评这个马克思列宁主义的武器。我们能够去掉不良作风,保持优良作风。我们能够学会我们原来不懂的东西。我们不但善于破坏一个旧世界,我们还将善于建设一个新世界。"3月25日,毛泽东等中央领导人与中央机关、人民解放军总部进驻北平香山,标志着中国革命的重心从农村转向城市。

On the morning of March 23, 1949, Mao Zedong led the CPC central officials out of Xibaipo Village to set out for Beiping (now Beijing). On their departure, Mao remarked to Zhou Enlai, "Today is the day we enter the capital to 'take our examination'." "All of us should pass; we will have no need to return," replied Zhou. Mao continued, "We will have failed if we return. We must certainly not become Li Zicheng. Let us all hope we achieve good results." Soon after, the Second Plenary Session of the Seventh CPC Central Committee was convened. At the meeting, Mao warned the entire Party, "Securing a nationwide victory is only the first step in a long march of ten thousand li. The Chinese revolution is great, but the road after the revolution will be longer, and the work greater and more arduous. This must be made clear now in the Party.

The comrades must be taught to remain modest, prudent, and free from arrogance and rashness in their style of work and must be taught to preserve the style of plain living and hard struggle. We have the Marxist-Leninist weapon of criticism and self-criticism. We can get rid of a bad style and keep the good. We can learn what we did not know. We are not only good at destroying the Old World, but also good at building the New." On March 25, Mao Zedong and the other leaders of the CPC Central Committee arrived in Beiping and set up their base at Xiangshan Hill, along with the staff members of the CPC Central Committee and the Headquarters of the PLA, marking the shift of the revolutionary focus from the rural to the city.

党的七届二中全会
The Second Plenary Session of the Seventh CPC Central Committee

在中国人民解放战争即将取得全国胜利的前夕,经过充分准备,中国共产党于1949年3月5日至13日在西柏坡中央机关食堂召开了第七届中央委员会第二次全体会议。出席这次全会的有中央委员34人,候补中央委员19人,列席会议的11人。毛泽东主持会议并做了重要报告。会议决定了以下几个方面的问题:

On the eve of the national victory in the People's War of Liberation, the Seventh Central Committee of the Communist Party of China held its Second Plenary Session at Xibaipo from March 5 to 13, 1949. Thirty-four members and nineteen alternate members of the Central Committee were present. Eleven attended the meeting in a non-voting capacity. Mao Zedong chaired the meeting and presented an important report. The session decided the following issues:

(一)确定了促进革命迅速取得全国胜利的各项方针

会议认为,今后解决国民党残余军队的方式,不外天津、北平、绥远三种:天津方式,即用战斗去消灭敌军的方式;北平方式,即和平改编国民党军队的方式;绥远方式,即暂时维持原状、以后再改编敌军的方式。会议认为,在进行军事斗争的同时,还必须积极开展政治斗争,无论在军事和政治斗争中,都应把原则的坚定性同策略的灵活性紧密结合起来。为了适应斗争的需要,必须培养大批革命干部,要把人民解放军看成培养干部的学校。

Ⅰ. Formulating policies to accelerate a nationwide revolutionary victory

The meeting agreed that from then on there were only three patterns for disposing of the KMT troops—the Tianjin pattern, the Beiping pattern or the Suiyuan pattern. The Tianjin pattern refers to the tactic of eliminating enemy forces through combat. The Beiping pattern refers to the tactic of compelling enemy troops to reorganize peacefully, quickly and thoroughly in accordance with the PLA system. The Suiyuan pattern is to deliberately keep part of the KMT troops wholly or nearly intact. The meeting held that, while engaging in military struggle, active political struggle must also be carried out. Regardless of whether in military or political struggles, it is important to tightly integrate firm principles with strategic flexibility. It is necessary to cultivate a large number of cadres to meet the needs of the struggle. We must look upon the PLA as a gigantic school for cadres.

(二) 决定将党的工作重心由乡村转到城市

会议认为,从1927年大革命失败到现在,由于敌强我弱,党的工作重心一直在乡村。在乡村开展武装斗争,发动农民实行土地革命,建立革命根据地,为夺取城市作好了准备。现在经过辽沈、淮海和平津三大战役后,敌我力量发生了根本变化,继续采取农村包围城市的工作方式已经不适应了。从现在起,党的工作重心,应该由乡村转向城市,实行由城市领导乡村的工作方式。当然城乡必须兼顾,必须使城市工作和乡村工作、工业和农业、工人和农民紧密地结合起来,巩固工农联盟。

Ⅱ. Shifting the Party's work focus from rural to urban areas

The meeting held that, from 1927 to the present, due to the fact that the enemy was still stronger than the people's forces, the center of the Party's work had been in the village—gathering strength in the villages, mobilizing peasants to carry out land reform, establishing revolutionary bases in order to take the cities. After the three major campaigns of Liaoxi-Shenyang, Huai-Hai, and Beiping-Tianjin, there was a fundamental shift in the balance of power, so the period of encircling the cities from the countryside has now ended. From then on, the

Party's work focus should be shifted from rural to urban areas, ushering in a new era where the cities led the countryside. Attention must be given to both cities and villages and it is necessary to link closely urban and rural work, industry and agriculture, workers and peasants, and thus further consolidate the worker-peasant alliance.

(三)强调要加强党的思想建设,防止资产阶级思想的腐蚀

会议认为,在伟大的胜利面前,党的骄傲情绪,贪图享乐的情绪可能滋长。为了预防这种情况的发生,会议号召全党同志要树立无产阶级的世界观,防止骄傲自满情绪。

Ⅲ. Strengthening the ideological construction of the Party and guarding against the corrosion of bourgeois ideology

The meeting held that the great victory may breed arrogance and hedonism. To prevent such situations, the meeting called on all Party members to establish a proletarian worldview and guard against feelings of arrogance and complacency.

七届二中全会是一次制定夺取全国胜利和胜利后的各方面政策的极其重要的会议。这次会议解决了中国共产党夺取民主革命的最后胜利和由新民主主义革命向社会主义革命转变的一系列重大方针问题;并为这种转变,在政治上、思想上和理论上作了重要的准备。

The Second Plenary Session of the Seventh CPC Central Committee was of great significance in that it formulated the program for nationwide victory and defined the basic policies the Party would adopt after the national victory. The plenary session solved a list of problems critical to the final national victory and the transformation from new-democratic revolution to socialist revolution and made important preparations for the transformation in political, ideological, and theoretical terms.

伟大的战略决战
The Great Strategic Offensive

1947年6月起,解放军三路大军挺进中原,展开进攻。至1948年8月,

国共双方的力量对比发生了进一步变化。人民解放军的人数上升到 280 万人,解放区面积也扩大了。从 1948 年 9 月 12 日至 1949 年 1 月 31 日,中共中央先后组织了辽沈、淮海、平津三大战役,基本上消灭了国民党的主力部队,解放了全国大部分地区,加速了全国解放战争胜利的到来。

From June 1947, the three forces of the PLA had fought their way to the Central Plain and lifted the curtain on the PLA's strategic offensive. By August 1948, the strength difference between the KMT and the CPC further changed, with the PLA growing to 2.8 million and the Liberated Areas expanding. From September 12, 1948 to January 31, 1949, the CPC Central Committee waged the three campaigns of Liaoxi-Shenyang, Huai-Hai, and Beiping-Tianjin, wiped out the main forces of the KMT, and liberated most parts of the country, which culminated in victory throughout the nation.

三大战役以后,国民党继续在长江南岸部署兵力,妄图凭借长江天险,阻止人民解放军渡江向南进发。1948 年 12 月 30 日,毛泽东在新年献词中发出"将革命进行到底"的号召,强调必须用革命的方法,坚决彻底干净全部地消灭一切反动势力。1949 年 4 月 21 日,毛泽东主席和朱德总司令发布向全国进军的命令。人民解放军在东起江阴,西至湖口,长达 500 多公里的江面上,分三路发起渡江战役。4 月 23 日,人民解放军占领南京,宣告延续 22 年的国民党反动统治覆灭了。毛泽东在看到这个捷报后,写下《七律·人民解放军占领南京》。

七律·人民解放军占领南京
钟山风雨起苍黄,百万雄师过大江。
虎踞龙盘今胜昔,天翻地覆慨而慷。
宜将剩勇追穷寇,不可沽名学霸王。
天若有情天亦老,人间正道是沧桑。

After three decisive campaigns, the KMT continued to deploy troops to the south of the Yangtze River, which was a natural barrier, in an attempt to prevent the PLA from marching southward. On December 30, 1948, Mao Zedong issued the New Year's message of "Carrying the Revolution Through to the End", emphasizing that all reactionary forces must be destroyed resolutely, thoroughly, wholly and completely by means of revolution. On April 21, 1949, Chairman Mao Zedong and Commander-in-Chief Zhu De issued an order to the army for a countrywide advance. The PLA divided into three columns and fought their way across the river that stretched for more than 500 kilometers, from Hukou in the west to Jiangyin in the east. On April 23, the PLA captured Nanjing, declaring an end to the reactionary KMT regime that had lasted for 22 years. On learning of the news, Mao Zedong wrote the poem "Capture of Nanjing by the People's Liberation Army".

Capture of Nanjing by the People's Liberation Army
(Translated by Xu Yuanchong)

Over the Purple Mountain sweeps a storm headlong;
Our troops have crossed the great river, a million strong.
The Tiger girt with Dragon outshines days gone by;
Heaven and earth o'erturned, our spirits ne'er so high!
With our courage unspent pursue the foe o'erthrown!
Do not fish like the Herculean King for renown!
Heaven would have grown old were it moved to emotions;
The world goes on with changes in the fields and oceans.

中华人民共和国成立
The Founding of the People's Republic of China

1949年9月21日至30日,中国人民政治协商会议第一届全体会议在北平(现北京)举行,会议决定成立中华人民共和国,选举毛泽东为中华人民共和国中央人民政府主席,朱德、刘少奇、宋庆龄等为副主席,决定把北平改名为北京,作为中华人民共和国的首都,以五星红旗为国旗,《义勇军进行曲》为代国歌。

The First Plenary Session of the Chinese People's Political Consultative Conference (CPPCC) was convened in Beiping (now Beijing) from September 21 to 30, 1949. The session decided to found the People's Republic of China and elected Mao Zedong as Chairman of the Central People's Government and Zhu De, Liu Shaoqi, Soong Ching Ling, and others as vice chairpersons. The session approved Beiping as China's capital and renamed Beiping into Beijing. It also adopted a national flag with five stars on a field of red and the "March of the Volunteers" as the new national anthem.

1949年10月1日下午2时,国家领导人宣布就职,任命周恩来为中央人民政府政务院总理兼外交部长,毛泽东为人民革命军事委员会主席,朱德为人民解放军总司令。下午3时,首都北京30万军民齐聚天安门广场,举行开国大典。毛泽东站在天安门城楼上向世界庄严宣告:"中华人民共和国中央人民政府今天成立了!"在礼炮声中,毛泽东主席亲手按动电钮升起了第一面五星红旗。接着举行了盛大的阅兵式和群众游行。

At 2 p.m. on October 1, 1949, the Central People's Government Council held its inaugural meeting and appointed Zhou Enlai as the Premier of the Government Administration Council and Minister of Foreign Affairs, Mao Zedong as Chairman of the Chinese People's Revolutionary Military Commission, and Zhu De as the Commander-in-Chief of the PLA. At 3 p.m., 300,000 civilians and members of the military gathered in Tian'anmen Square where a grand ceremony was held for the founding of the People's Republic of China. Chairman Mao Zedong solemnly proclaimed to the world, "The Central People's Government of the People's Republic of China is founded today." Chairman Mao pressed the button on the flagpole, and the red five-star national flag ascended over Beijing for the first time as fifty-four guns fired in salute. The celebrations that followed started with a grand military parade and then a mass procession.

中华人民共和国的成立,彻底结束了旧中国半殖民地半封建的历史,彻底结束了旧中国一盘散沙的局面,彻底废除了列强强加给中国的不平等条约和帝国主义在中国的一切特权,实现了中国从几千年封建专制政治向人民民主的伟大飞跃,也极大改变了世界政治格局,鼓舞了全世界被压迫民族和被压迫人民争取解放的斗争。实践充分说明,历史和人民选择了中国共产党,没有中国共产党领导,民族独立、人民解放是不可能实现的。中国共产党和中国人民以英勇顽强的奋斗向世界庄严宣告,中国人民从此站起来了,中华民族任人宰割、饱受欺凌的时代一去不复返了,中国发展从此开启了新纪元。

The founding of the People's Republic of China put an end to China's history as a semi-colonial and semi-feudal society, the state of total disunity that existed in the old China, the unequal treaties imposed on China by foreign powers, and to all privileges that imperialist countries enjoyed in China. Marking the country's great transformation from a millennia-old feudal autocracy to a people's democracy, it also reshaped the world political landscape and offered enormous inspiration for oppressed nations and peoples struggling for national liberation around the world. It has been proven through practice that history and the people have chosen the CPC, and that without its leadership, it would not have been possible to realize national independence and the people's liberation. Through tenacious struggle, the Party and the people showed the world that the Chinese people had stood up and the time in which the Chinese nation could be bullied and abused by others was gone and would never return. This marked the beginning of a new epoch in China's development.

第二节　红色故事
Section II   Red Stories

一个苹果也是纪律
The Firm Military Discipline

1948年秋,辽沈战役锦州攻坚战前夕,正值苹果成熟收获之际。在东北野战军的战前政工会议上,罗荣桓指着院子里果实累累的苹果树说:"要教育部队保证不吃老百姓一个苹果,无论是挂在树上的、收获在家里的、掉在地上的,都不要吃,这是一条纪律,要坚决做到。"

In the autumn of 1948, on the eve of the decisive Battle of Jinzhou during the Liaoshen Campaign, apples were ripe and ready for harvest. At the meeting before the battle, Luo Ronghuan (Political Commissar of the Northeast Field Army, PLA) pointed to the apple trees bearing a lot of fruits in the yard and said, "We must educate the troops to refrain from eating any apples of the civilians, whether they are hanging on the tree, harvested at home, or dropped on the ground. This is a discipline that must be resolutely enforced."

兴城攻克后,4纵10师29团一部奉命来到城西一个大果园执行任务。七班长执行任务结束急匆匆地赶回连队,一进果园,顺手就捡起一个落地果,刚想咬,便被司号员小丁看见了。小丁连忙喊道:"你干什么吃苹果?忘了决心吗?一个苹果也是纪律!"七班长一听,赶忙放下苹果,连声检讨。这时,二排长走过来带领大家将落在地上的苹果全部捡起,装在筐里,放在老乡家的窗户底下。打扫完果园,战士们便整队出发了。

After taking Xingcheng County, the 29th regiment of the 10th Division of the fourth column was ordered to come to a large orchard in the west of the county to perform a task. The head of the 7th squad hurriedly returned to the company after completing the task. Entering the orchard, he picked up an apple from the ground. It was noticed by the trumpeter Xiaoding just when he was about to bite. Xiaoding shouted, "How dare you? Didn't you forget the determination? Not to eat any one of the apples, that is our firm discipline!" The squad head put down the apple immediately and made self-criticism. At this time, the platoon leader came over and led the soldiers to collect all the fallen apples into baskets and put them under the window of the villagers' house. After cleaning the orchard, the soldiers set off.

老乡们回到果园,看到扫得干干净净的果园和窗下一筐筐的落地果,心里激动不已。他们望着解放军队伍远去的背影,不停地说:"真是一支仁义之师啊!"

很快,"不吃老百姓一个苹果"的事迹上报到东野总部,10师也因此荣获了"仁义之师"的奖旗。

When the villagers returned, they were very moved to see a clean orchard and the baskets loaded with fruits. As they watched the retreating figures of the troop, they couldn't help but exclaim, "It's really an army of benevolence and righteousness!"

Soon, the story was reported to the Headquarters of the Northeast Field Army and the 10th Division was thus awarded a pennant bearing "An Army of Benevolence and Righteousness".

小车推出大胜利
Triumph on Wheels

在气势恢宏的淮海决战前线和广大后方,各解放区人民掀起了一场轰轰烈烈的支前运动,其规模之巨大,任务之浩繁,动员人力物力之众多,为古今中外战争史上所罕见。淮海战役支前工作最动人的场面,是几百万的民工大军推着小推车运送粮食。"最后一把米,用来做军粮,最后一尺布,用来做军装,最后的老棉被,盖在担架上,最后的亲骨肉,含泪送战场。"老百姓们正是唱着这样的歌谣、推着小推车勇往直前冲向战场。

In the front and the rear of the Huai-Hai Campaign, the people of the Liberated Areas showed tremendous enthusiasm and ceaselessly provided enormous amounts of human and material support for the frontline, which was unprecedented in scale and unusual in the Chinese and world military history. It was the most heart-warming moment amid the support work at the frontline when millions of civilians pushed cartloads of food toward the front. "Donating the last handful of rice for the front; sewing the last meter of cloth into an army uniform; draping the last quilt over the wounded; tearfully sending the last child off to the battlefield." The civilians, singing these heartfelt ballads, were pushing their carts forward, bravely charging towards the battlefield.

淮海战役胜利后,华东野战军司令员陈毅曾深情地说:"淮海战役的胜利,是人民群众用小车推出来的。"据统计,淮海战役中,华东、中原、冀鲁豫、华中四个解放区前后共出动民工543万人,支前群众所用的小推车达41万辆。

After the victory, Chen Yi, commander of the PLA Eastern China Field Army, once gratefully remarked, "Victory of the Huai-Hai Campaign was delivered in pushcarts by the people." According to statistics, no less than 5.43 million laborers from Liberated Areas in East China, Central Plain, Hebei-

Shandong-Henan, and Central China were mobilized and up to 410,000 pushcarts were served in the Huai-Hai Campaign.

军旗卫士钟银根
Zhong Yingen: Soldier of the Color Guard

民权门位于天津东北面,战略地位非常重要,是攻打天津的重要突破口。16岁的战士钟银根担任旗手,他高举红旗引领着战友们冲锋在前,风驰电掣般冲上城头,将战前师首长授予该连"杀开民权门"的红旗插在了城头。

Minquan Gate in the northeast of Tianjin is the gateway to the city, holding strategic importance for the Tianjin Campaign. Zhong Yingen was a 16-year-old soldier of the color guard of the division, to which the division commander conferred a flag reading "Breaking Through into Minquan Gate". Raising the flag high, Zhong Yingen charged forward followed by his comrades, and placed the flag atop the city gate.

这面火一般耀眼的红旗刺痛了敌人,他们集中所有的火力向红旗射击,红旗被淹没在硝烟迷雾之中。在枪林弹雨中,钟银根失去双腿,身负重伤,但依然紧握红旗,倒了又插,连续4次。最后他用肩膀拼命地抵着旗杆,远远看去,他的身体就是旗杆。

The flame-like flag became an eyesore for the enemy, so they concentrated all fire on the flag and smoke curled over it. Even though Zhong was seriously injured and lost both his legs to heavy gunfire, he steadfastly gripped the red flag, falling and rising again, four times in succession. He leaned against the flagpole with his last gasp, appearing in the distance like a flagpole himself.

年仅16岁的钟银根在战友们的厮杀呐喊声中,慢慢地闭上了眼睛。在军旗卫士钟银根"四竖红旗"壮举的激励下,1连打退敌人20多次反扑,巩固了突破口,使后续部队顺利进入城内,为尽快解放天津创造了条件。

Amidst the resounding gunfire, Zhong died a heroic death at the tender age of sixteen. Inspired by his heroic deeds, No.1 Dagger Company repelled twenty counterattacks in a row, which strengthened the breach and paved the way for the subsequent advance and the liberation of Tianjin.

第三节 红色景点

Section Ⅲ Red Tourism Attractions

西柏坡中共中央旧址
The Former Site of the CPC Central Committee in Xibaipo

西柏坡中共中央旧址坐落在河北省平山县。西柏坡,原是一个普通的小山村,距平山县城 80 余公里,位于太行山东麓,滹沱河北岸,有 100 多户人家,河两岸土地肥沃,稻麦两熟。早在抗日战争时期,这里就是老革命根据地之一。1948 年,人民解放军开始了对国民党军队的战略进攻。当时距西柏坡仅 90 公里的华北重镇石家庄已被攻克,石家庄成为华北解放区的领导中心。

图 7-1 西柏坡中共中央旧址
Figure 7-1 The Former Site of the CPC Central Committee in Xibaipo

The Former Site of the CPC Central Committee in Xibaipo is located in Pingshan County, Hebei Province. Xibaipo, an ordinary 100-household village about 80 kilometers away from downtown Pingshan, sits astride the eastern foot of the rolling Taihang Mountains and on the northern banks of Hutuo River. The rich and fertile soil on either bank of the river makes it abound with rice and wheat. The history of Xibaipo as one of the old revolutionary base areas can be traced back to the War of Resistance Against Japanese Aggression. In 1948, the PLA launched a strategic offensive targeting the KMT. Back then, Shijiazhuang, only 90 kilometers away from Xibaipo, had been captured and became the command center of North China Liberated Area.

在全国胜利即将来临之际,中共中央、人民解放军总部离开陕北,于5月26日到达西柏坡。中共中央"五大书记"毛泽东、朱德、刘少奇、周恩来、任弼时齐集于此。自1948年5月至1949年3月,西柏坡中共中央旧址为中共中央和中国人民解放军总部驻地。

With nationwide victory in sight, the CPC Central Committee and the PLA Headquarters left northern Shaanxi and arrived at Xibaipo on May 26, thus the Five Secretaries of the CPC Central Committee including Mao Zedong, Zhu De, Liu Shaoqi, Zhou Enlai and Ren Bishi reunited here. From May 1948 to March 1949, it served as the Supreme Headquarters of the CPC Central Committee and the PLA.

1955年,因修建岗南水库,中共中央和解放军总部旧址及西柏坡村一起搬迁。1970年冬,在距原址北500米、海拔提高57米的地方开始对旧址进行复原建设。现在可以参观的中共中央旧址建筑面积2760平方米,占地16440平方米。主要有:毛泽东、朱德、刘少奇、周恩来、任弼时、董必武的旧居、中国共产党七届二中全会会址、中央军委作战室旧址、中央机关小学旧址等。复原基本保持了原貌,屋内陈设按原状进行了布置,展品主要是当年领袖们的办公和生活用品。

Due to the construction of Gangnan Reservoir in 1955, the Former Site of the CPC Central Committee and the PLA Headquarters, along with Xibaipo Village, were relocated together. In the winter of 1970, another new village patterned on the original site was built at the site 500 meters north of the original one and at the height of 57 meters above the original. To date, an area of 16,440 square meters with a total floor space of 2,760 square meters can be visited. They are the former residences of former Chinese leaders including Mao Zedong, Zhu De, Liu Shaoqi, Zhou Enlai, Ren Bishi and Dong Biwu, the Site of the Second Plenary Session of the Seventh CPC Central Committee, the Site of the Command Room of the Central Military Commission, the Site of Primary School Attached to the CPC Central Committee and others. The original appearance has been basically preserved. The rooms are furnished in the same way as the originals, and the exhibits mainly include office supplies and the basic necessities of the former leaders.

五大书记铜像
Bronze Statues of the Five Secretaries

1945年6月19日,中国共产党召开了七届一中全会,选举出毛泽东、朱德、刘少奇、周恩来、任弼时五位同志为中央书记处书记,史称"五大书记"。会议还选举毛泽东为中央委员会主席、中央政治局主席、中央书记处主席。从此以后至新中国成立初期,中共中央"五大书记"成为中国共产党的最高领导层。2009年8月25日,在西柏坡纪念广场上,从左至右,矗立起周恩来、刘少奇、毛泽东、朱德、任弼时五位书记的铜像。铜像下,是用鲜花摆出的黄镇将军手写体"新中国从这里走来"几个大字。

On June 19, 1945, Mao Zedong, Zhu De, Liu Shaoqi, Zhou Enlai and Ren Bishi were elected members of the Secretariat at the First Plenary Session of the Seventh CPC Central Committee, known as "the Five Secretaries". Mao Zedong was appointed Chairman of the CPC Central Committee, Chairman of the CPC Central Political Bureau and the General Secretary of the CPC Central Secretariat. From then on until the early years of the People's Republic of China, the Five Secretaries of the CPC Central Committee had been the paramount leaders of the CPC. Bronze Statues of Five Secretaries (from left to right: Zhou Enlai, Liu Shaoqi, Mao Zedong, Zhu De and Ren Bishi) were inaugurated on August 25, 2009 in Xibaipo Memorial Hall Square. Beneath the bronze statues, the handwritten words "Xin Zhong Guo Cong Zhe Li Zou Lai"[新中国从这里走来]

图 7-2　西柏坡纪念广场五大书记铜像
Figure 7-2　Bronze Statues of the Five Secretaries in Xibaipo Memorial Hall Square

(New China set off from here) penned by General Huang Zhen, were formed using fresh flowers.

西柏坡纪念馆
Xibaipo Memorial Hall

西柏坡纪念馆位于河北省平山县内,是解放战争后期中国共产党中央和中国人民解放军总部所在地,是解放全中国的最后一个农村指挥所。1958年,因修建水库,革命遗址搬迁。1970年开始,西柏坡中共中央旧址进行复原建设,复原总面积为16440平方米。1977年,新建西柏坡纪念馆,建筑面积为3344平方米。1978年5月26日,中共中央旧址和纪念馆同时开放。

Xibaipo Memorial Hall, located in Pingshan County, Hebei Province, is the seat of the CPC Central Committee and the PLA during the late period of the Liberation War, and also the last rural command post. In 1958, the revolutionary site was relocated due to reservoir construction. Since 1970, the Former Site of the CPC Central Committee has been restored, with a total area of 16,440 square meters. In 1977, Xibaipo Memorial Hall was built, covering an area of 3,344

图 7-3 西柏坡纪念馆
Figure 7-3 Xibaipo Memorial Hall

square meters. On May 26, 1978, both the Former Site of the CPC Central Committee and the Memorial Hall were opened to the public.

第一展室：走进西柏坡
Exhibition Room #1：Discovering Xibaipo

1947年初，国民党军队全面进攻解放区失败后，改为重点进攻陕北和山东解放区。3月18日，中共中央主动撤离延安。在枣林沟，中共中央决定：毛泽东、周恩来、任弼时等组成中央前委，继续留在陕北，指挥全国的解放战争；刘少奇、朱德等组成中央工委向华北转移，进行中央委托的工作。西柏坡位于河北省平山县中部。平山县具有光荣的革命传统、优越的战略位置、得天独厚的地理条件和良好的群众基础。同年5月，中央工委进驻平山县西柏坡。

In early 1947, the KMT troops failed in the all-out attack on the Liberated Areas and then shifted their focus to Northern Shaanxi and Shandong Liberated Areas. On March 18, the CPC Central Committee retreated from Yan'an and decided in Zaolingou that the Front Committee of the CPC headed by Mao Zedong, Zhou Enlai and Ren Bishi should stay in northern Shaanxi to command

图 7-4 西柏坡纪念馆第一展室
Figure 7-4　Exhibition Room #1

the Liberation War, while the CPC Central Working Committee led by Liu Shaoqi and Zhu De retreated to north China so as to better carry out the work assigned. Xibaipo is located in the middle of Pingshan County which has a glorious revolutionary tradition with favorable strategic locations, superior geographical position, and consistent grassroots support. In May of the same year, the CPC Central Working Committee moved to Xibaipo Village in Pingshan County.

第二展室：废除封建土地所有制
Exhibition Room #2: Abolishing Feudal Land Ownership

中央工委在西柏坡召开全国土地会议,领导解放区的土地改革运动和整党工作,冲击了几千年来的封建土地制度,提高了党组织的战斗力,为解放战争的胜利发展奠定了基础。

In Xibaipo, the CPC Central Working Committee held the National Land Conference to facilitate further advances in land reform, which uprooted the centuries-old feudal system from China. In conjunction with the land reform, Party consolidation was carried out to increase the Party's fighting capacity and provide an important guarantee for the success of the Liberation War.

图 7-5　西柏坡纪念馆第二展室
Figure 7-5　Exhibition Room #2

第三展室:指导晋察冀军事斗争
Exhibition Room #3:Commanding the Military Struggle in Jin-Cha-Ji

在中央工委的指导下,晋察冀野战军先后取得了青沧战役、大清河北战役、保北战役、清风店战役、石家庄(石门)战役的胜利,扭转了晋察冀军事斗争的局面。特别是石家庄的解放,使晋察冀和晋冀鲁豫两大解放区连成一片,为中共中央移驻西柏坡创造了有利条件。

图 7-6　西柏坡纪念馆第三展室
Figure 7-6　Exhibition Room #3

Under the leadership of the Central Working Committee, the Shanxi-Chahar-Hebei (shortened as Jin-Cha-Ji) Field Army won victories in the battles of Qingcang, Daqinghebei, Baobei, Qingfengdian and Shijiazhuang (Shimen), which reversed the course of the military struggles in the Shanxi-Chahar-Hebei District. The liberation of Shijiazhuang connected two liberated areas—Jin-Cha-Ji and Jin-Ji-Lu-Yu, providing favorable conditions for the relocation of the CPC Central Committee to this area.

第四展室：统一解放区的财经工作

Exhibition Room #4: Unifying the Financial and Economic Work of the Liberated Areas

根据中共中央指示，建立了华北财经办事处，逐步建立起财政管理的各项规章制度，使解放区经济有了较大的发展，为统一解放区的财经工作创造了有利条件。

图 7-7　西柏坡纪念馆第四展室
Figure 7-7　Exhibition Room #4

Under the guidance of the CPC Central Committee, the North China Financial and Economic Office was set up and financial management rules and regulations were established over time, which promote the economic development and provide favorable conditions for unifying the financial and economic work of the Liberated Areas.

第五展室:决战前夕
Exhibition Room #5: On the Eve of the Great Strategic Offensive

1948年春,全国战场形势发生了根本变化。为了更有力地领导和指挥全国的解放战争,中央前委毛泽东、周恩来、任弼时等东渡黄河,移驻西柏坡。在西柏坡召开的九月会议,为人民解放军与国民党军队进行战略决战,夺取新民主主义革命的胜利,从思想上、政治上和组织上做了重要准备。

图 7-8 西柏坡纪念馆第五展室
Figure 7-8 Exhibition Room #5

The spring of 1948 saw a radical change in the nationwide battle situation. In order to effectively command the Liberation War, Mao Zedong, Zhou Enlai, and Ren Bishi led the army eastward across the Yellow River into Xibaipo. The September Meeting convened in Xibaipo made important ideological, political and organizational preparations for the strategic offensive against the KMT troops to win the new-democratic revolution.

第六展室:大决战(1)
Exhibition Room #6: The Great Strategic Offensive (Ⅰ)

1948年9月12日到1949年1月31日,中共中央和中央军委组织指挥了辽沈、淮海、平津三大战役,歼灭和改编了国民党军队154万余人,摧毁了国民党赖以维持其反动统治的军事力量,加速了解放战争的胜利进程。

图 7-9　西柏坡纪念馆第六展室
Figure 7-9　Exhibition Room #6

From September 12, 1948 to January 31, 1949, the CPC Central Committee and the Central Military Commission waged the three campaigns of Liaoxi-Shenyang, Huai-Hai, and Beiping-Tianjin, wiped out and reorganized over 1.54 million KMT troops, and shattered the military forces upon which the reactionary KMT regime relied, thereby accelerating the victorious progress of the Liberation War.

第七展室:中国共产党七届二中全会

Exhibition Room #7: The Second Plenary Session of the Seventh CPC Central Committee

1949年3月5日至13日,中国共产党七届二中全会在西柏坡召开。全会确定了促进革命迅速取得全国胜利的各项方针;决定将党的工作重心由农村转到城市;强调要加强党的思想建设,防止资产阶级思想的腐蚀,并向全党提出了"两个务必"的告诫,为新中国的建立做了政治上、思想上和组织上的准备。

图 7-10 西柏坡纪念馆第七展室[原七展室——大决战(2)]
Figure 7-10 Exhibition Room #7

The Second Plenary Session of the Seventh CPC Central Committee was convened in Xibaipo Village from March 5 to 13, 1949. The meeting formulated the policies for winning a nationwide victory, decided a shift in the focus of the Party's work from rural areas to the cities, emphasized the importance of strengthening the ideological structure of the Party to guard against bourgeois influence, and articulated the "two musts" directive to the entire Party. Thus, the plenary session laid political, ideological, and organizational groundwork for the founding of New China.

第八展室:描绘蓝图
Exhibition Room #8:Drawing the Blueprint

西柏坡时期,以毛泽东为代表的中国共产党人以马列主义基本原理为指导,结合中国实际,确立了新中国的国体、政体,构建了中国共产党领导的多党合作和政治协商基本政治制度,制订了新中国经济建设方针,提出了新中国外交工作基本原则,规划了新中国文化教育事业。1949年3月,中共中央、中国人民解放军总部离开西柏坡,迁往北平。

During the Xibaipo period, Chinese Communists, represented by Mao

Zedong, guided by the fundamental principles of Marxism-Leninism, and in accordance with China's specific conditions, established the form of state and system of government for New China, constructed the basic political system of multi-party cooperation and political consultation under the leadership of the CPC, formulated the guidelines for New China's economic development, proposed the basic principles of New China's diplomatic work, and planned the advancement of New China's cultural and educational undertakings. In March 1949, the CPC Central Committee and the PLA Headquarters left Xibaipo for Beiping.

第九展室：难忘的岁月
Exhibition Room #9: The Unforgettable Years

中共中央在西柏坡组织指挥三大战役，召开七届二中全会，筹建新中国，同时也留下了许多动人的故事。青青的西柏坡岭，蓝蓝的滹沱河水，简朴的农家小院，到处记载着革命先辈工作、生活的足迹。领袖们的音容笑貌，战友的欢歌笑语，将永远成为人们缅怀历史的美好回忆。

In Xibaipo, the CPC Central Committee commanded the three decisive campaigns, held the Second Plenary Session of the Seventh CPC Central Committee, and made preparations for the establishment of New China, during which there were many touching stories. The lush green Xibaipo Ridge, the blue ripples of Hutuo River, along with the shabby farmyard, all witnessed the revolutionary forerunners' life and work here. The looks of the former leaders and cheerful chatters of comrades in arms will always be very fond recollections of those unforgettable years.

第十展室：走向复兴
Exhibition Room #10: The Road to Rejuvenation

重点介绍党和国家领导人以及社会各界、海内外知名人士到西柏坡的情况。历史的车轮，已经驶过了几十个春秋，毛泽东等老一辈无产阶级革命家在西柏坡描绘的新中国的蓝图已经变成现实。他们建树的丰功伟业和铸就的西柏坡精神，将激励人民为全面建设小康社会，加快推进社会主义现代化进程而不懈奋斗。

This exhibition room focuses on the visits to Xibaipo by party and national leaders, figures from all walks of society, and well-known personalities from both home and abroad. Over the past decades, the blueprint for New China drawn in Xibaipo by proletarian revolutionaries represented by Mao Zedong has been realized. Their great achievements and the "Xibaipo Spirit" they forged will continue to inspire the people to strive tirelessly for the comprehensive construction of a well-off society and to accelerate the process of socialist modernization.

专栏 7：西柏坡精神

Special Column Ⅶ: The Xibaipo Spirit

西柏坡精神是中国共产党人在革命时期铸就的伟大革命精神，党和人民的宝贵精神财富。在中国革命即将取得全国胜利的前夕，党中央在西柏坡召开具有伟大历史意义的七届二中全会，毛泽东同志告诫全党："务必使同志们继续地保持谦虚、谨慎、不骄、不躁的作风，务必使同志们继续地保持艰苦奋斗的作风。"

2013年7月11日，习近平总书记在河北省调研指导党的群众路线教育实践活动时指出：全党同志要不断学习领会"两个务必"的深邃思想，始终做到谦虚谨慎、艰苦奋斗、实事求是、一心为民，继续把人民对我们党的"考试"、把我们党正在经受和将要经受各种考验的"考试"考好，使我们的党永远不变质、我们的红色江山永远不变色。

The Xibaipo Spirit was forged by Chinese communists during the revolutionary period and will always be an invaluable spiritual asset to the Party and the people. With national victory of Chinese revolution in sight, the Seventh Central Committee of the CPC held its Second Plenary Session in Xibaipo. At the meeting, Mao Zedong warned the entire Party, "Comrades must be taught to remain modest, prudent, and free from arrogance and rashness in their style of work and must be taught to preserve the style of plain living and hard struggle."

When inspecting the mass line campaign in Hebei Province on July 11, 2013, President Xi Jinping called on the whole Party to further understand the essence of the "two musts". All Party members should remain modest, prudent and hardworking, seek truth from facts and serve the people wholeheartedly. Only in this way can we perform excellently on the "exam" set by the people and withstand tests facing the Party both now and in the future to keep the CPC's nature unchanged and ensure the color of red China will never change.

参考文献

References

专著、译著及论集

1. 埃德加·斯诺.西行漫记原名:红星照耀中国[M].董乐山,译.北京:中国人民解放军战士出版社,1979.
2. 蔡清富,黄辉映.毛泽东诗词大观[M].成都:四川人民出版社,2009.
3. 马克思,恩格斯.共产党宣言[M].陈望道,译.社会主义研究社,1920.
4. 方志敏.可爱的中国[M].北京:人民文学出版社,1982.
5. 光未然词,冼星海曲.黄河大合唱[M].北京:人民音乐出版社,1975.
6. 刘刚.踏上红色之旅[M].北京:中央编译出版社,2005.
7. 《红色之旅》编写组.红色之旅[M].郑州:中州古籍出版社,2005.
8. 冀昀.尚书[M].北京:线装书局,2007.
9. 罗广斌,杨益言.红岩[M].北京:中国青年出版社,1977.
10. 毛泽东.被敌人反对是好事而不是坏事(藏文)[M].北京:民族出版社,1964.
11. 毛泽东.毛泽东选集第2卷[M].北京:人民出版社,1958.
12. 毛泽东.毛泽东选集第3卷[M].北京:人民出版社,1958.
13. 毛泽东.毛泽东选集第1卷[M].扬州:苏中出版社,1945.
14. 习近平.习近平谈治国理政:第1卷[M].北京:外文出版社,2018.
15. 习近平.习近平谈治国理政:第2卷[M].北京:外文出版社,2017.
16. 习近平.习近平谈治国理政:第3卷[M].北京:外文出版社,2020.
17. 习近平讲党史故事[M].北京:中共中央党校出版社,2022.
18. 许渊冲.许渊冲英译毛泽东诗词[M].北京:中译出版社,2020.

19. 中国李大钊研究会.李大钊全集(第3卷)最新注释本[M].北京:人民出版社,2006.

20. 朱文通等.李大钊全集.第2卷[M].石家庄:河北教育出版社,1999.

21. 读图时代人文旅游编辑部.江山如此多娇:中国红色旅游指南[M].北京:北京出版社,2005.

英文专著、译著

1. Editorial Committee. A Concise History of the Communist Party of China [M]. Beijing：Central Compilation and Translation Press, 2021.

2. Editorial Committee. Xi Jinping Speech at a Ceremony Marking the Centenary of the Communist Party of China [M]. Beijing：Central Compilation and Translation Press, 2021.

3. Institute of Party History and Literature of the Central Committee of the Communist Party of China. Chronicle of the Communist Party of China (July 1921 – June 2021) [M]. Beijing：Central Compilation and Translation Press, 2021.

4. Snow, Edgar. Red Star Over China [M]. New York：Grove Press, 1968.

5. Tse-Tung, Mao. Selected Works of Mao Tse-Tung Volume 2 [M]. Beijing：Foreign Languages Press, 1965.

6. Tse-Tung, Mao. Selected Works of Mao Tse-Tung Volume 3 [M]. Beijing：Foreign Languages Press, 1965.

7. Tse-Tung, Mao. Selected Works of Mao Tse-Tung Volume 4 [M]. Beijing：Foreign Languages Press, 1961.

网络资源

1. https://ctext.org/shang-shu/great-plan

2. http://www.jgsgmbwg.com/about.php? cid＝3

3. https://en.theorychina.org.cn/

4. https://www.marxists.org/reference/archive/mao/selected-works/

5. http://www.rjjng.com.cn/

6. http://www.qstheory.cn/yaowen/2020-09/03/c_1126450023.htm

7. http://www.yagmjng.com/index.php/page/1.html

8. http：// www.xbpjng.cn/columns/6eceedc4-f105-4c13-84f3-9a7739ea6b96/index.html

9. https：// www.12371.cn/special/zgjs/

10. http：// www.81-china.com/

11. https：// www.zgyd1921.com/

12. https：// www.jgswh.com